THE GUINNESS BOOK OF INNOVATIONS

The 20th Century From Aerosol To Zip

THE GUINNESS BOOK OF INNOVATIONS

The 20th Century From Aerosol To Zip

Geoff Tibballs

DEDICATION

To Carol, Nicola and Lindsey

Editor: Beatrice Frei
Design and Layout: Stonecastle Graphics Ltd, Marden, Kent
Picture Editing and Research: Image Select International

First published in 1994 by Guinness Publishing Ltd

33 London Road, Enfield, Middlesex

Typeset in Ellington and Avant Garde
by Ace Filmsetting Ltd, Frome, Somerset
Printed and bound in Great Britain by
The Bath Press, Bath

A catalogue record for this book is available from the British Library

ISBN 0-85112-742-8

Introduction

In 1899 the director of the United States Patent Office boldly declared: 'Everything that can be invented has been invented.' He was a shade premature. The 20th century has been responsible for more innovations, great and small, than any other — aeroplane flight, space travel, radar, television, the jet engine, radio, penicillin, heart transplants, talking films, test-tube babies, the Open University, Kit-Kat, Clearasil, the list is endless. Most have enriched our lives, a few we could have done without. Have you ever seen anyone who looks good in a shell suit?

On the other hand, some inventions which we automatically think of as being modern — the anorak, the duvet, central heating, double glazing — actually date back to the 19th century or beyond. The anorak (or parka) was a beloved garment of Alaskan Eskimos while double glazing was originally incorporated in Hampton Court Palace to protect the stained glass windows.

As this century draws to a close, we wonder what startling discoveries the 21st century will bring. What will people be saying in 2094? — 'Do you remember when the first Martian corner shop opened?' 'Do you remember when we had postmen, trains and England won the Ashes?' 'What must it have been like before cars were powered by Bovril?' Perhaps somebody will produce scaffolding in pretty pastel shades, a quick-wrap supermarket bag that can be opened in less than half an hour or, of course, the long-awaited cure for the common cold. All I do know is that unless one of the innovations is a drug to increase life expectancy, none of us will be around to find out.

A 1910 advertisement extols the virtues of the new Thermos Jug, a cousin of the famous flask.

Action Man

God did not create boys to play with dolls. They played with train sets, toy soldiers and model racing cars. They would no more dream of playing with a doll than tidying their room — until 1964, that is. For in that year the American company Hasbro introduced a 12-inch doll aimed specifically at boys. His face, scarred on the right cheek, was, according to the manufacturers, 'comprised of the faces of 20 medal of honor recipients'. His name was G.I. Joe.

To the surprise of the American toy industry, this heroic figure dressed in Second World War uniform quickly caught on, appealing to a young public weaned on John Wayne and hamburgers. Such was Joe's impact that representatives of the British firm Palitoy were soon hot-footing it across the Atlantic to secure a licensing deal. Joe was duly anglicised to Action Man, a title influenced by the popular television series of the time, *Danger Man*. Among the names rejected was Ace 21, considered because the early doll had 21 individual parts.

Action Man stormed the British toy shops in January 1966 in the guise of soldier, sailor and pilot. His sturdy jaw, painted hair and moving joints were enough to sweep any girl off her feet — it was prudent to keep Sindy in a separate box. But all was not plain sailing. By 1969 the Vietnam War had caused a backlash against the doll in the US. War was a taboo topic and American toy shops were besieged by protestors bearing banners demanding: 'G.I. Joe Must Go'.

But Joe's demise did not affect Action Man who went from strength to strength in the 1970s during the course of which he acquired fibre hair, gripping hands and the 'Eagle Eye' (movable eyes produced by touching a lever at the back of his head). At the height of his fame, it was estimated that there was 1.3 of him for every boy in Britain, a somewhat curious statistic which indicated either that he was very popular or tended to break easily.

By 1984 over 350 different Action Man costumes had been produced including an astronaut, a Polar explorer, a Canadian Mountie and a French Foreign Legionnaire. The military range was such a success that regiments actually used to approach Palitoy with suggestions for Action Man uniforms. Bill Pugh, Action Man's guiding light, said: 'I remember an officer, driving an army jeep, came screeching to a halt outside our offices and personally asked me to represent his regiment — the 17th/21st Lancers. He produced a uniform, still the same as worn in the Charge of the Light Brigade. We duly obliged.' Other lines were less well received, notably the footballer, his demise hastened by the failure of the England team in the early 1970s.

By the start of the next decade, age was beginning to catch up with Action Man. Star Wars and He Man were all the rage. They made our hero look like Larry Grayson. In 1984 the unthinkable happened. Action Man was dropped. He'd had sand kicked in his face.

But you can't keep a good man down and eight years later he returned to the shelves with a new tough-guy image dedicated to fighting the forces of evil. Perhaps to reflect nineties man, it might have been more appropriate if he were pushing a supermarket trolley and wielding nothing more potent than a duster.

Adidas Shoes

Jesse Owens winning four gold medals at the 1936 Berlin Olympics; Muhammad Ali boxing his way to the World Heavyweight Championship; Franz Beckenbauer leading West Germany's footballers to victory in the 1972 World Cup. They all achieved sporting excellence in adidas shoes.

The famous footwear took its name from Adolf (known to all as 'Adi') Dassler who created his first sports shoes at Herzogenaurach near Nuremberg in 1920. From his small cobbler's workshop, he had sensed the opportunities for entering the hitherto untapped sporting market, setting out to produce a shoe which was durable, which would enhance performance and offer protection against injury. Production techniques were fairly primitive, the trimming being carried out on a strange bicycle-like machine driven by the muscle-power of one of Dassler's assistants.

(above) adidas sports shoes down the ages.
(right) You can't keep a good man down — Action Man is relaunched.

A

Nevertheless, success was not long in coming. Athletes wore Dassler shoes at the 1928 Amsterdam Olympics and four years later at Los Angeles, Arthur Jonath won the bronze medal in the 100 metres. But it was the next Olympiad which really plunged Dassler shoes into the limelight, Jesse Owens' unrivalled feat being supplemented by gold for the German handball team in Dassler handball boots. By 1937 Adi Dassler was producing shoes for 11 different sports.

Hardships caused by the war meant that when Dassler resumed operations in 1946, he was forced to make training shoes out of canvas from tents and rubber from fuel tanks. The following year, he founded adidas, beginning with 47 employees (there are now 10000). One of the new company's most significant innovations was that of screw-in rubber studs for football boots, allowing them to be changed at half-time if necessary.

The adidas three stripes have gone on to be worn by countless top sportsmen and women, including athletes Ann Packer, Allan Wells and Daley Thompson, footballer Gerd Müller, tennis champions Rod Laver and Steffi Graf and golfer Sandy Lyle. At the 1984 Los Angeles Olympics, no fewer than 259 medals were won in adidas. Over 280000 pairs of adidas shoes are now produced daily and exported to more than 160 countries. It seems Adi Dassler was right about there being an opening in the market for sports shoes.

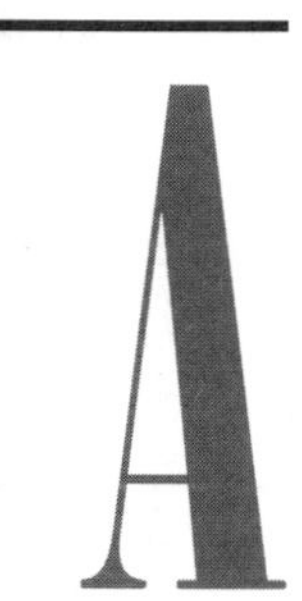

Aerosol

The idea of spraying water dates back to the fountains of ancient Rome, while in the 19th-century doctors used metal or glass phials, warmed in the hand to increase the pressure, in order to produce a spray as a local anaesthetic. Yet the aerosol was invented as recently as 1926.

That was when Norwegian engineer Erik Rotheim discovered that a product could be projected in a fine spray by introducing a gas or liquid into the container to create internal pressure. His patent, filed in October of that year, described the use of a pressure container fitted with a valve to dispense liquid soap, paint, insecticide and cosmetics.

The first commercial production of Rotheim's idea took place in Norway at the factory of the Oslo paint manufacturer Alf Bjercke where paint and polish aerosols were made on a small scale. Instrument maker Frode Mortensen then began manufacturing insecticides but none of these ventures took off and production ceased. In 1938 Erik Rotheim died at the age of 40.

For a while it seemed as if his work had died with him but it was the Second World War which created the urgent need for the aerosol. In 1942 more American servicemen died from infection and disease in the Pacific than were killed in combat. It was obvious that these disease-bearing insects had to be controlled quickly, a situation which gave impetus to develop the work of

A range of early British aerosols for killing insects and stale air (but not cage birds).

research chemist L.D. Goodhue and entomologist W.N. Sullivan who were employed on a programme for the US Department of Agriculture. Goodhue had been experimenting with aerosol insecticides since 1935 but had encountered a series of difficulties. In despair and faced with a meeting in Washington the next day to discuss the work programme, he returned to a previously abandoned idea on Easter Sunday 1941. Working alone in his laboratory, he placed a cage-full of cockroaches in a fumigation chamber and sprayed them with an aerosol containing insecticide. Within ten minutes, all of the cockroaches were on their backs.

The armed forces were enthusiastic and, after the prototype had been made more portable, a contract was signed in July 1942 for the manufacture of 'bug bomb' aerosols, as they were later christened by US troops. Around 50 million 'bug bombs' were made, some of which found their way on to the American civilian market as war surplus in the late 1940s. Businesses began to seek ways of exploiting the invention. The container of the 'bug bomb' was too heavy and costly and the valve too expensive for a commercial product but the problem was solved by modifying beer cans and fitting them with mass-produced plastic valves. Thus the first commercial delivery of 105 000 was made by Airosol Inc. in Neodesha, Kansas, on 21 November 1946. Within 40 years, world production had approached 7000 million aerosols annually.

Erik Rotheim never lived to see the impact of his invention, one which changed the world. But with current ecological scares, there are those who wonder whether it has been for better or worse.

Air Conditioning

As we sit in a pleasantly cool office on a sweltering summer's afternoon, we should pay homage to American Willis Carrier, the inventor of modern air conditioning.

Although crude experiments at cooling air date back many centuries (there was an attempt to treat the Houses of Parliament in 1837 by Englishman Jacob Perkins), it is Carrier who is rightly known as the father of air conditioning.

It was he who, in 1902, designed a 30-ton fan-cooled dehumidifying unit which was installed at the Sackett-Wilhelms Lithographing and Publishing Company in Brooklyn. Its purpose was to check the expansion and contraction of paper caused by varying weather conditions. However, the term 'air conditioning' was first coined by his fellow countryman Stuart Cramer in 1906 when he combined his dust filter with Carrier's device. The resultant machine drew in fresh air from outdoors, filtered and washed it, heated or cooled it and corrected any change in humidity. It was first employed in a textile mill to condition cotton rather than humans.

Carrier's work continued and in 1911 he came up with an air humidity graph which enabled him to calculate the air conditioning requirements for any given building. In 1928 the first air-conditioned office block was built — the 21-storey Milam Building in San Antonio, Texas. It provided a new degree of comfort for workers and meant that in many regions of the world the old sweatshop would eventually become a thing of the past.

Airfix

From the mid-fifties the name of Airfix has been synonymous with highly inventive construction kits of aircraft, ships, cars and railway accessories. Yet the company had originally been known as a manufacturer of combs and the first construction kit came about by financial dictates rather than design.

It was in 1948 that Airfix was commissioned to produce a promotional replica of a new tractor for Fergusson. Unable to afford delivery of the models complete, Airfix made them in kit form, moulded from acetate. So tight was the budget that the body of the tractor was made from broken-down fountain-pens bought as scrap and the tyres from the rubber core of waste cable. Nevertheless, this cost-cutting exercise proved amazingly popular and when it was decided to sell the tractors to the public, they were snapped up at 2s. 11d. a time. Airfix realised that they had inadvertently hit upon a winning idea. And they were quick to capitalise upon it.

The origins of Airfix can be traced back to 1939 when Nicholas Kove, a Hungarian Jew, formed a company to manufacture rubber toys filled with air. Since he had a penchant for words ending in 'ix' and wanted a name that would be listed near the head of trade catalogues, he settled on Airfix. But in common with so many other young businesses, Kove's was severely disrupted by the war. Due to a shortage of materials, he was forced into a new line of merchandise and began producing combs. By 1947 Airfix was the largest manufacturer of combs in the country, aided by Kove's introduction of the first injection moulding machine in Britain.

As the shackles of war were slowly released and the demand for combs declined with the repatriation of the grooming-obsessed American G.I.s, Airfix returned to toy-making. Following the triumph of the tractor, the company spotted the potential of injection-moulded construction kits made from the new plastic material called polystyrene DS. Woolworth's placed a huge order

Not quite ready for take-off. The many intricate parts which go to make an Airfix construction kit.

for the first kit — a model of Drake's ship *The Golden Hind*. Indeed, the order was so large, it took Airfix nine months to complete.

The Golden Hind appeared on the shelves in 1952, selling for 2s., followed over the next couple of years by the *Santa Maria*, HMS *Shannon* and the *Cutty Sark*. Two of Airfix's senior executives wanted to move away from ships into aircraft, but so reluctant was Kove to disrupt a winning formula that he made them agree to have the cost of the tooling, nearly £1000, deducted from their salaries if the venture failed. Their money was safe for in 1953 the resultant Spitfire aircraft, sold exclusively through Woolworth's, became a best seller.

Cars and buildings were next off the production line, the Airfix kits proving a particular boon to model railway enthusiasts. Numerous layouts were adorned by Airfix signal boxes, thatched cottages and station buildings. The kits were inexpensive, authentic and (often with a little paternal assistance whether sought-after or not) were fun to make and paint. And, providing they did not fall prey to a size 11 foot, they were remarkably durable.

Such was the quest for authenticity that one Airfix boss, seeing a 1930 racing Bentley cruising ahead of him through Wimbledon, accelerated his little A40, overtook the Bentley and forced it to a halt. The driver's fury only subsided when the Airfix man explained that he wanted to build a replica of the Bentley. The following Sunday afternoon, Airfix draughtsmen visited the proud owner's house and measured the car in minute detail!

Nowadays Airfix is part of Humbrol Limited, the paint manufacturers with whom the company has always been so inextricably linked.

Alcoholics Anonymous

It was as a young American soldier serving in France during the First World War that Bill Wilson started to drink. The effect was almost immediate. Although he landed a job as a stockbroker in New York, his drinking dragged him down. By 1931 it had become a serious problem. Despite the efforts of his wife Lois and the many promises and pledges made to her and to business associates, the compulsion to drink was too strong. Over the next three years, what had promised to be a brilliant Wall Street career rapidly deteriorated.

Then, in December 1934, languishing in hospital, Wilson underwent what he later described as an overwhelming and awesome spiritual experience. It led him to believe that there was an escape from drinking and that he could subsequently maintain his sobriety by helping other alcoholics. He began attending meetings of an association called the Oxford Group who, he had been told by a friend, often tried to help alcoholics. For six months he attempted to sober up those in a similar position to himself — but without success.

The following May, Bill Wilson embarked on a business trip to Akron, Ohio. The mission was a failure and, in despair, he contemplated turning to drink once more. Pacing up and down the lobby of the Mayflower Hotel, he was sorely tempted to buy a gin and, as he put it, 'be king for a night'. Fortunately, his willpower held firm and he reinforced his belief that the only salvation was to help others.

On the notice board in the hotel lobby, Wilson saw the name of the Reverend Walter Tunks and asked him whether he knew any local members of the Oxford Group. Receiving a list of nine or ten, Wilson tried to find a soul to save but without much luck. Nobody seemed available. With his search drawing to a close, one of the last names on the list, Mrs Henrietta Seiberling, finally came up trumps. 'I have just the man for you,' she enthused and recommended a friend — Dr Robert Holbrook Smith.

Smith (or Dr Bob as he came to be known) had been drinking steadily since his student days at the turn of the century. His alcoholism worsened yet he was able to function as a surgeon in Ohio, few of his colleagues realising how serious his illness was. Although he had attended meetings of the Oxford Group, he was reluctant to meet Bill Wilson and only agreed on Mrs Seiberling's insistence. On their way to the Seiberling residence, he told his wife he would not be staying more than 15 minutes. He stayed over six hours.

Smith was Wilson's first convert. By meeting and talking together, the pair found they could stay sober and their desire to help others led them to form Alcoholics Anonymous in that same year, 1935. Within two years, membership had reached 40 and by 1940, 2000. Then an American newspaper article caused a dramatic upsurge in interest. The post office box number of AA's little one-room office in New York was besieged with enquiries, as a result of which membership shot up to 8000.

In 1947 Alcoholics Anonymous came to England, the first meeting being held in a room at the Dorchester Hotel. Even though an advertisement placed in the *Financial Times* brought just two replies, the movement soon spread to the provinces and Scotland. Today Alcoholics Anonymous is a world-wide organisation with some 70 000 groups and over two million members in 115 countries — and all because Bill Wilson's business meeting in Akron turned sour.

Alka-Seltzer

In December 1928 an epidemic of colds and influenza swept across the United States. It was estimated that half of the population were affected. The pharmaceutical company, Dr Miles Laboratories, of Elkhart, Indiana, did not escape either. At the height of the epidemic, 25 per cent of the workforce were off sick.

One morning, A.H. 'Hub' Beardsley, a director of the firm, visited the offices of the local newspaper, the quaintly named *Elkhart Truth*. The managing editor, Tom Keene, explained that he had just received a distress call from a neighbouring newspaper, the *News-Times* of Goshen, requesting the loan of two linotype operators to stand in for those off sick. Keene was happy to oblige.

A whale with indigestion promoted Alka-Seltzer in 1949.

For his part, Beardsley was puzzled. In the current climate of ill-health, how could the *Truth* possibly afford to loan out its staff? Keene revealed that not one of the *Truth*'s employees had lost any time on account of colds and flu, adding that when a member of his staff showed signs of going down with a cold, he brought them into the office and dosed them up with aspirin and bicarbonate of soda with instructions to continue until the symptoms had passed.

Beardsley was suitably impressed and, on returning to the laboratories, asked the company's English chemist, Maurice Treneer, whether he could make an effervescent tablet containing bicarbonate of soda and aspirin. Within a week Treneer, a pioneer of effervescence, had done just that. In January 1929 the Beardsley family went on a Mediterranean cruise, taking with them a quantity of the new tablets. Beardsley later wrote: 'We had a very rough passage, with continuous storms, from the time we left Sandy Hook, until we arrived at Madeira. I found the tablets were wonderful for seasickness and colds. Someone brought on flu germs, and we had an epidemic of flu on board the ship. Two of the passengers died from pneumonia. I passed out these tablets, and had many compliments for them and thanks for their use.'

The product was known within Miles as Aspir-Vess, soon to be changed to Alka-Seltzer (because it was alkaline and when in solution it effervesced like the German Seltzer water).

In spite of the favourable tests, Beardsley recommended caution and did not begin marketing Alka-Seltzer until 1931. The company's first pharmacist, Harry Beaver, was even more guarded and feared that he had 'over-bought' when ordering five pounds of cotton to stuff into the tops of Alka-Seltzer bottles, which had to be corked and sealed in molten paraffin prior to the adoption of screw caps in 1936.

But skilled promotion ensured that America soon knew about Alka-Seltzer. Newspaper adverts invited readers to get a free drink of the potion at their drugstore and before long, Alka-Seltzer was sponsoring a number of popular radio shows, listeners being encouraged to 'Listen to it fizz!'. Alka-Seltzer was hailed as a cure for hangovers, headaches and even domestic quarrels which were put down to too much acidity in the body. In 1951 Miles introduced Speedy, a cute little character who waved a magic wand and who wore an Alka-Seltzer on his head and had another tablet for his body. Speedy was a mainstay of advertising throughout the 1950s, during which time Alka-Seltzer expanded its areas of sponsorship to successful television shows including *Laramie*, *The Flintstones* and *Bonanza*. It was shrewd placement for if anyone ever looked in dire need of a couple of Alka-Seltzer, it was Hoss Cartwright.

Aluminium Foil Milk Bottle Top

Beloved by milkmen, customers and blue tits alike, the aluminium foil milk bottle top has been around since 1914 when Josef Jonsson began production in Linkoping, Sweden. It was not until 1929 that it was introduced to the United Kingdom and even then it had to see off a determined challenge from the plucky little cardboard disc before it could claim the front doorstep as its throne.

In the 19th century milk was delivered first by milkmaids, bearing two large tubs on the ends of a wooden yoke carried across the shoulders, and then by milk perambulators or horse-drawn floats. The container used in the latter part of the century was a hand-can because, although some bottles filtered through, they were generally too expensive to produce.

But by 1920 cheaper methods of making bottles had been found and they entered widespread use, sealed with cardboard discs, many of which carried a simple — but touchingly personal — message. This ranged from 'Christmas and New Year Greetings' or 'God Save the King & Queen' to the more mundane 'Please Rinse Bottle and Return Each Day'. Since it was illegal to sell milk in open containers, the cardboard disc looked forward to a

The aluminium foil milk bottle top has become a familiar sight in the 20th century.

long and healthy future until the aluminium foil top barged its way onto the scene.

The reason the disc slipped was one of dishonesty. Milk bottles were expensive to replace and because those which bore cardboard discs were of universal size and shape, they could be illegally used by any despicable dairyman, regardless of the fact that it was not their dairy's name on the bottle. On the other hand, the foil-topped bottles were a different shape with a smaller mouth and were made in various types according to the method of capping. Thus the distributors were safeguarded against their bottles being kidnapped by rival dairies and so losses were restricted to natural breakage.

By 1944 over 90 per cent of the UK's bottled milk arrived with an aluminium foil top. The cardboard disc made a brief sentimental return for the 1953 Coronation with the message 'Let Us Drink a Health Unto Her Majesty' but it was soon consigned to the lactic wilderness once more. Surely there is a case for reintroducing it with a special message for blue tits: 'This Top Can Seriously Damage Your Beak'.

What some girls had to do to promote the company name . . .

Automatic Tea-maker

There is nothing new in man's desire for an extra 20 minutes in bed of a morning. The Romans craved a little more shuteye before a hard day's roadbuilding, the Vikings needed to build up their strength for another day of rape and pillage while Rip Van Winkle took it to ridiculous lengths. So from the moment tea became a universal drink, the search was on for a device which would make the morning beverage while man stayed in bed.

For many years the chosen device was woman until she, too, began to complain about the chore. Then in 1902 a Birmingham gunsmith, called Frank Smith, came up with a potentially hazardous contraption operated by a spring-wound alarm clock, set to the time the tea was required. The other principal component was a copper kettle which had a moving plate inside and was held in place by a trip wire. The kettle was brought to the boil after a pannier of methylated spirit was ignited by a striker plate coming into contact with a red-topped match. When the kettle boiled, the plate inside it shook, causing the kettle to tip and pour the boiling water into the teapot. At the same time, the clock struck and a striker plate moved across the top of the methylated spirit, thereby extinguishing the fire. It was advertised as: 'A clock that makes tea!'

Not surprisingly, Mr Smith's teamaker, which cost a princely 30s., failed to catch on and man's headache remained for another 30 years until the spread of electricity encouraged Brenner Thornton to invent the legendary Goblin Teasmade. Thornton designed its movement so that the current automatically heated the element in the special kettle at a certain time before the alarm was due to go off. When the water boiled, it decanted through a tube directly onto the tea in the pot and the current heating the element switched off. The weight of the water in the pot automatically turned on a light, setting off the alarm. It was not only relatively simple but also far safer than its predecessor since it did not rely on any precarious balancing acts.

Goblin immediately recognised its potential and put it on the market in 1937. Initially christened the Cheerywake, it was renamed the Teasmade under which name it sold for £5 15s. 6d., a price that included two earthenware cups, saucers, cream jugs and a sugar basin.

But as with any new concept, it took a while to convince everybody. Sales were slow, mainly because the retail trade did not understand how it worked. Many shop assistants were nervous about having to demonstrate its prowess to customers and, rather than make fools of themselves, preferred to secrete the Goblin Teasmade on the back shelves. Goblin solved the problem by despatching 250 demonstrators to stores throughout the country and by taking the Teasmade to every available exhibition.

Although some still thought it was just a clock on a tray, the Teasmade began to make a considerable impact in the 1950s. Its popularity was greatly boosted by television game shows such as *Take Your Pick* which, always on the lookout for relatively inexpensive but exciting items, made the Teasmade a regular prize. And hotels began to realise that the Teasmade could make things more pleasant for their guests and save their staff a lot of trouble at the same time. Indeed some people became so devoted to the new labour-saver that when redecorating the bedroom, they painted, or even wallpapered, their Teasmade to match. If only Rip Van Winkle had owned a Goblin Teasmade . . .

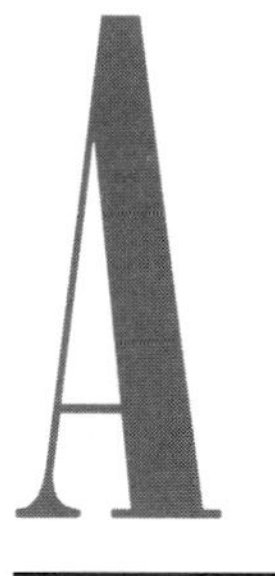

Avon

Back in 1880s America, David H. McConnell, an upstanding youth, spent his school vacations selling bibles. But he soon realised that the small samples of perfume which he gave out with the books were received with greater enthusiasm than the bibles themselves.

Sensing that the Lord was trying to tell him something, McConnell founded the California Perfume Company in 1886 and employed agents to sell his five perfumes — Lily-of-the-Valley, White Rose, Heliotrope, Hyacinth and Violet — on a door-to-door basis.

The venture was a tremendous success and led, in 1939, to a spin-off enterprise, Avon Products. The California Perfume Company factory at Suffern, New York, was set amidst rolling hills and verdant valleys and was said to have reminded McConnell of Shakespeare country. Thus he had used the name of Avon in a number of California Perfume Company products even prior to 1939.

The new company made Avon a household name. As the world returned to normality after the Second World War and women yearned for the little luxuries which they had been forced to forego during hostilities, the Avon lady, with her vast range of perfumery, was a welcome visitor. To the woman of the house, the sound of the door chimes meant only one thing — it was Avon calling. Such has been the impetus of this friendly phenomenon that the species has tended to breed at an alarming rate so that there are now over a million and a half Avon representatives operating in more than 100 countries.

That modern miracle, the Avon lady.

A

Babycham

The Showering family began brewing and cider-making at Shepton Mallet in Somerset towards the end of the 18th century. At one point, they diversified their talents to incorporate shoe-making and hotel-keeping. In 1932 the family business became a private limited company and the four brothers, Herbert, Arthur, Ralph and Francis, soon looked for other liquid lines to manufacture.

Shortly before the war, Francis Showering started his research into the fermentation of fruit juices and by 1949, he had produced a clear, naturally sparkling perry from pear juice. The product was test-marketed for three months in the Bristol area, using 600 licensed outlets. The results were highly encouraging and between 1950 and 1953, it won every first prize in every national competition at every major agricultural show in the country. Because of its success, the infant champion perry became the 'baby champ' and so Babycham was born. The name had the added advantage of suggesting champagne.

The much-loved Babycham chamois has now met the same fate as Bambi's mum.

Convinced they were onto a winner, Showerings marketed Babycham nationally in 1953 and staked everything on an inspired advertising campaign based on a spritely little baby chamois and the slogan: 'I'd love a Babycham.' The adverts caught the imagination of the public, particularly women and young people, to such an extent that a quota system had to be operated for 18 months before supply could keep pace with demand. And when commercial television came to Britain in 1955, the sight of the cute chamois skipping around the screen boosted sales still further.

Over the years public perception has tended to pigeon-hole Babycham as rather twee. It was not the sort of drink that the disco girls of the seventies and eighties were likely to order. Aware that the product needed dragging into the modern world, the Gaymer Group, who now market the perry, ran a television commercial in which a cool disco dude announced to his assembled worshippers that he would 'lurve a Babycham'. If that was not enough to shock traditionalists, in the summer of 1993 Gaymers announced that they were axing the baby chamois because it was too dated. A spokesman said: 'We like to think it has gone to that great advertising heaven along with George the Hofmeister bear and the Guinness toucans.'

Bacofoil

The year of 1962 saw the launch of the satellite Telstar, the first James Bond film, *Dr No*, the release of the film *Summer Holiday* . . . and the birth of Bacofoil aluminium foil.

The arrival of Bacofoil may have passed relatively unnoticed but it has subsequently proved itself a greater boon in the kitchen than either Messrs Connery or Richard.

Aluminium's commercial use dates from 1886 when American Charles M. Hall and Frenchman Paul Heroult independently invented the method of extracting the metal from its oxide by electrolysis. The process proved to be faster and much cheaper, as a result of which aluminium became less of a luxury and more suitable for industrial use. By 1912 aluminium foil (a thin sheet of aluminium) had taken over from tin. Although it eventually came to be used in milk bottle tops, its versatility did not really extend to the kitchen or the home in general until the 1960s when it became available in easy-to-handle rolls.

Non-toxic, strong, heat reflective, impermeable and able to withstand extremes of temperature, aluminium foil has since become the housewife's friend with the old chore of scrubbing roasting tins now largely a thing of the past.

More than 25 million rolls of aluminium foil are bought every Christmas and they are not just used for wrapping the turkey. Cake decorations, greetings cards and jewellery can all be made from foil. It is even recommended that girls make foil clothes to wear to fancy dress parties. Drivers have found it invaluable for protecting windscreens on frosty nights; gardeners make foil mobiles to keep birds off their fruit; and a foil nose shield, whilst not exactly the height of fashion on the beaches of the Riviera, will, if attached to sunglasses, prevent a dangerously burnt nose.

For the girl who has everything — a dress in Bacofoil.

Ball-point Pen

Few 20th-century inventions have proved as invaluable as the ball-point pen, yet few inventors made as little out of their brainchild in its infancy as Laszlo Biro.

Unlike his simple product, Biro was a man of many parts. A Hungarian hypnotist, sculptor and journalist, he was to be found in 1938 editing a government-sponsored magazine. On a visit to the printers in Budapest, he began to consider the virtues of transferring the principle of the printers' quick-drying ink to pens and that same year he patented his first basic prototype.

It was a crude affair that required considerable modification. Biro was able to achieve this by setting up a production company in Argentina after fleeing his native land to escape the approaching Nazi jackboot. His work on a writing implement that would not blot resulted in a patent on 10 June 1943 for a pen which combined a rotating steel ball-point with a minute capillary tube containing the ink.

Around this time Biro met Henry Martin, an Englishman who was visiting Buenos Aires on a mission for the British government. Martin instantly recognised the potential of the new pen in wartime, believing it to be ideal for air crews calculating navigations at high altitudes. It was also able to write on damp paper and at awkward angles and could write 200 000 words without refilling. Accordingly, Martin acquired the UK rights from Biro and in 1944 began producing ball-points for the RAF in a disused aircraft hangar near Reading. Employing a staff of 17 girls, Martin's company produced 30 000 pens that year.

Having sold out to Martin for the British market, Biro compounded the error by forgetting to patent his invention in the United States. It was a costly lapse since, hailing it as the 'first pen that writes underwater', Gimkel's of New York sold no fewer than 10 000 at $12.50 apiece on the first day of sale, 29 October 1945. The following year, Martin sold Biros to the British public at £2 15s. each. They were thus almost a luxury item, their cost amounting to a week's wages for the average office girl. Nevertheless, by 1949 sales of ball-points had surpassed those of fountain-pens. It was a state of affairs lamented by many traditionalists.

A further development occurred in 1958 when the French company BiC introduced the BiC Crystal, a disposable ball-point pen. Retailing at just 1s., it proved so popular that 53 million were sold in the UK in 1959. Over 12 million are now sold daily throughout the world.

Laszlo Biro died in 1985. He may not have made as much money as he should have done out of his invention but at least he had the satisfaction of knowing that his name had entered the vocabulary of countless households.

The announcement of the revolutionary new writing implement, the Biro.

Barbie Doll

Barbara Millicent Roberts has been going out with boyfriend Ken for 33 years. They have yet to marry. But far from being viewed as the spinster of the parish, a poor soul to be pitied, she is worshipped as a heroine throughout the world.

Better known as the Barbie doll, her worldwide income totals over £300 million per year. Since 1959 her makers Mattel have bought over 57 000 miles (91 000 km) of dress fabric for her wardrobe — enough to stretch from London to Sydney three times. And she has got through more than a billion pairs of shoes. She makes Imelda Marcos look like Sandie Shaw.

It was while watching her daughter Barbie play with paper dolls that Ruth Handler, who with husband Elliot founded Mattel, came up with the idea for the Barbie doll. She said: 'I was fascinated with the way my daughter and her friends projected themselves through teenage and adult-style paper dolls.'

Barbie made her debut in New York on 9 March 1959 but was considered too adult by many toy buyers. For while it was deemed acceptable for Marilyn Monroe and Jayne Mansfield to show their curves to the masses, the thought of a child's doll having a well-rounded figure raised a few eyebrows. New York's *Village Voice* called her 'Boobs in Toyland'. Ruth Handler conceded: 'The toy buyers didn't care for Barbie at first. And many of them did not order the doll. They did not think mothers would buy a doll with breasts.'

But although further complaints were to follow about Barbie's materialistic attitude in that she constantly needed to replenish her wardrobe, she steadily caught on and in 1961 found someone to buy clothes for her when she met a new boyfriend at a dance. Having named Barbie after her own daughter, it was only natural for Ruth Handler to christen the boyfriend after her son Ken. Just as Barbie's chest created a headache for Mattel, so did Ken's private parts — or lack of them.

Ruth Handler recalled: 'It was a conscious decision to make the Ken doll without genitals. That was a discussion between the designers and me which I lost. The men all felt Ken shouldn't have genitals. I wasn't sure. I argued for a little bump and we did get a little bump as time went on!'

Poor Ken needed all the help he could get. Skinny to the point of anorexia, he hardly measured up to every girl's dream guy. Consequently he disappeared for a few years in the sixties, returning with rippling muscles and a new trendy hairstyle to reflect his new outdoor, fun-loving image. No longer did he look as if he spent his weekends studying railway timetables.

Meanwhile, Barbie was having to come to terms with the Swinging Sixties and the Twiggy-inspired slimmer

B

The old serious-looking Barbie. She has had plenty to smile about since.

figure. Barbie refused to join the permissive society, always keeping Ken at arm's length. Their relationship never progressed beyond coffee.

A few facelifts later and Barbie is still going strong. Her love of fast cars and exotic holidays have outraged feminists who see her as a stereotyped bimbo, conveniently forgetting that in her time she has been a doctor, a pilot, an astronaut, a TV news reporter, a business executive and an Olympic gold medallist. In all, over 600 million Barbie dolls have been sold worldwide and for every second of every day, two Barbie dolls are sold somewhere in the world.

Girls take part in competitions to choose the best Barbie lookalikes while collecting has become a real craze in the United States with original Barbies valued at nearly £2000, blondes apparently being more valuable than brunettes. Irina Creaser shares her home in West Virginia with a husband and over 700 Barbie dolls. She enthuses: 'Barbie is tall and haughty with long slim legs, perfect hair and pouty red lips that seem to make a come-on.' But she feels that too much is made of the doll's figure. 'People say if Barbie were life-size she'd keel over or not be able to see her shoes, but that is rubbish.'

Bathroom Scales

Some would consider the bathroom scales to be just about the worst invention of the 20th century. With the possible exception of a pet hamster, what other household object can immediately plunge one into the depths of despair just by standing on it?

Invented in 1910 by the German company Jas Ravenol and marketed under the name of Jaraso, bathroom scales remained a luxury item until the 1960s. Then, in 1964, the Hanson Scale Company introduced the first scale with a digital display, the tell-tale figures which shattered the dreams of women who wanted to look like Twiggy and men who longed to be Charles Atlas. For them, there was no justice in these scales.

Belisha Beacon

The advent of the motor car brought death and destruction to the roads of the world. Pedestrians accustomed to nothing more lethal than a horse-drawn carriage suddenly found themselves confronted by seemingly uncontrollable, racing machines. As they attempted to cross busy thoroughfares, they knew how the average hedgehog feels today.

One of the problems as far as Britain was concerned was that absolutely anyone could buy a car, get in and drive it. It was not until 1931 that a prospective driver had to sign a declaration of physical fitness. Mr Magoo would have been in his element. One American state came up with the novel legislation that any motorist who killed a pedestrian had to spend an hour alone with the corpse. A more practical solution to the number of accidents was the creation of special pedestrian crossings — when introduced in Paris, they had seen annual road deaths drop from 292 to 237 despite a considerable increase in the volume of traffic. Thus, at the suggestion of the London Traffic Advisory Committee, a pedestrian crossing, indicated by a square white sign on a post bearing a cross, a directional arrow and the words PLEASE CROSS HERE, was established at London's Parliament Square in December 1926. By the following August, a further 16 posts had been erected around Piccadilly Circus and neighbouring streets, the crossings being marked with two parallel white lines painted across the road. In 1933 these were replaced with a herring-bone pattern of white lines and the square sign was ousted in favour of a large circular sign marked with the letter C.

In spite of the new experimental measures plus the introduction of compulsory driving tests and the Highway Code, deaths from road accidents ran at the alarming rate of 22 a day in the UK by 1934. In one week in July, 148 people were killed and no fewer than 5778 injured. Figures from Paris indicated that 61 per cent of road accidents were the fault of pedestrians and so the UK Minister of Transport, Sir Leslie Hore-Belisha, issued a notice to instruct users of pedestrian crossings. 'Pedestrians must not obstruct a vehicle proceeding in the general line of traffic movement, i.e. straight ahead, but vehicle traffic turning at right angles must give way to pedestrians using the marked crossings.' Pedestrians breaking these rules were liable to a fine of 5s. Safety First campaigns were also set up. Among their recommendations were that pedestrians should not read newspapers while crossing roads nor should they drop parcels in the middle of busy streets, presumably something which no one would choose to do anyway.

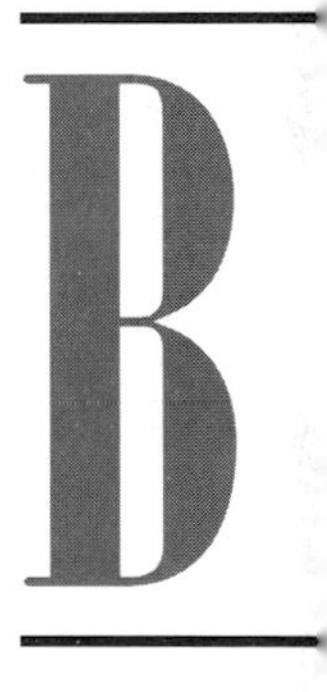

In September 1934 Sir Leslie introduced a new type of pedestrian crossing, marked by studs on the road and yellow beacons. He declared: 'There should grow up the habit of crossing the road at the stipulated points provided, and in the minds of motorists there should be the habit of expecting pedestrians to be crossing at those points.' In an attempt to demonstrate their safety, Sir Leslie marched Canute-like across these 'pedestrians' sanctuaries' as he called them. However, he was occasionally forced to speed up his dignified walk when motorists showed little signs of stopping — even for the Minister of Transport. Indeed, drivers held the crossings in such contempt that they were in the habit of verbally abusing any pedestrians caught using them.

The first beacons were erected in Kensington Road, West London. A letter-writer to *The Times* had suggested calling them 'Beleacons' but on 13 October 1934 another correspondent, Mr H. Lang Jones from West Dulwich, suggested that they should be called 'Belisha Beacons' in honour of their instigator. The original beacons were made of glass but served as a target for stone-throwing delinquents and were soon replaced with painted aluminium globes. Then in July 1952, nine months after the arrival of Zebra Crossings, plastic beacons with winking lights were introduced.

As for Sir Leslie, he continued to crusade for road safety, even appealing to Church leaders for their support. One of his more ingenious ideas was for speeding drivers to be brought to a halt by police cars armed with gongs. Many a car chase must have sent hotel guests scurrying into the dining-room thinking dinner was about to be served . . .

Bikini

B

When the American government announced in 1943 that the amount of fabric used in women's swimwear should be reduced by one-tenth as part of its policy to eliminate wartime textile wastage, it could scarcely have believed that these stringent measures would result in the birth of such a carefree garment as the bikini.

Until then, swimsuits had been one-piece but designers decided to make the required cuts in the midriff, thus creating the two-piece. The *Wall Street Journal* reported: 'The saving has been effected — in the region of the midriff. The two-piece bathing suit now is tied in with the war as closely as the zipperless dress and the pleatless skirt.'

The new fashion reached the eyes and ears of two French couturiers, Jacques Heim and Louis Reard. Both set about drastically minimising the two-piece. Heim was first to act, designing the Atome (so-called because of its size) to be sold in his beach shop at Cannes. In the summer of 1946, bathers at Cannes saw a message scrawled in the Mediterranean sky which read: 'ATOME — THE WORLD'S SMALLEST BATHING SUIT'. But within three weeks, the skywriting planes were airborne again as Reard unveiled his creation: 'BIKINI — SMALLER THAN THE SMALLEST BATHING SUIT IN THE WORLD'.

Reard wanted to display the daring two-piece at a Paris poolside fashion show but none of his regular models would wear it. So he had to recruit the services of a dancer from the Casino in Paris, Micheline Bernardini. And so on 5 July 1946, in a cotton swimsuit printed with a newspaper design and comprising less than one square foot of fabric, Mlle Bernardini catwalked into history. Reard had christened it the 'Bikini' to express the idea of 'the ultimate', the fashion show being held just four days after the US had detonated the atomic bomb at Bikini Atoll.

The world's fashion correspondents could scarcely believe their eyes. The bikini was described as 'the most meagre swimsuit a woman could wear without being arrested' and 'the garment that revealed everything about a girl except her mother's maiden name'. For her part, Mlle Bernardini received 50 000 fan letters. One United States clothes manufacturer, concerned that no single company should have a monopoly on making bikinis, declared: 'We all have a right to know how so little material can conceal so much.'

However, he was not speaking for his nation as a whole. The Americans were generally horrified at the monster which their government had inadvertently helped to create. Other US maunfacturers told Reard: 'American women would be scandalised and would never wear such a crazy thing.' They even trotted out that doyenne of the swimsuit, Hollywood star Esther Williams, to voice her disapproval. 'They come off in the water,' she complained. 'If you can't swim in them, what good are they?'

For the next ten years, the bikini led something of an underground existence, discussed in hushed tones like something on the black market. The stores along New York's Fifth Avenue refused to display it in their windows but did concede to stocking it inside. To wear a bikini in public was to risk the wrath of fellow sunbathers and the authorities alike — in 1950 the police admonished a wearer on Hampstead Heath, claiming that her outfit did not 'conform to regulations'. *Newsweek* magazine said that bikinis 'had a record of bans and secret sales second only to *Lady Chatterley's Lover*'. As more avant-garde designs appeared (one hi-tech fashion guru fixed propellers to each breast, another made a swimsuit out of porcupine quills), the bikini remained largely for private consumption only.

Towards the end of the 1950s, greater affluence brought about an increase in the number of private swimming pools which in turn led to an upsurge in the demand for bikinis. Leading fashion magazines such as *Harper's Bazaar* finally gave their seal of approval and by the summer of 1960, American beaches were awash with bare midriffs. In another three years, *Newsweek* was able to report: 'The bikini, long the scarlet woman of the $200 million-a-year US swimwear industry, is unmistakably moving toward respectability.' It had been a slow but worthwhile journey.

An itsy-bitsy, teeny weeny, non-yellow polka dot bikini adorns a cover of Disc Parade magazine.

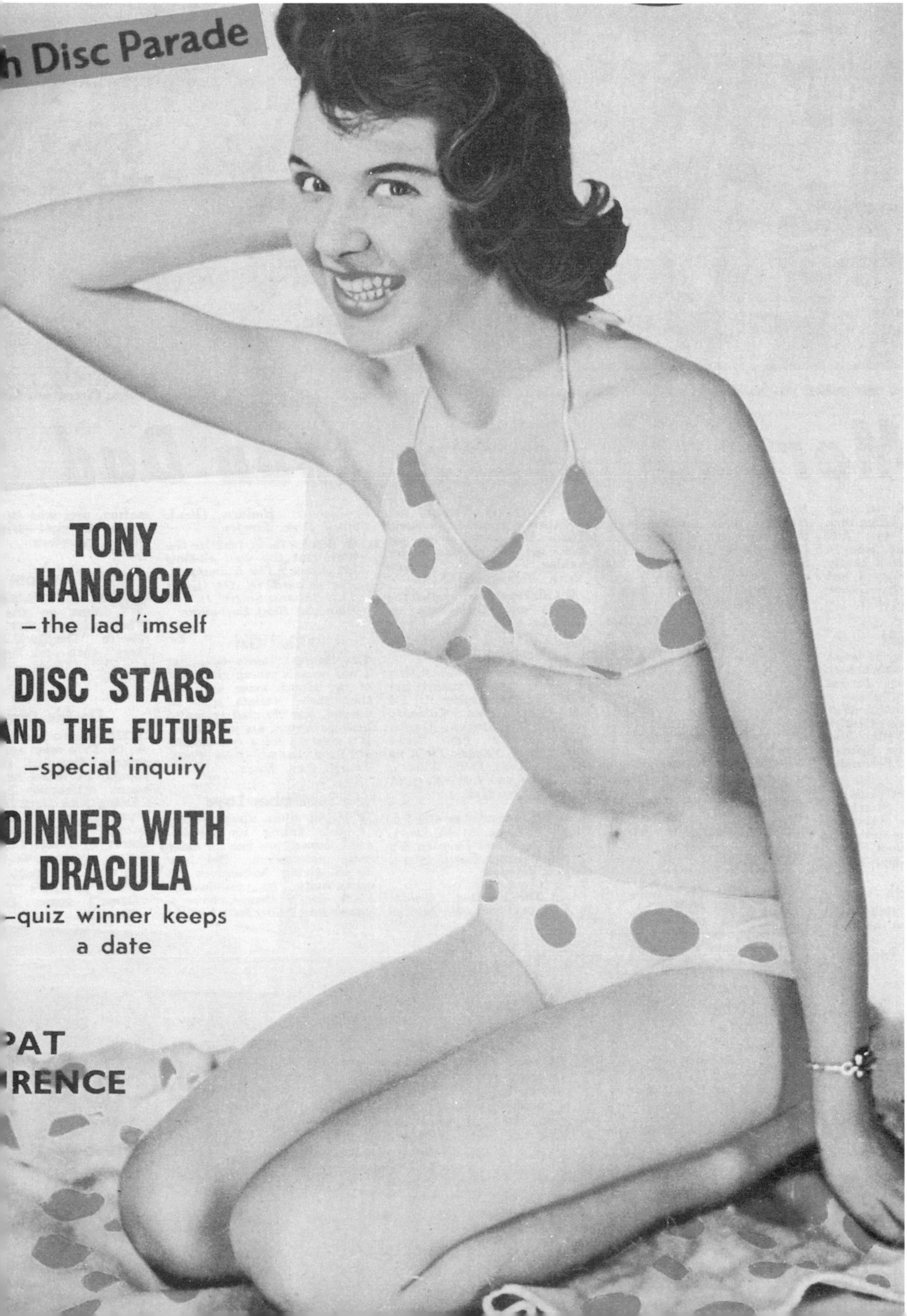

h Disc Parade

TONY
HANCOCK
–the lad 'imself

DISC STARS
ND THE FUTURE
–special inquiry

DINNER WITH
DRACULA
–quiz winner keeps
a date

PAT
RENCE

B

The Bisto kids celebrated 75 years in 1985.

B

Bisto

Like so many great ideas, Bisto was conceived over dinner. Not the plush interiors of the Savoy or the Dorchester but a more humble abode in West Hartlepool where Mrs James McRobert and Mrs George Patterson sat down to discuss the bane of a woman's life — lumpy gravy.

Their husbands were the secretary and manager respectively of the Cerebos company whose works at nearby Greatham produced Cerebos table salt and a wide range of food products. But there was nothing on the market to facilitate the process of gravy-making and so over the dinner table one evening, the ladies asked their men folk whether they could not produce something that would brown, season and thicken all in one go.

The task was delegated to the company chemist, a Mr Bowman, and after exhaustive tests, he came up with a dry powder which, when mixed with water and blended with the juices in the roasting tin, produced a thick, well-seasoned rich brown gravy. Cerebos knew they were on to a winner but needed a catchy name. Toying with various combinations of the initials of the selected slogan — 'Browns, Seasons, Thickens-in-One' — they came up with Bisto.

The dawning of Bisto was announced in a full-page advertisement on the front of the *Daily Mail* on 4 February 1910. Packets were 1d. and tins 3½d. and 6½d.

Advertising continued to spread the word and in 1919, illustrator Will Owen created a poster featuring two ragamuffin children, ecstatically sniffing the aroma wafting from a hot pie and uttering the words, 'Ah! Bisto'. The Bisto Kids had arrived. They have gone on to become a cartoonist's dream. Among the faces they have worn over the years have been Hitler, Stalin and Margaret Thatcher. So popular were they between the wars that Cerebos kept a stock of Bisto Kids costumes at the factory to loan to anyone entering a fancy-dress contest.

Following a spell out of the limelight, the Kids have returned while Bisto has maintained its place at the head of the gravy-making market. But would it have been so mouth-wateringly successful had the anagram-solver of 1910 come up with Botsi?

Blood Bank

The first blood transfusion in man took place as long ago as 1667 when Dr Jean Denis transfused the blood of a lamb into a young Parisian. Later the same year, Drs Lower and King transfused blood from a sheep into a certain Arthur Coga in London, no doubt giving rise to fears of internal bleating.

Both patients recovered and Mr Coga received 20s. for his co-operation and delivered an address in Latin to the Royal Society on his experiences. However, the following year when calf's blood was transfused to a patient who subsequently died, the dangers of transfusing animal blood to man were realised.

In the wake of successful human transfusions, Dr Karl Landsteiner of Vienna demonstrated in 1900 that blood from two people could only be mixed successfully if their individual blood groups matched. Two great advances occurred during the First World War as a result of wartime pressure on the medical profession to save lives. Firstly, it was found possible to prevent blood clotting once it was removed from the body by mixing it with sodium citrate. Secondly, it was proved that blood could be preserved in a safe condition for short periods in a special refrigerator, which meant that it was no longer essential to transfuse blood immediately after its collection.

Thus the stage was set for the development of civilian transfusion services and in 1921, four members of the British Red Cross Society in London, led by Dr Percy Oliver, volunteered to give blood at King's College Hospital. This was the start of the world's first voluntary blood donor service. Demand was but a trickle at first with only 26 requests for blood in 1924 but within five years, that figure had risen to 5333.

The logical next step was the formation of a blood bank. The first blood bank was set up at the Sklifosovsky Institute, Moscow, by Professor Sergei Yudin in 1931, followed six years later by another at the Cook County Hospital, Chicago. The first civilian blood bank in the United Kingdom opened at Ipswich in 1938.

Thousands of men and women saved lives by acting as voluntary blood donors during the Second World War and since the start of the National Blood Transfusion Service in Britain in 1946, the number of blood donations has risen from under 400 000 to over two million.

Book Token

The book token is one of the convenience gifts of the 20th century. It means that no longer are you likely to receive unsuitable tomes from well-meaning relatives — a complete encyclopaedia of gardening despite the fact that you only have a window box or *The Tales of Peter Rabbit* even though you are 42.

The idea for book tokens was first thought of in 1926 by Harold Raymond of the publishers Chatto & Windus but it attracted little support from booksellers. Finally in 1932 the National Book Council pressed ahead and introduced them with the slogan: 'The Gift is Mine, The Choice is Thine.' One feels that if the book token can survive a slogan like that, it can survive any recession in the publishing trade.

Boutique

Until 1955 clothes shopping had been a soulless experience for young people. Drab designs in drab shops served by ferocious, matriarchal assistants. It was enough to make naturism fashionable. Then along came the first boutique and buying clothes would never be the same again.

In its literal meaning of 'little shop', the boutique can be traced back to 1933 Paris where Lucien Lelong opened one in his couture house, selling less expensive versions of his classic designs. But the modern boutique as we know it — the trendy establishment catering principally for the younger shopper — originated 22 years later with Mary Quant's Bazaar in King's Road, Chelsea.

The daughter of a Welsh schoolteacher, Quant had always been interested in clothes. At the age of five, she had cut up bed spreads to make clothes. Later, as an art student, she made all her own outfits and, after working for a milliner, set up Bazaar with her future husband Alexander Plunket Greene and financial adviser Archie McNair. In their first week, they took five times more money than expected.

Initially they bought their merchandise from manufacturers but Quant was disappointed with the produce. She wanted young people, who were 'tired of wearing essentially the same as their mothers', to have fashions of their own and quickly realised that the only way she would be able to put her dreams into practice was by creating her own line of clothing. She began by buying patterns and altering them and by attending 'a few frantic evening classes in cutting'. Such was her limited knowledge of the fashion industry that instead of purchasing material wholesale, she bought it over the counter at Harrods of all places. Turning her bedsitter into a workshop and employing a handful of sewing women, Quant began to produce the designs she wanted, although she was still left in the position of having to sell one day's output of dresses before being able to afford to buy the next day's materials.

LADY JANE of
CARNABY ST
LONDON W.1.

(left) London's Carnaby Street was a mecca for men's and women's boutiques in the 1960s.

From these precarious beginnings, Bazaar grew to the point where a second store was opened in Knightsbridge in 1961. Mary Quant described Bazaar as 'a kind of permanently running cocktail party'. George Melly called it 'the one true pop manifestation in the years between rock and the Beatles'.

The Beatles were regular customers in the Swinging Sixties as Mary Quant's bold, adventurous fashions became the toast of the world. 'Paul McCartney used to come in and buy our clothes all the time,' says Quant. 'So did the rest of the Beatles. I remember John Lennon in a soft leather cap, and George Harrison and Patti Boyd buying their wedding clothes.'

Others were quick to cash in on the boutique boom. Biba, Bus Stop, Top Gear, Miss Selfridge and many others sprang up to cater for teenagers who for the first time had money to spend. Carnaby Street, once a scruffy London back alley, became the fashion mecca for young men (John Stephens had opened the first male boutique there in 1957). The prices were such that youngsters could afford to buy new clothes every week, all purchases taking place against the conducive buying background of the pop sounds of the day.

Looking back, Mary Quant says: 'It was very much an era of men and women dressing together, unlike before when women had shopped alone. The look was saying: "Isn't life terrific? Isn't life fun? It's great to be young."'

Boxing Gumshield

Although mouth guards are known to have been worn by the boxers of ancient Greece around 1200 BC, the modern gumshield dates from 1902 when it was invented by London dentist Jack Marks. The first fighter to wear one regularly was former featherweight champion Ted 'Kid' Lewis from 1912. Without it, the likes of Brian London would never have been able to keep their good looks but it did create a problem for Ralph Walton in a 1946 bout with Al Couture at Lewiston, Maine. Walton had just risen from his stool at the start of the fight and was still adjusting his gumshield in his corner when Couture knocked him out. The fight was officially over in 10½ seconds . . . including the 10-second count.

Boy Scouts

Robert Baden-Powell had always been keen on jobs for the boys. As a general of cavalry at the relief of Mafeking in 1890, he had used uniformed boys to great effect as messengers and workmen, thereby freeing adults to fight. He was interested in transferring his beliefs to peacetime and while inspecting the 21st anniversary parade of the Boys' Brigade in April 1904, it occurred to him that military drill held less appeal to a boy than some of the outdoor pursuits which he held dear. In despair at the sight of 'thousands of boys and young men, pale, narrow-chested, hunched-up, miserable specimens, smoking endless cigarettes', he set out to make them active and healthy. Convinced that the nation was suffering from the growth of 'shirkers' and boys who were 'mostly drifting towards hooliganism for want of a helping hand', Baden-Powell planned to train them to use powers of observation, to learn simple skills, to help others and to get out into the fresh air.

Accordingly, at the start of August 1907, BP (as he became known) took a party of 20 boys, collected from a mixture of Public Schools and London slums, on a week's camping expedition to Brownsea Island in Poole Harbour. It was the first Scout camp. He gave them the motto: 'Be prepared'.

The publication of his best-selling manual *Scouting For Boys* outlined his aims 'to help in making the rising generations, of whatever class or creed, into good citizens or useful colonists'. A rousing early Scout song summed up their philosophy:

> 'When you're marching, marching, marching
> Keep your eyes on everything,
> You must note each sound, every track upon the ground,
> And the cool, clear swing of the bird upon the wing.'

Baden-Powell supervises a Boy Scout at the Alexandra Palace Rally in 1922.

By 1914, there were over 150 000 Boy Scouts in Britain. They played an invaluable role during the First World War, helping to bring in the harvests, serving in soup kitchens, carrying government messages, guarding railway bridges and generally keeping eyes peeled for enemy spies since rumours were rife about German maids with guns secreted in their hand luggage.

Since 1907 over 250 million boys have joined the Scout movement throughout the world. No less an observer than H.G. Wells expressed his approval of the end product of Baden-Powell's training programme. Wells described 'a new sort of little boy, a most agreeable development of the slouching, cunning, cigarette-smoking, town-bred youngster, a small boy in a khaki hat, and with bare knees and athletic bearing, earnestly engaged in wholesome and invigorating games . . . I like the Boy Scout.'

Brassiere

Almost as many people claimed to have invented the bra as to have seen the Loch Ness Monster. Parisian shop owner Herminie Cadolle came up with a forerunner in 1889. And just after the turn of the century young French couturier Paul Poiret produced the *soutien-gorge* to achieve breasts that, as he so poetically put it, 'rise forth from the bodice like an enchanting testimonial to youth'. Monsieur Poiret, who was not one to undersell himself, later wrote: 'It was in the name of Liberty that I proclaimed the fall of the corset and the adoption of the brassiere . . . It is unthinkable for the breasts to be sealed up in solitary confinement in a castle-like fortress like the corset, as if to punish them . . . Yes, I freed the bust.'

But the person who is generally credited with inventing the modern bra is Mary Phelps Jacob, an American socialite living in Paris, who later became better known as Mrs Caresse Crosby. It was in 1913 that Mary Jacob, rebelling against restrictive whaleboned corsets and bodices and unhappy with her silhouette in a particular dress, asked her maid to tie two handkerchiefs to a length of ribbon to act as supports for her breasts. She wore the impromptu creation to a party where it was so popular that she was persuaded to make copies for her friends. She called it the Backless Bra but her attempts to market it were unsuccessful and later, after marrying the first of her three millionaire husbands, she sold the patent to manufacturers Warner Bros.

However, the brassiere developed without her and by 1916 that emobodiment of refinement, *The Lady*, said of brassieres: 'The French and American women all wear them and so must we.' The garment remained essentially a cover for the bare bosom and was not really used to enhance the breasts until the 1930s when cup sizes and padded bras were introduced. Then in the forties and fifties, Hollywood stars such as Jane Russell, 'sweater girl' Lana Turner (who wore tight-fitting jumpers over bras reinforced with stiffening points), Marilyn Monroe and Jayne Mansfield all showed women what they could aspire to with the right bra. In the 1960s the Playtex Cross Your Heart Bra vied for support with the Gossard Wonderbra. There were even cherry-flavoured edible bras for public consumption in the wife-swapping seventies.

The bra has often been more popular with men than women. Originally considered a symbol of women's freedom, it is ironic that in the 1970s the bra itself was sacrificed on the altar of feminism in the name of Liberty.

Beauty that is Yours Sincerely

Cosmetically speaking, you can assume a superficial beauty that is a tribute to the cleverness of modern beauty aids and treatments. . . . BUT, the lasting charm of *natural* loveliness is dependent on a healthy skin, a clear complexion and the absence of tired muscles, taut nerves, wrinkles and "sag." The Pifco Vibratory Massager, used as a part of your daily beauty treatment, will prove both pleasant and beneficial. It helps to keep you slim and trim, promotes a healthy scalp, affords relief for tired feet and many muscular aches and pains.

59/6
Tax 14/6

PIFCO
ELECTRIC VIBRATORY
Massager

Obtainable at good-class Chemists, Electricians and Stores. Write for illustrated folder and name of nearest stockist to: Dept. 33, Pifco Ltd., Watling Street, Manchester 4.

The Pifco Electric Vibratory Massager was the ideal companion to the brassiere.

Breathalyser

Perhaps the most remarkable thing about the breathalyser was that it was so long in coming. After all, its forerunner, the drunkometer, had been designed by Dr R.N. Harger back in 1938 and was introduced at the end of that year by the Indianapolis Police Department.

Yet it was not until 8 October 1967 that statutory breath tests arrived in Britain, the first being carried out on an unnamed youth involved in an accident near Bristol a few minutes after midnight. Anybody found guilty was liable to a fine of up to £100 or imprisonment and an automatic one-year driving ban.

The Minister of Transport, Barbara Castle, called it 'the start of a social revolution' but not everyone shared her enthusiasm, notably publicans who envisaged a marked decline in trade. The Hatfield Hotel in Lowestoft quickly came up with a solution by laying on a free bus service for customers.

Brillo Pad

In 1913 a New York salesman peddling Wearever Aluminium door to door discovered that housewives were experiencing difficulties cleaning his aluminium pots and pans satisfactorily. He explained his dilemma to his brother-in-law who was a manufacturer of costume

A housewife demonstrates the cleaning power of a Brillo Pad.

B

Denis Compton epitomised the clean-cut sporting image of Brylcreem in the early 1950s.

jewellery and had worked with all types of metals. The jeweller came up with the idea of a combination of a special soap and metal fibres to carry out the twin jobs of dissolving grease and food particles and of removing them speedily but gently, without damaging the utensils.

It proved most effective and so the jeweller approached a lawyer — Milton B. Loeb — with the aim of forming a company to manufacture and sell the new product. It was Milton Loeb's lucky day.

Loeb suggested the name Brillo and when the Brillo Manufacturing Company was formed, he became first treasurer and then president. From its factory in Brooklyn, Brillo produced a special cake of red soap plus loose wads of metal wool. These were the original Brillo Pads.

In 1928 Brillo Pads were imported to the UK by businessman Stanley A. Bevin and 11 years later, with Bevin as managing director of the new British subsidiary company, a factory was built on London's North Circular Road. Unfortunately, the building of the plant coincided with the start of the Second World War. Soap was rationed and while steel wool was produced, most of it was used for camouflage purposes. Like so many other vital commodities, the Brillo Pad went 'under the counter'.

Production of the pads restarted in 1946 but soap remained rationed until 1950. Neverthless, sales of Brillo Pads received a sizeable boost when the company decided to expand distribution beyond the hardware trade to include the grocery business. Thus many more shops were able to stock Brillo Pads.

The Brillo Pad we know and love today — the soap pad — was not developed until 1951 and even then for the first few years, women preferred the old arrangement of buying the ordinary pads with a tablet of soap. What changed matters as far as Britain was concerned was the introduction of Independent Television in 1955. Brillo were one of the first advertisers and the public immediately took to the new soap pad they saw on their screens. And housewife and Brillo Pad have lived happily ever after.

Brylcreem

It was all Denis Compton's fault. Throughout the 1950s, it seemed compulsory for the male population of this land to wear half a ton of Brylcreem on their heads in the belief that it would turn them into a great sportsman like the Arsenal footballer and England cricketer whose immaculately groomed hair embodied the product's advertising campaign. Such a quantity did many men wear that it was far more likely that they would involuntarily slide off the pillow in the middle of the night and end up on the floor writhing in agony, a sporting career in ruins!

A mix of brilliantine and cream (hence the name), Brylcreem was first marketed in 1928 by the County Chemical Co., Birmingham, whose proprietor, Wilfrid Hill, had asked his chief chemist to formulate a new-style hair cream which would differ from the brilliantines, gums and oils which were prevalent at the time. The resulting product, which contained no gum or starch, was originally sold only to hairdressers. It was so successful that by 1935 annual sales were running at two million, this despite the fact that no money had been spent on advertising. Instead, tens of thousands of gallons of Brylcreem were given free to hairdressers for use in their shops.

When George Royds was appointed advertising agent in 1935, he stated his objectives thus: 'Our first aim was to secure the goodwill of the barber and at a later stage create a masculine image that would appeal to millions of everyday people — football fans, sportsmen etc . . . One must go to the barber to have one's hair cut. He has a captive audience and his views on matters relating to the hair can very easily influence the purchaser . . . He was the king pin on which to hang our campaign.'

Consequently, early advertising depicted everyday scenes in a barber's shop. The intervention of war dealt a severe blow to many products but was a positive boon to Brylcreem whose advertising concentrated on RAF officers wearing Bryclreem on their hair. Thereafter, all young RAF types became known as the 'Brylcreem Boys'.

In 1946 Denis Compton signed up with Brylcreem. It promised him 'a clean scalp, free from unsightly dandruff', large flakes of which might otherwise have dislodged his bails at an inopportune moment. Beneath a photograph of Compton wielding the willow ran the line: 'Men people look to — use Brylcreem.'

Sales soared, the new tub (available in 1954 for 1s. 8d., 2s. 6d. or 4s. 6d.) proving particularly popular. By 1961 over 100 million were sold each year. Although changing hairstyles led to a decline in the youth market (how many hippies did you see doing the 'Brylcreem Bounce'?), Brylcreem is still very much with us, even if few of those who now wear it harbour any realistic dreams of scoring the winning run against Australia at Lord's.

Camcorder

When choosing a future husband, there are a number of points a bride has to consider. Will he treat her well? Will he provide for her? And above all, how will he look on the wedding video?

For these days the camcorder is as much an essential part of a wedding as the ring. A couple from Torquay actually restaged their daughter's £20 000 nuptials simply because the original video film was fuzzy.

Introduced by Sony in 1982 and championed by the unlikely figure of Jeremy Beadle, the camcorder has taken over our lives. With some three million camcorders in the UK alone, it is virtually impossible to visit any tourist attraction without being berated for wandering into shot by some budding Martin Scorsese.

Some take it even further. Police called to a traffic accident on the Santa Monica Freeway near Los Angeles found one of the drivers involved recording their arrival on his camcorder. To their amazement, he asked them to go back and 'arrive' again — this time with full lights and sirens. And he flatly refused to be arrested until someone filmed the handcuffs going on.

Not only has camcorder man no shame but there appears to be no limit to his powers. Editing programmes are now available for home videos which can, for example, change the colour of your car or your child's hair. You can buy ready-made videos of popular American tourist spots, insert yourself into them and pass them off as your own holiday videos — even if you spent the entire fortnight on a camping site outside Rhyl.

Experts believe that it is only a matter of time before people start hiring actors to play themselves, their wives and children in home videos of life's magic moments. You could go to Sainsbury's with Julia Roberts or make Macaulay Culkin do his maths homework. So if you see Tom Cruise on Blackpool beach with his trousers rolled up and a knotted handkerchief on his head, you'll know

Cartoon Film

Such cinematic superstars as Donald Duck, Bugs Bunny and Tom and Jerry might all have remained on the drawing board but for one man — J. Stuart Blackton. For it was English-born Blackton, a former cartoonist and reporter for the *New York World*, who, in 1906, produced for the Vitagraph Company of New York the world's first cartoon film.

Entitled 'Humorous Phases of Funny Faces', it depicted an artist (the hand of Blackton) drawing a man and a woman on a blackboard. The majority of the illusions were created by use of simple cardboard cut-outs although there was some genuine animation at the start of the film in sequences which showed the couple rolling their eyes and then the man obliterating the woman with puffs of smoke from his cigar.

The face of the Nineties — Camcorder Man.

A rival claimant for the title of first animator was Spaniard Segundo de Chomon who, in 1902, translated foreign title cards in his Barcelona home. It was said that one day he was shooting some cards but failed to notice that a fly had alighted on them until the film was developed and projected. The irregular exposure rate made it seem as if the fly was jumping around on screen and this apparently gave Chomon the idea for animation. However, the fact that his first film, *El Hotel electrico,* was not released for another six years suggests that his thoughts may well have been influenced by Blackton.

Another pioneer of cartoons was Frenchman Emile Cöhl who invented the match-stick character Fantôche. A trait of Cöhl's work was the way in which drawn figures metamorphosed into something completely different. Thus a woman would become angry, her head would fall off and turn into a parrot — and all 60 years ahead of Monty Python.

Among early animal characters were Gertie the Dinosaur and Old Doc Yak, the latter's tail-coat and striped trousers being a rare example of sartorial elegance in a goat. Even if animals in cartoons are blessed with amazing powers of recovery, it has not always been plain sailing. Tom and Jerry were pilloried in the 1970s for 'mindless violence' while Mickey Mouse was banned at the very start of his career. After seeing a preview of Mickey's first film in 1928, MGM boss Louis B. Mayer refused to put Walt Disney under contract because he thought pregnant women would be frightened of seeing a ten-foot high rodent on screen!

Cash Dispenser

On 27 June 1967 a small machine installed at the Enfield branch of Barclays Bank heralded what has been described as the most important development in personal finance this century. It was the world's first cash dispenser.

Invented by John Shepherd-Barron, developed by De La Rue and officially opened by comedy actor Reg Varney, the trailblazing Barclaycash machine operated on a voucher system. These vouchers were supplied in packs of ten and issued free to approved customers only, each of whom was allocated a personal code number. The maximum withdrawal at a time was £10.

The world's first cash dispenser installed at Barclays Bank, Enfield, in 1967 and the plaque which commemorates the event.

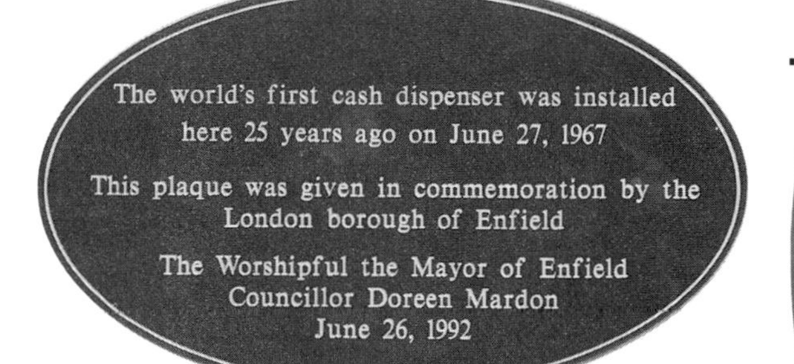

C

Five other Barclaycash machines were installed as part of the pilot scheme (at Hove, Ipswich, Luton, Peterborough and Southend) and so successful did they prove that 24-hour cash soon spread to the whole country. In 1975 the first ATM (Automatic Teller Machine) was introduced at Oxford. Plastic cards replaced the vouchers, cardholders were issued with PINs (Personal Identification Numbers) and the withdrawal limit was increased to £50.

Today 'holes in the wall', as they have been fondly termed, can be found all over the world — there are over 18 000 in the UK alone. The ceiling has been raised to £200 a day, Barclays calculating that their machines dispense £2000 per second over the busy Christmas period.

But like all great inventions, the cash dispenser has been subject to teething troubles, not always of its own making. Just as the original machines were prone to attacks from chewing gum, so the introduction of protective shields in the 1980s brought a new set of problems. Customers sometimes forgot to pick up their shopping and valuables as well as their cash and there were instances of fish and chips and even a set of false teeth trapped behind the shield!

C

Catseye

Yorkshireman Percy Shaw was a man of simple pleasures who enjoyed nothing more than a drink at Rose Linda's, a hostelry at Queensbury, on the hills above his house in Halifax. What he did not enjoy was the hazardous drive home, down a winding gradient with only a rickety wooden fence between the road and a steep drop over the side.

One foggy night in 1933, Shaw had a particularly hair-raising journey home. With headlights hopelessly ineffective on such occasions, he was forced to follow the tramlines in the middle of the road but that night the tramlines had been removed and he was only prevented from going over the edge by the reflection from a cat's eyes.

'When the tramlines were taken up from that hill,' said Shaw later, 'I knew I had to do something. I wanted guiding home from Rose Linda's.'

He set about modifying the lenses used in road signs, having furtively removed a few in the name of research. 'I must have put them in the road 1000 different ways. It was all a matter of trial and error.'

Eventually he hit upon the winning formula and in 1935 formed Reflecting Road Studs Ltd, building a new factory at Boothtown, Halifax, in the grounds of his house to produce his invention. Each 'eye' is a lens of crystal glass, set so as to catch a car's headlights. The rubber pad from which the catseyes shine is clipped into a cast iron base, buried in the road. The pad's hollow walls are cut so that when a car rides over it, rubber eyelids close, wiping away any dust and on wet days, washing the eyes.

Shaw received his first order for 36 studs for a pedestrian crossing at Baldon in Yorkshire and then in 1937 the Ministry of Transport laid an experimental 5-mile stretch of road using ten different types of reflective studs. After two years, the only ones still in full working order were Percy Shaw's catseyes.

As orders poured in, Shaw's factory produced half a million catseyes a year. Many were for export since Shaw did not trust foreigners and therefore would not permit manufacture under licence overseas.

A self-made millionaire, Percy Shaw retained that quintessential British eccentricity. He never married and lived in the same house from the age of two right up until his death in 1976, aged 86. He owned a Rolls-Royce and had four television sets in the lounge yet the house possessed neither carpets nor curtains. He believed that carpets retained unpleasant smells and cigarette ash while curtains would deny him the view of his beloved Yorkshire. His favourite programmes were wrestling and Moira Anderson, a combination rarely spoken of in the same breath. Even the factory bore testimony to his unusual business methods. When it was built, he made sure that the workmen spared the sycamore tree he climbed as a child. And this building, manufacturing a worldwide product of paramount importance to road safety, still operates with a tree poking through the roof.

Cellophane

In 1908 Dr Jacques Edwin Brandenburger, a Swiss chemist, invented a film from regenerated cellulose that was both thin and flexible. The new film was named cellophane ('phane' meaning 'showing through') and manufacture was undertaken by a French company, La Cellophane, in 1912.

Prior to the First World War, which temporarily halted further development, cellophane was primarily used for wrapping luxury articles. Indeed the early cellophane was an expensive item itself and was not even moisture-proof.

Resistance to moisture was finally achieved in 1926 through the work of Charch and Prindle, two chemists with the American firm Du Pont, who added a thin layer of varnish to the film. As a result, cellophane was soon in great demand for wrapping sweets and cigarette packets. The first major brand of cigarettes to use cellophane was Craven A, followed in the early 1930s by Kensitas and Player's. In their advertisements, the

Love is . . . discussing the joys of cellophane.

manufacturers of these brands underlined the greater protection and improved appearance offered by wrapping in cellophane, Kensitas going so far as to demonstrate their wrapped packs in water. There was no danger of soggy cigarettes with cellophane.

An important innovation of the time was the tear-tape, first introduced by Wrigley's chewing gum in 1931 and which consisted of a cellulose strip laminated to the film wrapper. So popular did it become that four years later, Cavender's Gold Leaf cigarettes brought out a red tear-tape for easier location on the pack.

Today cellophane is used for wrapping a multitude of items and has been joined in the market-place by newer materials, resulting from research into plastics. Thicker cellulose film has been employed for wrapping prepacked fruit since the early 1950s while an even more recent development has been that of clingwraps. Usually made of PVC (polyvinylchloride), these are strong and shrink-tight, making them ideal for wrapping foodstuffs. Clingwraps were first introduced commercially in the United States in 1958, marking the entry of vinyls into the field of packaging, and by 1962 that country had produced 23 000 tons of PVC film. It has since proved invaluable in wrapping sandwiches, covering dishes in the refrigerator and even making last night's leftovers look palatable.

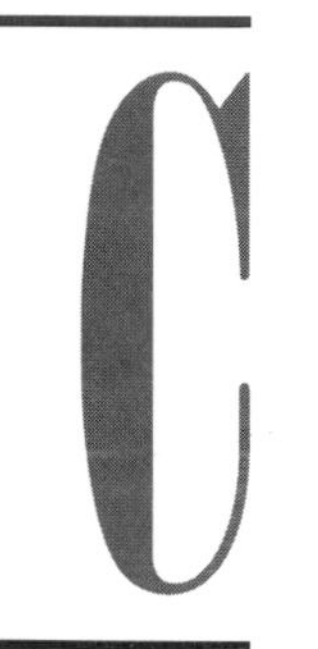

Chanel No. 5

Probably the world's most famous perfume was created in 1921 by Frenchman Ernest Beaux. He submitted various samples to French fashion queen, Gabrielle 'Coco' Chanel, and it was the fifth which she chose. So she decided to name her new fragrance after this number which, in any case, had apparently always brought luck to the one-time orphaned peasant girl.

It certainly did here for Chanel No. 5, launched in Europe in 1921 and in the United States four years later, soon became a symbol of elegance with a fragrance described as 'utterly seductive'. It developed into a worldwide best-seller, buyers attracted by the design of the bottle which was a perfect reflection of the style which made her international reputation and by the suggestion that Mlle Chanel had tried and rejected four other fragrances before deciding that this was the one which was good enough to market. Realising this, she followed No. 5 with No. 19 and No. 22 but neither achieved anything like the same success. It was a gimmick that worked only the once.

The famous bottle, Chanel No. 5.

An early choc ice from Wall's.

Choc Ice

On leaving the University of Nebraska, Christian K. Nelson teamed up with another young man to purchase a small confectionery store in Onowa, Iowa. One day in 1921 a small boy came in to the shop and was undecided whether to buy an ice cream cone or a bar of chocolate.

The boy's lengthy deliberations gave Nelson food for thought. It occurred to him that the boy really wanted to buy chocolate and ice cream but could not afford both. Since neither item was expensive at the time, Nelson was convinced that there should be some way of satisfying the child's desire without requiring him to make two purchases.

So, Nelson experimented over a period of several months, initially using milk chocolate bars as a coating for the ice cream and then adopting the more traditional chocolate coating we know today. Satisfied with the latter, he put the world's first choc ice on the market in the autumn of 1921, christening it the Eskimo Pie.

With the major advantage of not sticking to the wrapper like plain ice cream, Nelson's startling new invention was a great success. It soon spread to Europe where in June 1926 the British ice cream industry's monthly magazine eulogised: 'Coating ice bricks with chocolate is certainly one of the brain waves in ice cream history. That two sweetmeats of such dissimilar natures and at such different temperatures as ice cream and melted chocolate could be induced to amalgamate into a comfortably stable and marketable article is something in the nature of a miracle.'

Cluedo

Could that upstanding military gentleman Colonel Mustard be leading a double life? When he ventures abroad, does he swap his tweeds and army boots for a floral dress and stilettos? For in Switzerland he is known as Madame Curry. Then again his colleagues also travel under a number of unusual aliases. In France the Rev. Green changes profession to Dr Olive; Miss Scarlett calls herself Fröken Röd in Scandinavia; and in Brazil the chameleon-like Professor Plum becomes Professor Black. The names may change but in Cluedo the language of murder is international.

The world-famous whodunnit board game was devised by English solicitor's clerk Anthony E. Pratt in 1944. Mr Pratt, who described himself as 'an introvert full of ruminations, speculations and imaginative notions', joined forces with his wife, a competent amateur artist. She did the drawings and it is on her designed board that the game is still played today.

After spending hours perfecting the mechanics of the game, Mr and Mrs Pratt visited Waddingtons in Leeds to discuss the possibilities for its manufacture. They were accompanied by their friends, Mr and Mrs Bull, who had already invented a successful game, Buccaneer. Waddingtons personnel were invited to join the four in the first public game of Cluedo which was played in the office of Norman Watson, the then managing director, in 1947. He sat and watched and almost immediately recognised a winner.

Due to post-war shortages of various materials, the game was not finally launched until 1949. But it has more than made up for lost time, being sold in 73 countries with sales exceeding 50 million sets worldwide. Enough rope has been included in these sets to encircle the world (over 47 000 miles/75 000 km)! With six characters, six weapons and nine rooms, there are a potential 324 different murder combinations.

Even though no self-respecting criminal would any longer be seen armed with a piece of lead piping, the game has managed to retain its appeal. In 1990 the first World Cluedo Championships took place in Torquay and amateur sleuths can take part in live Cluedo weekends. Cluedo has been the subject of a British TV game show, a stage play and a Hollywood movie, starring Tim Curry and Madeline Kahn. The film was entitled 'Clue' — in the USA, the game is known as 'Clue' and in Brazil 'Detective'.

Another curiosity is that in America, the perpetual victim, Dr Black, is known as Mr Boddy. And thereby hangs the biggest mystery of all. While millions have discovered who committed the murder (personally I find it is usually Rev. Green), where and by what means, nobody has the faintest idea why the unfortunate Dr Black was killed in the first place.

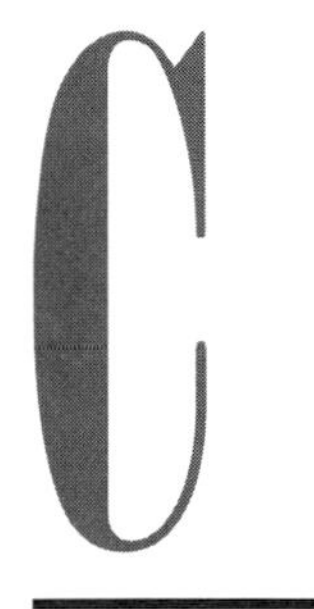

CLUEDO — SUSPECT CARDS and MURDER VICTIM

United Kingdom	Mrs. Peacock	Miss Scarlett	Mrs White	Col. Mustard	Rev. Green	Prof. Plum	Dr. Black
Belgium / France	Mme. Pervenche	Mademoiselle Rose	Mme. Leblanc	Colonel Moutarde	Dr. Olive	Prof. Violet	Dr. Lenoir
Netherlands	Mevr. Peacock	Mej. Scarlett	Mevr. White	Kolonel Mustard	Dominee Green	Prof. Plum	Dr. Black
Germany	Baronin von Porz	Fräulein Ming	Frau Weiß	Oberst von Gatow	Herr Dir. Grün	Prof. Bloom	Der Hausherr
Switzerland	Capitano Azurro Capitaine Azurro	Evelyne Rose	Fräulein Weiss	Madame Curry	Professor Verde Professeur Verde	Dr. Dunkel	Herr Kludo Monsieur Cluedo
Italy	Signora Pavone	Miss Scarlett	Signora Bianchi	Colonello Mustard	Dottor Verde	Prof. Plum	Dr. Black
Portugal	Sra. de Corte-Real	Menina Isabel	Senhora Ana	Coronel Monteiro	Dr. Pacheco	Prof. Brandão	Doutor Neves
Spain	Profesora Rubio	Srta. Amapola	Sra. Prado	Marqués de Marina	Sr. Pizarro	Dr. Mandarino	Dr. Lemon
Greece	Ka. Pagoni	Dis. Floga	Ka. Aspru	Si. Mustardas	Aid. Prasinos	Kath. Damaskinos	—
Sweden / Finland / Denmark	Fru Blå	Fröken Röd	Fru Vit	Överste Senap	Pastor Grön	Prof. Plommen	—
Norway	Baronesse von Blauw	Frk. Ming	Fru Witt	Oberst Gulin	Direktør Grønn	Prof. Blom	—
South Africa	Mrs. Peacock	Miss Scarlett	Mrs. White	Col. Mustard	Mr. Green	Prof. Plum	Dr. Black
Australia / New Zealand	Mrs. Peacock	Miss Scarlett	Mrs. White	Col. Mustard	Rev. Green	Prof. Plum	Dr. Black
Philippines	Mrs. Peacock	Miss Scarlett	Mrs. White	Col. Mustard	Mr. Green	Prof. Plum	Mr. Boddy
Brazil	Dona Violeta	Srta. Rosa	Dona Branca	Cel. Mostarda	Sr. Marinho	Prof. Black	Dr. Pessoa
*Canada French	Mme. Peacock	Mlle Scarlett	Mme. White	Col. Mustard	M. Green	Prof. Plum	M. Boddy
English	Mrs. Peacock	Miss Scarlett	Mrs. White	Col. Mustard	Mr. Green	Prof. Plum	Mr. Boddy
USA	Mrs. Peacock	Miss Scarlett	Mrs. White	Col. Mustard	Mr. Green	Prof. Plum	Mr. Boddy
USA (Spanish Rules)	Sra. Pavorreal	Srita. Escarlata	Sra. Blanco	Cor. Mostaza	Sr. Verde	Prof. Ciruela	Sr. Caddaver

*Canada: Bilingual cards, board, notes, rules.

Compact Cassette

One of the principal challenges in the development of the tape recorder during the 1950s was to reduce its size and thereby increase its versatility. After all, it would have taken a spy of gargantuan proportions to have concealed a huge old-fashioned tape recorder about his or her person.

The first step was taken around 1958 by RCA who put the cumbersome open reel of tape inside a sealed plastic box. This largely eliminated tape entanglement and also offered instant loading and unloading. However, the box was still horribly unwieldy and RCA's tape cartridges were superseded in 1963 by a true compact cassette introduced by the Dutch firm Philips.

At one-sixteenth of the size of the RCA cartridge, the Philips cassette was a veritable breakthrough. The first compact cassette, the C60, was launched at that year's Berlin Radio Show and gave 30 minutes' playing time per side. The cassette was blank (pre-recorded versions came later) and whilst it proved satisfactory for recording speech, it left a lot to be desired when recording music. Many of these problems were eliminated with the advent of the Dolby system (invented by American Raymond Dolby) which considerably reduced the surface hiss on cassettes.

Philips introduced the first cassette recorder — the Model 150 Carry-Corder — in 1964. It was the first real battery-operated portable tape recorder, previous so-called portables having required large batteries which were eaten up extremely quickly. Although just too large to fit in a pocket, the Model 150 slotted neatly into an attache case.

In order to encourage the spread of the new system throughout the world, Philips allowed other manufacturers to use its patent free of charge. The compact cassette was to make motoring — and spying — infinitely more comfortable.

Compact Disc

From looking forward to working to a ripe old age, the long-playing record has found itself unceremoniously forced into early retirement. No speeches of thanks for services rendered, no golden handshake — just a mass clearing of the decks and a realisation that future public appearances will be restricted to church bazaars and car boot sales.

The reason for the swift demise of the LP is the advent of the compact disc. Although the compact disc had barely been heard of ten years ago, it has certainly not been a story of overnight success. Philips began working on the concept of a laser disc as far back as 1969 but the company's efforts only started to come to fruition when it pooled its resources and knowledge with Japanese giants Sony. For while Philips created the video disc system, it was Sony who researched the error correction circuitry which helps to ensure proper sound reproduction even when the disc is subjected to fingerprints or dust.

In 1980 the digital audio system, to give it its proper title, was unveiled by Sony at the Japan Audio Fair. At first, the discs were referred to as digital audio discs but the acronym of DADs was slow to catch on and so they became known instead as compact discs (CDs).

Carrying some 75 minutes' uninterrupted playing time (no need to switch sides like an LP), the grooveless 12 cm discs had the added benefit of being virtually indestructible. Not only were they said to be immune to scratches (the plague of their predecessor), it was claimed that you could walk on them or even smear them with honey without causing any damage. But above all, the sound quality was infinitely better. Celebrated conductor Herbert von Karajan declared of the new system: 'All else is gaslight.'

The compact disc player was finally launched in Japan in October 1982 although the silver disc was not available commercially until the following year. The price of the playing decks was between £450 and £549 — twice as much as a good hi-fi system — and so not surprisingly the compact disc was slow to catch on. Perhaps not all music-lovers saw the benefit of being able to smear honey on their favourite recordings.

In 1986 Dire Straits' 'Brothers In Arms' became the first CD to sell a million copies worldwide. From that point on, the rise of the compact disc has been irresistible. Devotees of the LP have reluctantly been forced to concede defeat in the vinyl countdown.

Contraceptive Pill

In 1941 American Russell Marker discovered *lithospermum ruderale*, a plant that contained the hormone progesterone and which for centuries had been used by the Mexicans as a contraceptive. Nine years later, Dr Gregory Pincus of the Worcester Foundation for Experimental Biology at Shrewsbury, Massachusetts, commenced research on behalf of the Planned Parenthood Movement to produce a form of contraceptive that would be 'harmless, entirely reliable, simple, practical, universally applicable and aesthetically satisfactory to both husband and wife'.

Over the next five years, Pincus and his colleague, Dr John Rock, worked on an oral contraceptive from progesterone and oestrogen. The first serious testing of the new pill was carried out in 1956 at San Juan in Puerto Rico where 1308 women involved in a slum-clearance project volunteered to act as guinea pigs. At the end of a three-year trial period, only 17 of the 830 women still taking part had become pregnant. There was also an attempt to try the Pill out on men but after one subject developed swollen testicles, the idea was scrapped.

The first Pill, Enovid 10, produced by the G.D. Searle Drug Company of Skokie, Illinois, was marketed commercially in the United States in August 1960. Meanwhile in the United Kingdom, Searle were conducting tests on 50 Birmingham women. Since the only previous contraceptive available was the cap, there was no shortage of volunteers, all of whom had to be married with at least one living child and had to have sex at least once a week. On 30 January 1961 the Pill became available in the UK and by June 1963 it was available on prescription.

Needless to say, its arrival greatly disturbed the guardians of morality. Although it assisted enormously in the liberation of women, the Pill was seen in many quarters as a passport to promiscuity. The Family Planning Association adopted a wary stance, refusing to offer advice on contraception to single women unless they had either an engagement ring or a date for the wedding!

An early advertisement for birth control.

But the most far-reaching condemnation came from the Catholic Church. In 1965 Pope Paul VI told the United Nations General Assembly that its task was 'to make certain that there is enough bread at the banquet of life' and not that of 'stimulating birth control by artificial means'. The Papal opposition to the Pill was emphasised in the encyclical 'Humanae Vitae' of 1968 but surveys revealed that a large percentage of Catholics were defying the edict.

The Pill has remained a highly controversial innovation, both on health and moral grounds, but not all ladies have been able to express their views on it with such eloquence. Take Tanya, a hippopotamus at Amsterdam Zoo, who was put on the Pill because of her unfortunate tendency of squashing her offspring to death. Alas, the Pill had no effect and could not prevent Tanya giving birth for the 16th time.

Cordless Phone

On 17 June 1946 a mobile telephone commercial service was introduced by the Southwestern Bell Telephone Company of St Louis, receivers being put in the cars of two subscribers, the Monsanto Chemical Company and a contractor, Henry L. Perkinson. The following year, US Ambassador James Clement Dunn was able to speak in Milan on a car phone to Vincent Impellitteri, the president of New York City Council, to celebrate Marconi Day at the Milan Fair.

In conjunction with Fidelity, British Telecom launched the 'Hawk', Britain's first cordless phone in April 1983. Costing £170, it operated via a radio linking the mobile extension set with the customer's phone line which could be anything up to 600 ft (180 m) away. This offered the enormous benefit of allowing the user to make and take calls while lounging in the bath, a corner of the house previously immune to Bell's invention.

As the go-getting eighties progressed, the arrival of car phones and mobile phones meant that business could be conducted absolutely anywhere — on a train, in a traffic jam, up a tree. Whole deals have probably been sealed while queueing for the checkout at Marks & Spencer. The telephone even infringed on the field of sport. In 1989 it was reported that a number of dropped catches at a cricket match in Hampshire were attributed to fielders answering calls on their mobile phones!

Correction Fluid

At first sight, any link between the Monkees pop group and correction fluid would appear to be negligible. But a fact no doubt hidden from their fans was that the white wonder liquid was invented by Bette Nesmith Graham, mother of former Monkee Michael Nesmith.

When she was 17, Bette applied for a job as a secretary with a Dallas law firm even though she could not type. But the company liked her, packed her off to secretarial school and by 1951, she was working as an executive secretary at the Texas Bank and Trust. Her typing was still hopeless, particularly when confronted with one of the new electrical machines, but rather than risk losing her job, she thought up an ingenious way of covering up her mistakes.

She had once helped out with the design of the windows at the bank and had observed how the lettering artists always painted over any errors. 'So I decided to use what artists use. I put some tempera waterbase paint in a bottle and took my watercolour brush to the office. And I used that to correct my typing mistakes.'

Over the next five years, Bette willingly came to the rescue of colleagues in similar distress with her white 'Mistake Out' liquid. The formula was improved with a little help from the chemistry teacher at Michael's school and in 1956 Bette offered her invention to IBM. They rejected it and so, changing the name to 'Liquid Paper', she began a cottage industry, using the family kitchen as a laboratory and the garage as a bottling plant. The bottles themselves could hardly be described as uniform, many being old ketchup and mustard containers filled by Michael and his pals. Even so, by the end of 1957, she was selling 100 bottles of Liquid Paper a month.

Soon correction fluid became big business. One of the leading brands today is Snopake, early advertisements portraying a pretty, smiling secretary supported by the caption: 'She may seem perfect . . . but wait until she has the new Snopake.' Apart from those who thought it was nail varnish, correction fluid was greeted gleefully by typists who could suddenly repair mistakes without the boss even noticing. For many years, substantial quantities of Snopake were sold to the British government, they obviously making more mistakes than most.

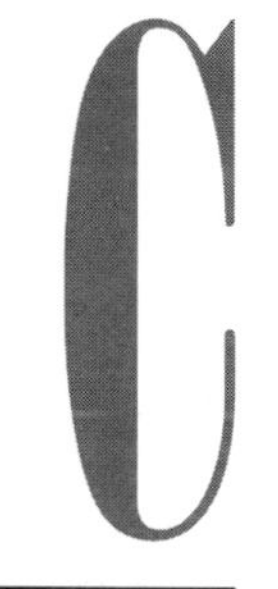

Correction fluid, that essential item of office equipment.

Credit Card

That invaluable piece of plastic, the credit card, was invented by American Ralph Scheider in 1950. Operating in New York, it permitted the cardholders, who were all members of a special Diner's Club, to eat in 27 of the city's restaurants and pay later.

The scheme was so simple that others were bound to follow suit and in 1958, the Bank of America came up with the first bank card, the Bankamericard. In the same year, American Express was launched in the US although it did not allow settlement in sterling until it arrived in Britain on 10 September 1963. At that time, some 3000 establishments in the UK already accepted American Express cards but only for those who could pay their accounts in dollars. As far as the British were concerned, an American Express card was very much a luxury item. To join cost £3 12s. 0d. a year but more prohibitive was the stipulation that members had to earn a minimum of £2000 per annum, a sizable amount in those days.

Nevertheless, it was successful enough to alert the British banks and on 29 June 1966, Barclaycard was born. Cards were sent out to one million customers with 30 000 retailers agreeing to join the scheme. Fears were expressed that credit cards would raise prices but Mr R.J. Knight, manager of the domestic division of Mercantile Credit Bank, confidently predicted: 'It has been estimated that by the year 2000 credit cards will have taken over and money will only be used as petty cash.'

Such faith seemed misplaced as, to put it mildly, the new form of credit was a slow burner. By the end of the year, only an additional 5000 retailers were prepared to accept Barclaycard, leading one Barclays executive to comment that it was 'met with a tidal wave of indifference'. To add to Barclays' woes, no computer was large enough to deal with all the vouchers which came into the Barclaycard offices so they had to be flown to Germany for processing. Not surprisingly, therefore, the entire operation initially ran at a loss. It is fair to say that in that respect at least, times have changed.

Crossword Puzzle

As a child in Liverpool, Arthur Wynne had remembered his father entertaining him with a Victorian parlour game called 'Magic Square'. So when Wynne emigrated to America and landed a job in the Tricks and Jokes Department of the *New York World*, he called upon his childhood experiences to devise what he called a 'word-cross'. The first one appeared on 21 December 1913 beneath the word 'FUN' since it was set on the 'Fun' page of the paper.

To be honest, the 32 clues were not exactly demanding. Among the examples were 'What bargain hunters enjoy', 5 letters (sales), 'A boy', 3 letters (lad) and 'An animal of prey', 4 letters (lion). Whilst it may not have taxed today's *Times* commuter expert for more than one station, Wynne's puzzle proved sufficiently popular with his readers for him to be asked to compile more. Readers began to send in their own examples and by January 1914, the name had changed to 'cross-word'.

In 1921 Margaret Petherbridge assumed the role of editing the *New York World*'s crosswords and it was she who introduced the single-number clue, replacing Wynne's '5–6' style. The following year, in February 1922, the new word sensation came to Britain where *Pearson's Magazine* described it as 'a new form of puzzle in the shape of a word square', adding enthusiastically: 'These new word squares are having a tremendous vogue in America just now.'

The craze reached the ears of American publishers Simon and Schuster who, in 1924, brought out a book of 50 crosswords which came with a free pencil and rubber. Unable to resist such bounteous gifts, the American public turned the book into a best-seller although it is interesting to note that Simon and Schuster had been so concerned about its possible failure that they had published it under the name of the Plaza Publishing Company, Plaza being the name of their telephone exchange.

By now, the crossword had replaced mah-jong as America's most popular game. It made its debut in a British newspaper when the *Sunday Express* printed a crossword sold to them by one C.W. Shepherd on 2 November 1924. The introduction read: 'Here is the great new pastime which it may be predicted with confidence will be the rage of England as soon as it becomes known.' Sadly, Mr Shepherd had bought the crossword from the United States and had failed to notice that one of the answers was the American spelling 'honor'. The day before publication, the *Sunday Express* asked him to alter it to the British spelling which necessitated a multitude of changes to the puzzle. And in the end, the paper decided to leave out that clue altogether! Mr Shepherd tried not to get too down . . .

The surge of the crossword continued unabated. An American railway company put dictionaries in carriages to assist the perplexed. On 1 July 1925, *Punch* magazine observed that the crossword had been 'the dominant feature of our social life in these last six months. Its appeal to the British bosom has been universal. It touched all classes, because it made demands upon a modicum of intelligence common to them all'. Perhaps this was why it was popular with politicians, Stanley Baldwin declaring himself a fan.

But as with most crazes, this one had its downside and soon there were reports of two New York magistrates having to ration addicts to a maximum of two puzzles a day after the defendants had been found guilty of neglecting to support their families. The President of the British Optical Association feared that crosswords might cause eye strain and headaches although this claim was countered by the Chicago Department of Health who believed that solving crosswords gave people a mental stimulus which was good for their health and happiness. However, a 1925 Broadway revue entitled 'Puzzles of 1925' featured a scene in a 'Crossword Puzzle Sanatorium' for those who had been driven insane by the craze. In Britain at least, the crossword was largely despised by intellectuals. When even *The Times* succumbed on 1 February 1930, the newspaper received numerous protests about lowering of standards. One correspondent wrote: 'I hate to see a great newspaper pandering to the modern craze for passing the time in all kinds of stupid ways.' *The Times* attempted to maintain a degree of respectability by printing crosswords in Latin and Greek. When the same paper held its first National Crossword Competition in 1970, it attracted 33 000 entries.

Arthur Wynne's first 'word-cross' puzzle

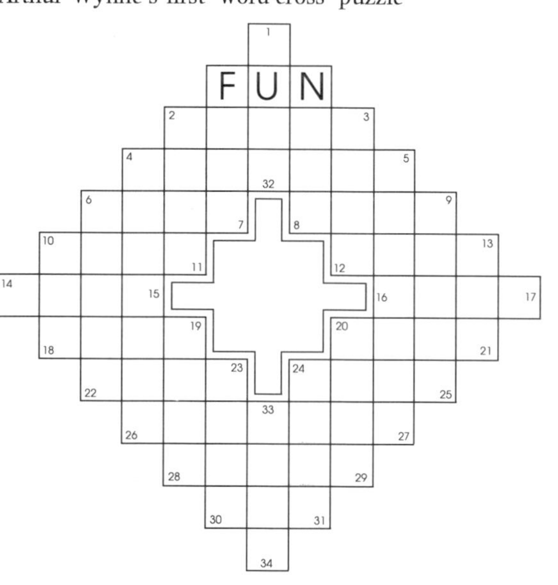

2–3. What bargain hunters enjoy.
4–5. A written acknowledgment.
18–19. What this puzzle is.
22–23. An animal of prey.
26–27. The close of a day.
28–29. To elude.
30–31. The plural of is.
8–9. To cultivate.
12–13. A bar of wood or iron.
16–17. What artists learn to do.
20–21. Fastened.
24–25. Found on the seashore.
10–18. The fiber of the gomuti palm.
6–22. What we all should be.

6–7. Such and nothing more.
10–11. A bird.
14–15. Opposed to less.
4–26. A day dream.
2–11. A talon.
19–28. A pigeon.
F–7. Part of your head.
23–30. A river in Russia.
1–32. To govern.
33–34. An aromatic plant.
N–8. A fist.
24–31. To agree with.
3–12. Part of a ship.
20–29. One.
5–27. Exchanging.
9–25. To sink in mud.
13–21. A boy.

It was probably the advent of the cryptic clue, pioneered by the likes of Edward Powys Mathers (alias 'Torquemada' of the *Observer*), which finally earned the crossword approval from even the upper echelons of society. Queen Mary expressed her interest while Queen Elizabeth II is said to be an admirer of the *Daily Telegraph* puzzle and Princess Margaret has won prizes for completing the crossword in *Country Life*. Anyone who doubts the addictive nature of the 'word square' should consider the tale of the Fijian woman who wrote to *The Times* in May 1966 informing them that she had just completed their crossword from the issue dated 4 April 1932.

Detergent

Where hard water prevails, scum-forming soap is not always the most efficient of cleansing agents. Thus a significant step forward in the easing of the washday blues was the discovery of synthetic detergents.

The Belgian A. Rechler was one of the first to reveal the superior cleaning power of chemical detergents in 1913 but it was another three years before a product became commercially available. Then, with soap in short supply because of the war, the Germans brought out Nekal A. Since it needed rubbing, Nekal A was not very good at actually removing dirt which was seen by some as something of a drawback in a detergent. In fact, it found its niche in the textile industry for washing wool.

The growth of the oil industry in the 1930s resulted in detergents made from a mineral source but the shortage of oils and fats caused by the Second World War necessitated the exploration of new fields. (Ironically, one of the main uses of detergents nowadays is for breaking up oil slicks at sea.)

In 1942 a liquid synthetic detergent, Teepol, appeared on the market, followed two years later by Lissapol N, the first synthetic detergent to be made from coal gas. Whilst these products were suitable for light-duty washing (woollens or crockery), they could not handle heavy-duty items such as whites, sheets or pillowcases.

In the early 1950s, detergents manufactured from a petroleum derivative, alkylbenzene, appeared on the market and rapidly established themselves as viable alternatives to soap and soap powders. Then in the 1960s, the biological revolution came to Britain whereby enzymes were added to detergents to help remove blood and other awkward protein stains. There were even products to remove 'those unmentionable stains'. The washday blues were banished for good.

Dettol

In the years following the First World War, concern was expressed about the high rate of illness and death from puerperal sepsis (childbirth fever) and in the late 1920s the British government's Minister of Health appointed a committee of eminent obstetricians to investigate the problem. One of the chief anxieties surrounded the use of antiseptics in midwifery. Most of the antiseptics of the time were poisonous irritants and the committee reported in 1932 that the most commonly used antiseptic was too irritating to the skin for routine use and in solution was too weak to kill microbes.

Happily, during the committee's deliberations, a new product was undergoing a two-year clinical trial at a London maternity hospital, the results of which showed a reduction of over 50 per cent in cases of puerperal sepsis. The product was called Dettol.

Non-poisonous, non-staining and kind to the skin, Dettol was launched in 1933 by Reckitt & Sons. Hailed as 'The New Safe Germicide', the 1s. bottle with the familiar sword on the label bought lasting protection 'even in the hands of a child'. It was an undiluted success, considered such an essential part of the war effort that production was switched from Hull on the east coast to a less vulnerable spot at Skipton in North Yorkshire. As well as its widespread application in military hospitals, Dettol was used in the Women's Services as an antiseptic addition to hair shampoo and many people even enjoyed putting it in their baths.

As Dettol began to serve animals as well as humans, it was also exported overseas (in South America it is known as Espadol). In France they advised: 'Tuez les germes d'infection septique avec Dettol.' And whether it be in leper settlements in the tropics or Antarctic expeditions, the sign of the sword has been a symbol of safety the world over.

A 1930s promotion for Dettol.

Digital Watch

One of the products that resulted from the compact electronic revolution of the 1960s was the digital quartz watch in which the time is kept by tiny quartz crystals oscillating at 32 768 cycles per second.

Experiments with liquid crystal devices were conducted throughout the sixties, primarily by John Bergey, an engineer at the Hamilton Watch Company, Lancaster, Pennsylvania. In 1966 George Theiss, president of a small electronics company in a suburb of Dallas, saw an LED (light emitting diode) display and immediately knew that this was the display required to construct a digital electronic watch. Soon he teamed up with engineer Willy Crabtree and together they produced the world's first digital wrist watch — the Pulsar — in 1971.

The quartz mechanism means that the most digital watches gain or lose is five seconds a month, making them more accurate than anything produced in 500 years of mechanical timekeeping.

Dinky Toy

For many boys raised in the fifties and sixties, there was only one thing to spend your pocket money on — Dinky toys. The splendid range of vehicles captured the imagination of millions and made the Dinky toy a veritable British institution.

It was in 1932 that Meccano Ltd introduced a small series of 'modelled miniature' vehicles, intended purely as accessories for the company's blossoming Hornby train sets. There were six in total — a motor truck, delivery van, tractor, tank, sports car and sports coupé. When these were snapped up by eager youths in short trousers, Meccano wasted no time in meeting public demand and in 1934 the Dinky line was born. Among other early vehicles were an ambulance (1934), Daimler (1935), Rolls-Royce (1935), Chrysler 'Airflow' Saloon (1935), Mercedes Benz (1936) and Austin 7 (1936). In 1937 a collection of six British cars cost 5s. 6d., single models being available for 9d. or 1s. One of the original

A display of early Dinky toys.

1934 models, a Pickford's van, was sold in 1978 for £370.

Through the 1930s Dinky toys spread their wings to include ships of the British Navy, aircraft and military vehicles in camouflage colours. Dinky also attempted to break into the girls' toy market with Dolly Varden's range of dolls' houses and furniture but this venture proved spectacularly unsuccessful.

With sales boosted by *Meccano Magazine*, Dinky enjoyed a halcyon period during the 1950s and 1960s. When the Liverpool factory eventually closed in 1979, over 1000 different Dinky toys had rolled off the production line. Now manufactured in Spain, the name of Dinky still holds a universal appeal. In 1993 a mint condition two-tone Foden tanker, purchased in the 1950s, was sold to a Californian at a Guildford auction for a world record £4830.

Directory Enquiry in London answer customers' calls in 1949.

Directory Enquiry

Credit where credit is due. It used to be said that in Britain at least, you could cook a three-course meal while waiting for Directory Enquiry to answer. But stung by the criticism, the service has improved enormously to the point where operators now pounce upon the caller with the hunting instinct of the average menswear salesman.

Directory Enquiry was first introduced in New York on 1 April 1906. In the UK, local information desks dealt with queries at first but it was something of a haphazard affair and the arrangement was eventually abandoned. A more specialised service was instituted and Directory Enquiry staff in London were issued with the following information: The London Telephone Directory (incidentally the 1884 edition had included the names of W.S. Gilbert and Sir Arthur Sullivan); a card index of addition and alteration to the directory since the last issue; a card index of ex-directory subscribers; an

D

'Official' Telephone Directory (for official use only); a telephone directory of government departments; and Kelly's London Directory (used when just the address was known). Not only did having to look through a list of names in a directory cause severe eye strain, it was also exceedingly time-consuming, particularly with the supplementary cards. And in the early 1930s, there were in the region of 400 alterations and additions a day to the London Directory. In 1933 it was calculated that the average time to solve an inquiry was 130 seconds — and this was a marked improvement!

At first, Britain had boy operators but these were deemed to be 'too high-spirited' and were replaced by genteel women who had to be at least 5 ft 3 in (1.59 cm) tall (so as to reach the top of the switchboard) and have no speech impediment or accent. Applicants had to be single and were expected to resign if they got married. The rallying advertising call emphasised that this was a job for a gal of breeding, adding as an extra inducement: 'Here indeed is an occupation to which no heavy-handed father could object.' Unless of course he had to hear the torrent of abuse his daughter was sometimes subjected to by impatient callers.

D

Disc Jockey

In some quarters, disc jockeys are considered to be just about the lowest form of human life, in company with used-car salesmen, tabloid journalists and estate agents. But it was not always so and Britain's very first disc jockey, Christopher Stone, the Oxford-educated son of a vicar, possessed a distinctive style that earned him a place in public affection.

He landed the job by being in the right studio at the right time. It was Compton Mackenzie who should have been making the historic broadcast but he had gone off on an expedition and so his place was taken by Stone, his brother-in-law. Thus on 7 July 1927, Christopher Stone presented records from the BBC's Studio 3 at Savoy Hill.

In the early days, Stone, who grew to detest the term 'disc jockey', was not paid for his endeavours but instead was permitted to plug *The Gramophone* magazine which he edited in association with Mackenzie. Becoming sensitive to such blatant promotion at an early age, the BBC later withdrew the plug and agreed to pay Stone five guineas a time in lieu. On his death in 1965, *The Times* wrote: 'He set a fashion in broadcasting and pioneered the curious and exclusive profession based on the simple act of spinning a disc on a turntable and talking amiably and informatively about it.'

Stone himself had once said: 'I never had any words written down. I insisted on being free to meander along in my own fashion and tell a few personal stories prompted by the records I played.'

Christopher Stone's era was a far cry from 1992 when a Connecticut teenager became so infuriated with a disc jockey playing the same record over and over again that he went to the studio and shot him dead.

Discotheque

The modern successor to the dance hall derives its name from the French for 'record library'. The French were very much the pioneers of these new establishments and as early as 1962, the youth of Paris were demonstrating the dance craze of the time, the Twist, in small, dimly lit premises.

By the mid-sixties, discotheques had crossed the Atlantic where they tended to be little more than sleazy taverns with a juke-box and a scantily clad dancer in a cage. This was not what the British later came to expect from the High Street Top Rank. Besides, where would you find a cage in Watford?

The music played was traditionally black (Tamla Motown or soul) until the disco boom of the 1970s encompassed groups such as the Bee Gees and films like *Saturday Night Fever*. John Travolta's performance in that movie inspired the first World Disco Dancing Championships held in London in 1978 and won by Japan's Takaaki Dan. It also inspired a new mode of discotheque behaviour. No longer were girls happy to shuffle around their handbags while boys debated whether another trip to the bar might mean missing out on the rush for the 'slow one'. Instead, the dance floor resembled a dodgems track with exhibitionist youths launching into frenetically choreographed routines, contorting themselves into positions whereby they were in serious danger of being garrotted by their own cheap medallions. There was no room for the couple who merely wanted a slow smooch — they were shunted out of the way. It was the end of civilisation as we know it.

Disposable Nappy

One of the greatest revolutions in babycare in the 20th century has been the post-war switch from towelling nappies to disposable paper models which, at their most basic, consist of a shaped, absorbent pad of cellulose pulp. Recent figures indicate that in many countries 90 per cent of nappy changes are made with disposables, the figure in France being as high as 98 per cent. Yet in 1956 disposables held less than one per cent of the market.

A few products were around at that time, including Drypers and K.D.'s in the United States while in the UK, Paddipads had been introduced by Robinsons of Chesterfield back in November 1949. But because of their prohibitive price and tendency to leak, these paper nappies were only bought by mothers in an emergency.

It was in 1956 that Vic Mills, Director of Exploratory Development for Procter & Gamble in the US, looked after his newborn grandchild for a period. He hated cleaning nappies and asked some of his researchers to examine the practicality of paper versions which were worn inside plastic pants. The resultant product, featuring an absorbent pad, was tested in Dallas. It was an unfortunate choice. With an average maximum air temperature of 93°F (34°C), few mothers used plastic pants which made their offspring feel uncomfortable and brought them out in heat rashes.

Undeterred, the research team came up with a new, improved product. But to obtain the go-ahead for further market testing, they had to gain the approval of Gib Pleasants, the company's Vice-President of Research. Pleasants had initial reservations but was so impressed by the demonstration that, with words which will surely go down in the history of the disposable nappy, he ordered: 'Test that new diaper.'

The new model was duly tested in Rochester, New York, in March 1959, using both a tape-on and pin-on design. The latter, in particular, was enthusiastically received, parents considering it to be as good, if not better, than cloth nappies. So Procter & Gamble set about designing the machinery necessary for mass production. It was an exercise fraught with difficulties. Glue dripped everywhere and congealed with the dust from the wadding to block up the equipment.

At this stage, the prospective product still had no name. Tads, Solos and Larks were all rejected in favour of Pampers and in December 1961, Pampers were tested in Peoria, Illinois. Again the outcome was less than satisfactory for while mothers approved of Pampers, they did not like the price of 10 cents each. A price reduction to 6 cents plus better production methods brought about the breakthrough which Procter & Gamble were seeking and the disposable nappy began to make sizable inroads into towelling territory.

Yet even as late as 1980 there was some public resistance, principally because disposables did not yet have leg elastics and so leaks were often an occupational hazard. However, the technology of the 1980s solved this and other problems. Ultra nappies were introduced in 1987, enhanced by a substance called supersorber, a granular material able to absorb up to 28 times its own weight of water (compared to cellulose pulp which only absorbs up to four times its weight).

Nowadays, with Boy/Girl Pampers and models tailored to meet every stage of development, any baby would be proud to be seen out in a disposable nappy.

Disposable nappies have proved a boon for babies and parents alike.

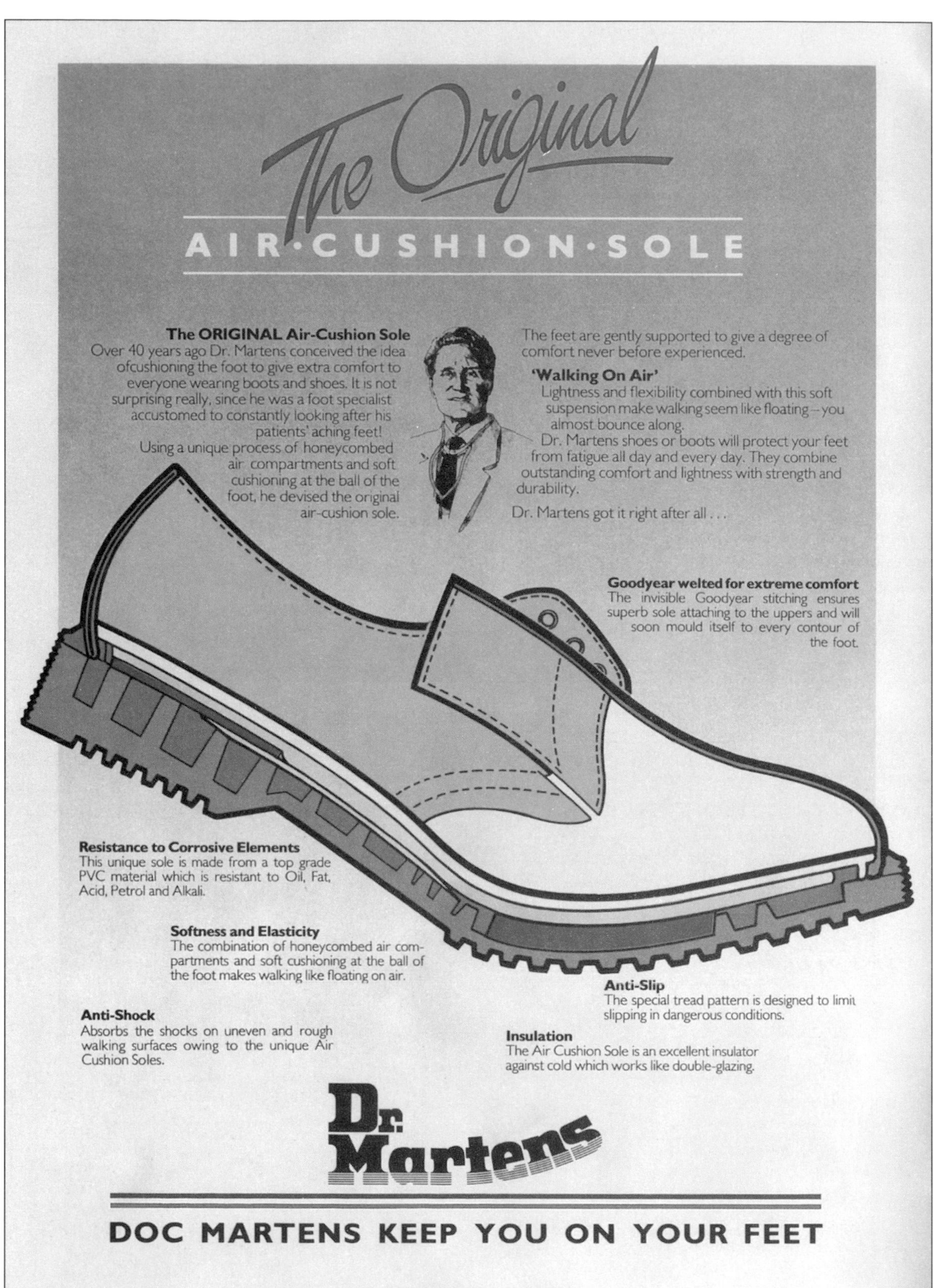
The Original
AIR·CUSHION·SOLE
The ORIGINAL Air-Cushion Sole
Over 40 years ago Dr. Martens conceived the idea of cushioning the foot to give extra comfort to everyone wearing boots and shoes. It is not surprising really, since he was a foot specialist accustomed to constantly looking after his patients' aching feet!
Using a unique process of honeycombed air compartments and soft cushioning at the ball of the foot, he devised the original air-cushion sole.
The feet are gently supported to give a degree of comfort never before experienced.
'Walking On Air'
Lightness and flexibility combined with this soft suspension make walking seem like floating – you almost bounce along.
Dr. Martens shoes or boots will protect your feet from fatigue all day and every day. They combine outstanding comfort and lightness with strength and durability.
Dr. Martens got it right after all . . .
Goodyear welted for extreme comfort
The invisible Goodyear stitching ensures superb sole attaching to the uppers and will soon mould itself to every contour of the foot.
Resistance to Corrosive Elements
This unique sole is made from a top grade PVC material which is resistant to Oil, Fat, Acid, Petrol and Alkali.
Softness and Elasticity
The combination of honeycombed air compartments and soft cushioning at the ball of the foot makes walking like floating on air.
Anti-Slip
The special tread pattern is designed to limit slipping in dangerous conditions.
Anti-Shock
Absorbs the shocks on uneven and rough walking surfaces owing to the unique Air Cushion Soles.
Insulation
The Air Cushion Sole is an excellent insulator against cold which works like double-glazing.
Dr. Martens
DOC MARTENS KEEP YOU ON YOUR FEET
R. GRIGGS & CO. LIMITED
Wollaston, Wellingborough, Northamptonshire. Telephone: Wellingborough (0933) 665381 Telex No: 311219

D

Doc Martens

To most of us, Doc Martens are readily associated with the British 'bovver boy' image of the early 1970s, a menacing accessory worn with skinhead haircut and braces. The mere sight of the thick-soled boots brought fear to High Street and football terrace alike. The police would wait outside soccer grounds and confiscate the laces in the belief that no serious kicking could then take place. In April 1970 an Old Bailey judge went as far as to say: 'The mere wearing of such boots constitutes possessing offensive weapons.'

By a curious geographical twist, the boot which was to become such an unwelcome feature on the mean streets of industrial Britain was conceived on the gentle slopes of the Bavarian Alps. It was there in 1945 that Klaus Maertens, a Munich doctor, injured his foot while skiing. To alleviate the pain of walking, he made himself a very special pair of shoes. Using old tyres, he constructed soles that had air trapped within closed compartments, thereby cushioning the foot. The result was so effective that within two years they were patented and developed commercially by Maertens and an old student friend, Dr Herbert Funck.

The first orthopaedic shoes produced by Dr Maertens were made out of materials left over from the end of the war, notably sponge rubber and Igelit. The latter, which was generally used to repair old aircraft, was welded around the sponge rubber to ensure a smooth sole. They were manufactured in the town of Seeshaupt near Munich by what can only be described as an enthusiastic bunch of amateurs, including an organ builder, a musician and a locksmith.

By the late fifties, Maertens' shoes and boots were selling well throughout Germany, mainly in ladies' styles, and the two doctors considered expanding overseas. Maertens wanted to license production in the UK but the only footwear company interested was that of R. Griggs & Co. Ltd, Wollaston, Northamptonshire, who specialised in vulcanised rubber soles. The others regarded the product as a short-lived gimmick. Anglicising the name to 'Dr. Martens', Griggs thus brought out the first UK pair on 1 April 1960.

Griggs started selling the new 'Air Wair' shoes with bouncing soles to industry, the police and the Post Office, emphasising the durable qualities and resistance to oil, fat, acids, petrol and alkali. It was the eight-eyelet cherry red model which caught the attention of the 'bovver boy' but although the skinhead has long been consigned to the cult graveyard, Doc Martens have maintained a hold on the youth fashion scene. They have been customised by the addition of jewellery, girls wear them with frilly lace tops and they have partnered the creations of leading international fashion designers. They are even adored by Japanese tourists who make pilgrimages to London just to stock up on Doc Martens.

(left) The original Doc Martens — a far cry from the bovver boot beloved by skinheads.

Drambuie

Few products have been shrouded in as much secrecy as Drambuie. Although not commercially produced until 1906, the world-famous liqueur actually dates back to the Jacobite rebellion of 1745 and that romantic Scottish hero, Bonnie Prince Charlie.

On the run from the English, following his defeat at the Battle of Culloden and with a £30 000 price tag on his head, the Prince was offered refuge on the Isle of Skye by Captain John Mackinnon of Strathaird. Resisting the temptation to cash in on his house guest — in those days £30 000 was more than anyone could hope to earn in a lifetime — Mackinnon maintained the secrecy of the Prince's whereabouts. On parting, the Prince, with no valuables about his person, could only show his gratitude by revealing to Mackinnon the secret of his personal liqueur. He called it Drambuie, taken from the Gaelic 'dram' (drink) and 'buidh' (pleasing).

For the next 150 years, the Mackinnons kept the secret of Drambuie. But when Malcolm Mackinnon left Skye to become a partner in an Edinburgh whisky firm, he took with him the mystery recipe. Experimenting with jelly bags and copper pans, it took him two weeks to make sufficient Drambuie to fill a dozen bottles.

(above) Drambuie, a 20th-century innovation which owes its origins to Bonnie Prince Charlie.

It would be fair to say that when Drambuie finally went on sale to the public, orders came at a trickle rather than a flood. Only a dozen cases were sold in the first year. But Mackinnon persevered and by 1916, Drambuie had been accepted into the cellars of the House of Lords. If it was the First World War which saw the breakthrough for Drambuie — many Scotsmen stationed in France began to order it — it was the Second which severely halted production. With restrictions placed on the availability of fine old whiskies, an integral part of Drambuie, Mackinnon had no option but to limit its output. And he never saw production return to normal for he died before the end of the war.

Drambuie has since gone from strength to strength. It is served on the great transcontinental trains, on major shipping lines and on the world's airlines. It is sold everywhere from the Arctic wastes of Northern Canada to the southern tropics.

The company is still run by the Mackinnons and to the wife of the chairman falls the traditional responsibility of preparing the special essences that go into Drambuie. To this day, that recipe is known only to the Mackinnon family. It remains one of the world's most closely guarded secrets.

Durex

Italian anatomist Gabrielle Fallopius published the first known description of a condom back in 1564. It was made of linen cut to shape. However, the majority of early condoms were made from animal intestines which led Casanova, surely the finest advert imaginable for the product, to complain: 'I do not care to shut myself up in a piece of dead skin to prove that I am perfectly alive.'

For their part, the Japanese wore condoms made from tortoiseshell or thin leather until the development of the vulcanisation of rubber in 1844 changed the mating habits of a lifetime.

In the early part of the 20th century, most condoms were imported from Germany but in 1932 the first manufactured condom appeared when the London Rubber Company launched Durex, its name being derived from its three prime requisites: Durability, Reliability and Excellence.

When the Second World War broke out, the irony was that a number of British soldiers would be preparing for action stations, wearing German condoms. But German supplies were soon cut off and it was left to LRC to triple the output of Durex and thus cope with the insatiable appetite of the allied armed forces.

In 1957 Durex introduced the first lubricated condom and naturally enough the Swinging Sixties witnessed the arrival of vending machines, discreetly placed in gents' lavatories until in 1992, following the lead of Europe, they came out into the open at Nuneaton Bus Station.

Each Durex condom can hold approximately 40 litres of air, equivalent in volume to nine gallons of water, before bursting. It is calculated that nowadays over 40 million couples use sheaths regularly. In Japan they are sold door-to-door while such was the demand in that well-known fleshpot, Macclesfield, that the drains were blocked by thousands of used condoms. Something to look forward to is the musical condom which has already been patented in the United States. It is tone-sensitive and apparently any tune can be recorded. 'Johnny Remember Me' might be appropriate.

Something for the weekend, sir?

An early example of Elastoplast packaging.

Elastoplast

Children of the fifties will testify that the worst part about any cut or graze was having the Elastoplast removed afterwards. The fabric had that uncanny knack of seeming to take half your skin with it, as well as systematically plucking every hair from the surrounding area. And it always left that unsightly black square that took about a week to scrub off.

The common belief was that Elastoplast had been devised by the Spanish Inquisition as a method of torture for occasions when neither the rack nor the burning hot coals had the desired effect. In truth, it was developed at Hull in 1928 by Horatio Nelson Smith, nephew of the founder of a pharmaceutical group.

Sceptics thought the new elastic adhesive bandage would be too costly but it found favour with a young surgeon who discovered that bedridden patients with varicose ulcers were able to move around with the support of the bandage. In an inspired move, Smith had 40 000 copies of an article detailing the benefits of Elastoplast printed and circulated among the medical profession. He took Elastoplast to every consultant in London's Harley Street and as doctors tried it out, they became aware of its qualities.

Elastoplast soon earned widespread use as a post-operative dressing and became invaluable for the treatments of wounds and in sprains and fractures. In South Africa, miners were made to have their injuries dressed with Elastoplast at the end of every shift. It was so successful in cutting down septic injuries that its usage spread far beyond the original vision of treating varicose veins and ulcers.

After the war (which stretched resources enormously), Smith and Nephew introduced waterproof Elastoplast. But it was the arrival of the user-friendly lightweight Airstrip in 1959 which eased the agony for wounded offspring.

Today Elastoplast is manufactured in five continents (it is known in many countries as Tensoplast) and is a major seller everywhere. What's more, the cure is no longer more painful than the injury.

Electric Blanket

In days of yore, one of the most popular varieties of bedwarmer among the wealthy was the human kind. It was common practice for the maid to be asked to snuggle down between the sheets beforehand and take the chill off, a situation which is believed to have given rise to the 'early night' for husbands. English Prime Minister W.E. Gladstone preferred a stone bottle containing hot tea which he proceeded to drink the following morning!

For the first half of this century, rubber hot water bottles held sway, sometimes backed up by an electric fire in the bedroom. Then, on 9 October 1946, the Simmons Company of Petersburg, Virginia, brought out the world's first electric blanket. Thermostatically controlled, it retailed for $39.50.

The electric blanket seemed a comfort which many could do without, particularly in Britain where it arrived in the 1950s. The major fear surrounded its safety. The first models were marketed without safety devices and a survey by the Fire Protection Association revealed that in 1956 electric blankets and other bedwarmers were responsible for more than 2600 of the fires reported to British insurance companies. Over a three-year period, electric blankets had caused 20 deaths.

As safety measures have been tightened, the electric blanket has become an essential part of bedding on cold winter nights. In the 1950s a mysterious surge of electricity in unoccupied houses in America was eventually traced to the one-night visit of tramps whose most important item of luggage was their electric blanket which they carried around from house to house.

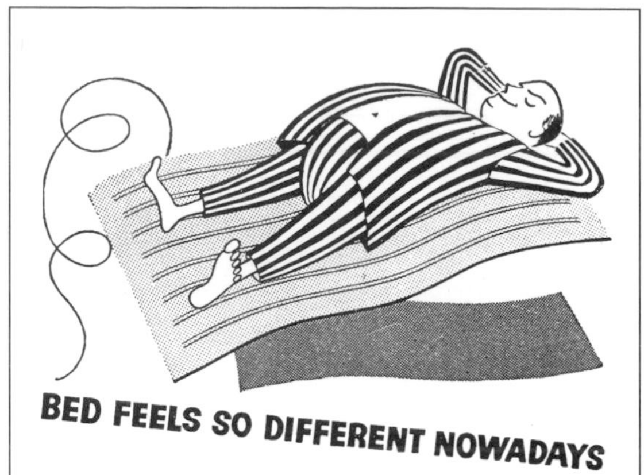

If you haven't relaxed on a Warmabed Electric Blanket you can't imagine the sheer bliss of it! Warmabed Electric Blankets are expertly made from 100% Pure Wool, everything about them is absolutely first class. They give a benison of cosy warmth—soon you'll forget about chilly dampness, there won't even be a memory to shudder at! A Warmabed Electric Blanket is your warm friend for life.

Warmabed
ELECTRIC BLANKETS

are supplied in 100% Pure Wool, in pink, periwinkle blue, honeysuckle or willow green.

3 sizes :—JUNIOR ... £4 14 6
SINGLE ... £8 10 0
DOUBLE ... £12 5 7
(All prices include Purchase Tax)

GOOD HOUSEKEEPING INSTITUTE GUARANTEE

Ask to see the Warmabed Electric Blanket Regulators from 55/-.

In case of any difficulty in obtaining locally, post coupon for illustrated brochure and address of nearest stockist.

NAME ....

ADDRESS ....

MODERN ELECTRICAL INDUSTRIES LIMITED
KNOTTINGLEY, YORKSHIRE IH

(above) To sidestep public fears over the safety of electric blankets, manufacturers chose to emphasise the luxury aspect.

Electric Dishwasher

Surprisingly for an item which we always think of as ultra-modern, the dishwasher was invented as long ago as 1855. But it bore little resemblance to the labour-saving device we know today. For a start it was manually operated, a handle being turned to thrash a cradle of dirty dishes through water. Indeed it was almost harder work than the time-honoured method of doing the dishes, with the result that few housewives were interested in the new apparatus despite the comforting words of *Scientific American* magazine which promised: 'The use of the machine constitutes no danger whatsoever to either man or dish.' That the man of the house was anywhere near the dishwasher is worthy of mention in itself.

The development of the electric motor at the start of this century led to a trickle of electric dishwashers from 1912 although manual models still existed in greater abundance. One of the earliest electric machines was introduced by brothers Willard and Forrest Walker of Syracuse, New York, but it, too, relied heavily on the human hand since the motor was only used to drive the water over the dishes. The Walker brothers had previously produced a dishwasher powered by a combustion engine, the sort of contraption that most women would actively ban from the kitchen!

Little progress was made between the wars. What electric models there were usually had to be filled by a kettle. The machines, which were top-opening at first, were inefficient cleaners and had an alarming tendency to break down full of boiling water. The 1926 manual *Housecraft* termed them 'a useless investment'.

The automatic dishwasher, in theory a true labour-saver, finally came to the United States in 1940 but even so only a million had been sold by 1951. Just when it seemed that the electric dishwasher would never gain public acceptance, improved detergents in the fifties saved the day. At last, the housewife could see an effortless way of getting her finest crockery sparkling clean and be sure that her 36-piece dinner service would not come out as a 72-piece.

(right) The New Colston Mark IV dishwasher, as seen in Housewife magazine of September 1964.

ADVERTISEMENT

In even the happiest marriage, money can become a vexing question. Love doesn't differentiate between spendthrifts and budgeters, and sometimes marriage guidance counsellors—occasionally the law—have to sort out the tangle.

Has a wife the right to save out of the housekeeping?

A neighbour announced to her husband recently that she intended to spend three weeks' holiday with a friend in New York. When he wanted to know where the money would come from, she said she'd saved £200 from the housekeeping. He hit the roof.

Men have taken their wives to court for less. And it certainly doesn't indicate a particularly close relationship when a woman will so deceive her husband—or find such deception necessary

But when wives let their hair down in a girls-together session, they'll admit that they use some of the housekeeping for pin-money. In some cases, it's the recognised thing. A set sum covers housekeeping, clothes, the lot. In others, a woman just assumes the right to whatever she saves by clever catering. It's only when she always provides mince instead of steak and pockets the difference that trouble's brewing.

Clever women with generous husbands can stretch the housekeeping to some point. Save from their allowance to benefit themselves and their families—by investing in a New Colston Mark IV fully automatic dishwasher.

PUSH-BUTTON HELP

The New Colston dishwasher releases you permanently from the drudgery of washing up. It does it all—completely automatically. Washes, rinses twice and power-dries . . . at the touch of a button! And that means a saving of an hour a day—the 20 minutes after each meal it takes to wash up for the average family.

All *you* do is put the dirty plates, cups and saucers, glasses, cutlery, dishes, smaller pots and pans straight into the Colston. No need to rinse first! The front-opening door and glide-forward racks make loading and unloading easy—there's no bending or lifting.

Press the button, and the Colston takes over. It measures the right amount of water and heats it to 145°F—hotter than hands can bear. Then it mixes in a special germicidal detergent, and sprays every piece with a unique, two-directional washing action that removes every particle of food, grease and stain. Even dried-on egg and mustard, and lipstick smears, disappear!

Then the New Colston rinses *twice*, in two changes of clean water, and finally power-dries with hot air before switching itself off. It even cleans itself as it operates.

In fact, Colston automatic dishwashing is a good deal more hygienic than most manual methods and the machine has been awarded the Certificate of the Royal Institute of Public Health and Hygiene.

Worried about breakages? Don't be! Precious glass and china are safer than in your hands at the sink. Only the water moves.

And the Colston is quite safe to use when there are children about. The machine stops automatically if the door is opened.

RIGHT IN SIZE—RIGHT IN PRICE

There's room for a New Colston Mark IV dishwasher in every kitchen. It takes 40 pieces of china and 45 pieces of cutlery in one load, but is very compact. It can stand free, needing no special plumbing (no installation costs), or can easily be built in with other kitchen fitments.

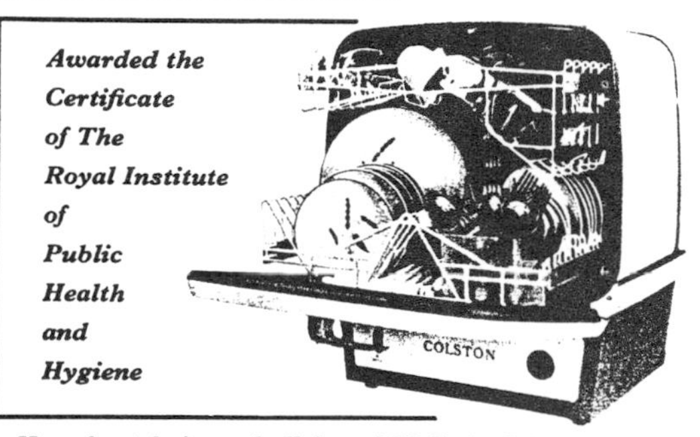

How about design and efficiency? Well, the Colston has been selected by the Council of Industrial Design for the Design Centre in London, and has been chosen by the Electrical Development Association for their List of Recommended Appliances, and awarded the Certificate of the British Electrical Approvals Board.

Yet, with all this, the New Colston costs far less than any other fully automatic dishwasher—just 75 gns. or easy terms. You get an excellent 12 months' guarantee with factory-trained engineers providing quick and efficient service, and there is an economical maintenance plan.

GOOD INVESTMENT

It's worthwhile investing in a New Colston Mark IV fully automatic dishwasher—whether you buy it as a household necessity or budget for it out of the housekeeping. So take the first step towards a washing-up free future—send for a free colour booklet giving you full details. Post the coupon today!

NEW COLSTON washes up so clean even dried-on egg disappears

To: Colston Appliances Ltd., Dept. HW3, High Wycombe, Bucks.
Please post me the free colour booklet on the New Colston Mark IV fully automatic dishwasher.
(BLOCK LETTERS PLEASE)

NAME..........

ADDRESS ....

.... COUNTY..........

0-60

17

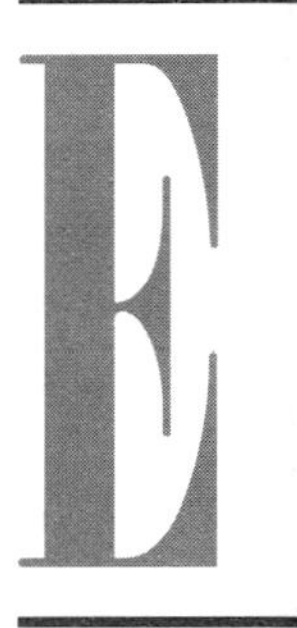

Electric Guitar

American Lloyd Loar paved the way for the familiar vibrant sound of the electric guitar by inventing the first microphone to be specially adapted for a guitar in the early 1920s. His fellow countryman Adolph Rickenbacher later had the idea of placing the microphone on the back of the instrument and connecting it to a loudspeaker. The outcome was Rickenbacher's Electro Vibrola Spanish Guitar which was made out of bakelite and which struck its first chord in 1935.

However, the first true electric guitar did not appear until 1947 when guitarist Merle Travis asked Paul Bigsby to design one for him. The following year, Leo Fender, a name which became synonymous with the electric guitar, marketed the Broadcaster and in 1950, the Telecaster. The Stratocaster (designed by Fred Tavaras) came on the scene in 1954 to help create a sound lapped up by that remarkable fifties innovation, the teenager. It was not a universal welcome. Parents frowned upon electric guitars, considering them to be a symbol of immorality, and some dance halls banned the loud, twangy sounds.

Even guitar masters such as the Shadows' Hank Marvin occasionally found difficulty adjusting to the electric guitar.

In his early days, he nearly electrocuted himself when the strings accidentally touched the microphone. 'There was a bang and a flash and the strings were all burnt at the edge,' he recalled. 'I hadn't known anything about electric guitars but after that experience, I quickly learned.'

The late Jimi Hendrix, arch exponent of the electric guitar.

Electric Kettle

Although an electric kettle sat on display at the Chicago World's Fair of 1893, it was not seriously marketed until the 1900s. Even then, in company with other electrical appliances available at the time, it existed as little more than a toy for the idle rich. Sensible folk boiled water over a coal fire. It was cheaper and there was no risk of electrocution. Of course for the wealthy, these considerations were immaterial — servants were expendable.

Early electric kettles were particularly hazardous affairs. A metal plate was bolted to the base with the plate heated by bare-wire filaments sealed in a separate compartment. So it was necessary to heat the base of the kettle as well as the water which was not only inefficient but highly dangerous. All in all, it was scarcely surprising that these kettles took 12 minutes to boil — there was no such thing as a 'quick cuppa' in those days.

This system remained in operation until 1921 when Bulpitt and Sons of Birmingham introduced the 'Swan', a kettle with an immersed element, the sleeve of which was soldered into the body of the kettle. It raised the efficiency of heating from under 50 per cent to nearly 100 per cent. Another significant step was the automatic cut-out featured for the first time in the 'Magnet' kettle, produced by GEC in 1930. Here the plug was fused so that if the base of the kettle overheated, the fuse melted and the current stopped. A more refined system, the one in use today, was adopted from 1955 with the marketing of a model with a thermostat which automatically switched off the kettle when the water reached boiling point. Alas, the smooth sound of progress meant goodbye to the curious array of buzzers, whistles or flashing lights which had adorned previous electric kettles.

Electric Razor

If anyone deserved to invent a memorable household appliance, it was Samuel L. Bligh of Pennsylvania. In 1900 he unveiled his ingenious 'beard grinder', an early attempt at mechanising the process of shaving. In truth, it relied more on pedal power than anything else. The shaver pedalled frantically on a sewing machine, the belt from the driving wheel of which passed over a wooden roller coated with emery, thus rotating it at high speed. The roller in turn was moved around the user's face, wearing away the stubble. Although the gallant Mr Bligh emphasised that neither soap nor water were needed, his device suffered from the fact that you could only have a shave where there was a sewing machine nearby.

Englishman G.P. Appleyard played his hand in 1913

with a patent outlining 'a power-driven shaving appliance'. It consisted of a fixed cutter with finely serrated edges and a reciprocating blade which, he said, 'may be rotated or oscillated and actuated manually, mechanically or electrically'. Appleyard's idea floundered principally because the tiny electric motors which he required were not yet readily available.

In the wake of these two failures, it was left to an American, Colonel Jacob Schick, to patent the first widely accepted electric razor in 1928.

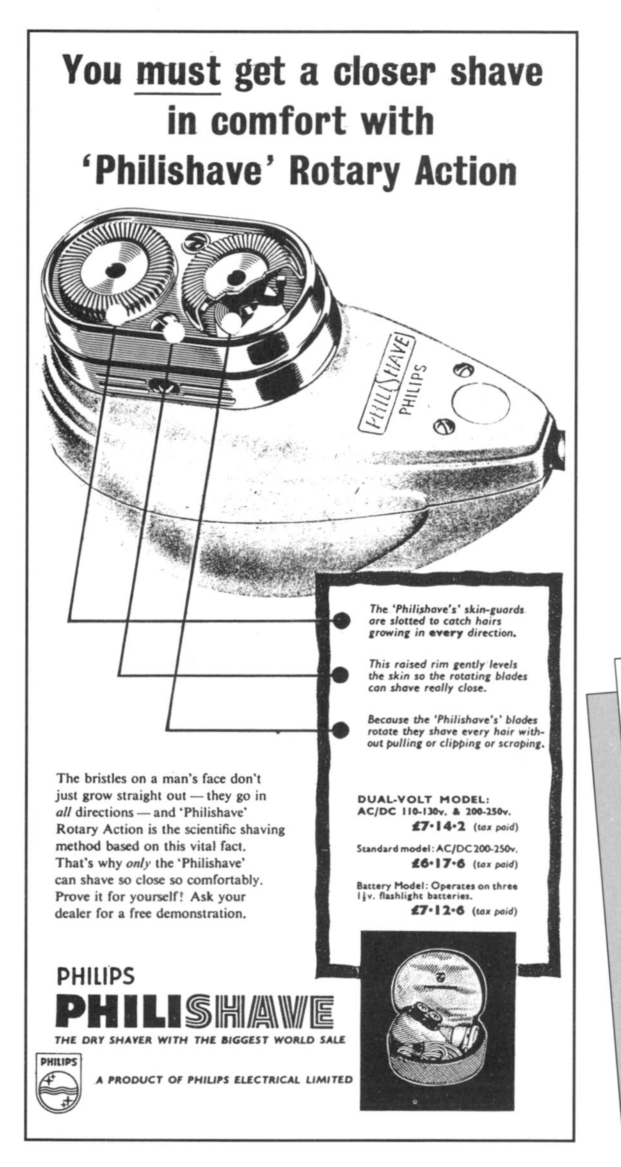

(above) The Philishave electric razor, 1957.

Electric Toaster

At the start of the 20th century, toasting was very much a manual exercise, performed in front of an open fire. The toaster had a long wooden handle connected to two wire squares between which the bread was held before the flames. It was thus only a marginal improvement on the old toasting fork.

One interesting device was the toast crisper which, with a spirit burner and covering hood, prevented the newly toasted bread becoming cold and soggy before consumption.

The first electric toaster was made by the General Electric Company (GEC) and went on sale in the United States in 1913. Its heating element, composed of bare wires wound around strips of mica, glowed red hot but could only toast one side of the bread at a time. The 'Universal' of 1923 (manufactured by the American firm of Landers, Frary and Clark) was more advanced and turned the bread to cook the second side.

Without a thermostat, these models were not to be trusted and burnt toast became an occupational hazard. The problem was eased in 1927 by the invention of the automatic pop-up toaster, designed by Charles Strite, a mechanic from Stillwater, Minnesota. But for some years it was only the American palate which benefited from this breakfast breakthrough since the new toaster did not transfer to the UK until the 1950s. In the meantime, the resourceful British had learned to camouflage their scorched toast with Marmite.

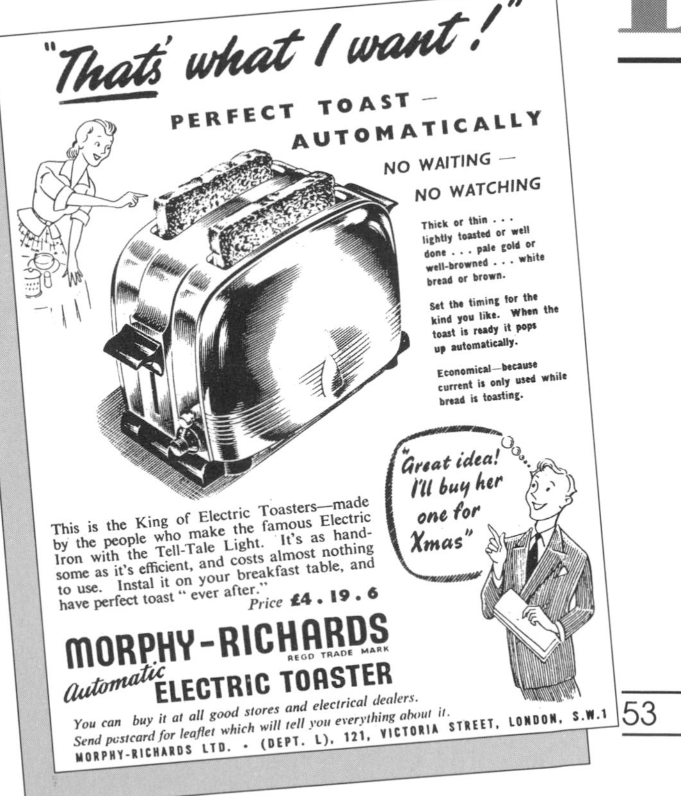

(right) The perfect Christmas gift for 1951 – a Morphy-Richards electric toaster.

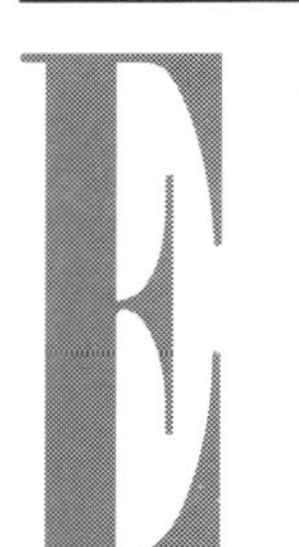

Electric Washing Machine

Of all the household items that have been lost to automation, few are so mourned as the washboard and mangle. The washboard had the bonus of doubling-up as an interesting musical instrument while the mangle somehow oozed rustic charm as it squeezed the drops of moisture out of the Monday wash.

It is extremely doubtful of course whether women share such nostalgic feelings. For years they have been trying to remove the toil of washday which in the 19th century was said to be as exhausting as swimming five miles of energetic breaststroke. In those days, the most common method of washing was to agitate the clothes with a wooden dolly (a curious device which resembled a cross on a milking stool). Mechanisation was touched upon with gas-powered or steam-driven washing machines but these tended to tangle the clothes in an unravellable web or, at worst, rip them to shreds.

As with other electrical devices, it was the introduction of the electric motor which showed the way forward and in 1907, American engineer Alva J. Fisher designed the world's first electric washing machine, the Thor. Manufactured by the Hurley Machine Corporation of Chicago, it used the motor to drive a belt which in turn moved the dolly, attached to the lid of the machine, backwards and forwards.

The early machines were understandably crude, being plugged into nothing more refined than an electric light socket. The attachments were rarely earthed and, because they were usually to be found beneath the machine, fell prey to dripping water. Nevertheless, manufacturers were quick to extol the virtues of their products, promising that 'the whole of the week's laundry can be washed, wrung and made ready for drying within the hour'. It was also claimed that the cost of the electricity needed to run the machine amounted to no more than 1d. a time.

The big boom in electric washing machines took place in the 1920s, coupled with a change in the position of the dolly. It was now placed upside down in the bottom of the machine, causing the clothes instead of the water to be pushed to and fro. This system, the forerunner of the modern fins and paddles, was far more effective at removing dirt.

In 1929, 84 per cent of new washing machines made in the US were electric. Britain lagged behind because the spread of electricity throughout the land was painfully slow. Even by 1939 not all homes in the UK had electricity. Even so, some models were available for the privileged few. The 1929 Harrods catalogue sang the praises of the Magnet Electric Washing Machine, priced

The ultra-modern 'Blighty' automatic washing machine, as seen at the Woman's Exhibition of 1923.

£42 0s. 0d., offering: 'Washing day without labour. Saves time and money. Washes six sheets or their equivalent in 15 minutes.' And there was more. 'Attachments are available for the machine so that it can be used for making ice-cream, mincing and sausage making, knife cleaning, making butter etc . . .' One wonders how many men later discovered sausage meat in their shirt-sleeves.

Apart from the lack of availability, the price of electric washing machines restricted their growth in Britain between the wars. A typical 1930s machine with mangle attached cost around £20, the equivalent of six to seven weeks' wages. Naturally, that was no bar to royalty and a Hotpoint was chosen for King George V's Jubilee House. He and Queen Mary were obviously impressed by the advertisement which enthused that it cleansed 'the dirtiest garments yet without fear of damage to the daintiest of lingerie'.

The launch of the twin tub in 1957 and the arrival of the automatic washing machine in the sixties revolutionised washday. There was no longer a place in society for the washboard and mangle. We will remember them.

Emergency 999 Service

In November 1935, five women died, trapped in a blazing house in London's Wimpole Street. A neighbour who dialled 'O' to summon the Fire Brigade complained that the brigade eventually arrived before the operator had answered. Clearly a more expedient method of dealing with emergency calls needed to be adopted.

Experiments, whereby callers had their eyes shut and sat in uncomfortable positions, revealed that the number 999 was the simplest to dial. It was also the only number which did not necessitate the complete redesign of the dial in telephone kiosks since it was essential that no money should be required to summon the emergency services. *The Times* added its support to the choice of digit, pointing out that it was a dignified number, one short of a cool 1000 with good solid associations such as the 999 years' lease. The newspaper added: 'OOO, besides taking longer than any other in the dialling, would suggest too pointedly for a brave man's use an Oh! Oh! Oh! of terror.'

When a caller dialled 999, a large red lamp glowed over the switchboard and a loud buzzer sounded like a klaxon horn. Such were the decibels emitted by the latter that one newspaper described it as 'a special buzzer which would do justice to the *Queen Mary* or any other liner in distress'. In the trial period before the new service came into existence, some girl operators fainted and had to be carried out when they heard the buzzer. This rather defeated the object. It was even suggested in the press that the buzzers were disturbing the peace of people living in the vicinity of the exchanges. Something had to be done quickly, so when a bright soul discovered that putting a tennis ball in the mouth of the buzzer muffled the noise, Post Office headquarters immediately ordered local engineers to go out and buy tennis balls and stuff them into the buzzers until a better scheme was devised!

The service was finally introduced to London only in July 1937. Within four hours, in the dead of night, a Mr Stanley Beard of Elsworthy Road, Hampstead, heard a noise outside his house and spotted a man's foot. His wife instantly dialled 999 and asked for 'police'. Seconds later, radio patrol cars raced to the spot and within four minutes, 24-year-old labourer Thomas Duffy was detained near Primrose Hill. He was duly charged with attempted burglary. Under the melodramatic headline: 'SHE IS FIRST TO

The light above the switchboard warns the operator of a 999 call.

DIAL 999', the *Daily Sketch* wrote: 'If a gunman invades your home in the night, if you wake to find your house on fire, if someone is ill or hurt and an ambulance is needed — RUSH TO THE TELEPHONE AND DIAL 999.'

By the end of the first month, 13 000 genuine 999 calls had been made. The following year, the service was introduced to Glasgow, the war then preventing further progress until 1946 when Belfast, Birmingham, Bristol, Edinburgh, Liverpool, Manchester and Newcastle were added to the list. Inevitably, some callers misused the new service. One of the earliest 999 calls was from a woman reporting that a wild goose crossing the road at Marble Arch was holding up the traffic . . .

Escort Agency

These days, the escort agency has acquired something of a nudge-nudge-wink-wink reputation. But it was not always thus. The very first such organisation was more likely to introduce clients to an heir to the throne than to a double-glazing salesman, making the most of his wife's visit to her sick sister. Run by Mrs Horace Farquharson and operating out of 31 Dover Street, London, from 1937, it was called the S.O.S. Bureau and was aimed at those who needed a suitable companion for a social function. For £3 an evening, Mrs Farquharson, who was extremely well connected, could obtain as an escort the younger son of a peer, someone who could presumably be relied upon not to slurp the gravy. Her brochure also offered presentations at court, £5000 securing the patronage of a Duchess, £3000 that of a Marchioness.

Espresso Coffee Machine

One of the many crazes which swept through Britain in the 1950s owed its origins to Italian Achille Gaggia who in 1946 invented the espresso coffee machine. The machine, which could prepare concentrated coffee quickly by passing steam through a filter, became immortalised in a string of coffee bars, starting in London's Soho and eventually spreading across the UK. The first was the Moka Bar in Frith Street, named after the original make of espresso machine, the Moka Express. Other popular venues included the Coffee Inn on Park Lane, the Boulevard in Wigmore Street, the Mocambo in Knightsbridge and a chain of Kardomah houses.

The decor of the coffee bars was usually tiles, wickerwork, bare bricks and tropical vegetation, topped by the statutory juke box. For once merchant seaman Thomas Hicks had embarked on a successful musical career as Tommy Steele after being seen playing at the 2 I's coffee bar while on shore leave, these establishments rapidly earned a reputation as *the* place for young singing hopefuls to be discovered. Before long, customers had to battle through a throng of agents just to get served.

Eurovision Song Contest

Did you know that 'La La La', Spain's 1968 entry, contained no fewer than 138 la's? That in 1974 plotters planning a military coup in Portugal used the playing of the country's Eurovision entry on radio as the signal for tanks to move in? Or that in protest at the four-way tie in 1969, Norway, Sweden, Finland, Portugal and Austria refused to take part the following year?

These are just a few highlights of the chequered career of the Eurovision Song Contest, an event which over the last 38 years has brought pleasure to millions although not always for the right reasons. Most viewers skip the songs, particularly the ones about Greek peasants rounding up herds of mountain goats on lonely October evenings while dreaming about their loved one working in a restaurant in Walsall, to focus on the giant voting scoreboard in the hope that one country will manage to score the dreaded *nul points*. Norway sang their way into Eurovision immortality in 1978 by being the first nation not to receive a single vote from the other participants. For the record, the pioneering song was 'Mil Etter Mil' sung by Jahn Teigen.

The first Eurovision Song Contest took place in Lugano, Switzerland, in 1956. Only seven countries entered, Switzerland winning with 'Refrains'. Song titles have ranged from the banal 'Ding Ding A Dong', 'A-Ba-Ni-Bi' and 'Boom Bang-a-Bang' to Germany's 1964 epic 'Man Gewöhnt Sich so Schnell an Das Schöne'. The Italians and French have pulled out more than once, complaining that the standard was too low, while when asked whether he would compete again, the United Kingdom's 1992 entrant, Michael Ball, replied: 'I'd rather stick needles in my eyes!' Occasionally, big stars do emerge from the Eurovision such as the Swedish supergroup Abba and . . . er . . . um. Well there was Abba.

In 1967 Sandie Shaw became the first British winner after singing 'Puppet on a String' in bare feet. Sixteen years later, Spain's Remedios Amaya tried the same gimmick. He came last with *nul points*. That's showbusiness.

False Eyelashes

Legendary American film-maker D.W. Griffith spared nothing in the creation of his 1916 silent epic *Intolerance*. Among the cast of 60 000 (the publicity for the movie claimed 125 000) was actress Seena Owen playing Princess Beloved. Griffith wanted her to have long eyelashes that brushed her cheeks, to make her eyes sparkle, and so he asked a wigmaker to prepare the world's first false eyelashes.

Human hair was woven through the warp of a 24-inch (61 cm) strip of fine gauze and at the start of each day's shoot, two small sections were cut from the end of the strip and gummed to Miss Owen's eyelids.

The result was suitably mystical but although the $575 000 production was acclaimed by the critics, it proved a disaster at the box office, leaving Griffith with massive debts. One school of thought suggested that he would have been better off patenting the false eyelashes.

Fan Club

Fan clubs are big business these days. Everyone from Madonna to Mickey Mouse has one, employing countless secretaries to answer questions from an adoring public.

The first official fan club, The Keen Order of Wallerites, was founded in London around 1902 by worshippers of celebrated actor/manager Lewis Waller. Members' badges depicted Waller resplendent in powdered wig as Monsieur Beaucaire on one side while the other bore his favourite flower, a pansy. The club boasted a list of rules which made the Ten Commandments seem optional. Members were expected to be at every first night (or face the consequences) while only the club secretary was permitted to address Waller personally. Soon a rival fan club, the True-to-Trees, was established to honour Beerbohm Tree.

In time, stage artists such as the above were eclipsed in public esteem by the burgeoning breed of movie stars. By the end of the First World War, 'America's Sweetheart' Mary Pickford was receiving an average of 18 000 letters a month. Some fans showed no shame. One wrote to Kathlyn Williams in 1916: 'Dear Miss Williams, You are my favourite moving picture actress. I would appreciate it so much if you would give me one of your old automobiles, any one, I wouldn't care how small.'

Fibre-tipped Pen

The idea for a new form of writing instrument was conceived by Pentel chairman and founder Yukio Horie in the late 1950s. He wanted a product that had a smooth black line, traditionally associated with Japanese brush characters, and which needed only minimum care and uncomplicated maintenance. Three years went in to the development until in 1962 Pentel's revolutionary Sign Pen was launched in Japan.

The Sign Pen utilised a water-based ink fed through a capillary system so that when it was used on writing paper, further ink was drawn through the fibre tip, ensuring a smooth flow at all times, even when writing at an angle or upside down.

For the overseas market, the Sign Pen was first exhibited at the 1963 Chicago Stationery Products Show where it received a tremendous response. A sample was given to President Kennedy who was so impressed that he immediately instructed his personal aide to scour Washington in search of Sign Pens. To seal its arrival on the world scene, the Sign Pen was named Product of the Year by *Newsweek* magazine that year. It remains a best-seller to this day.

(right) The fibre-tipped pen — a breakthrough in writing and art work.

Stuffy critics referred to the fish finger as the 'lowest common denominator' while journalists struggled to name the new concept. 'Food with built-in maid service' and 'ready prepared' were among the attempts before *The Guardian* hit upon 'convenience food' in 1960.

The fish finger profited from the fact that its arrival coincided with that of Independent Television in Britain. The sight of the perky *poissons* in the orange breadcrumbs lit up our screens accompanied by slogans such as: 'The happiest way to eat fish.' Their best-known salesman was the advertising creation 'Captain Birds Eye', played by Canadian actor John Hewer. When the old sea-dog was dropped from the campaign in 1971, *The Times* granted him the unprecedented accolade of an obituary. Reports of the captain's death were somewhat premature, however, as he rose again from the sea-bed three years later.

Although in the immediate aftermath of the Cod War, pound for pound, fish fingers cost more than smoked salmon, they have continued to occupy a place in the heart of our freezers. Scientific boffin Magnus Pyke called them the greatest food revolution since the discovery of fire and sales still top £100 million a year.

F

'Captain Birds Eye' (right) livened up the face of fish fingers in the late 1960s.

Fish Finger

It is difficult to imagine life before the fish finger. Somehow it always seems to have been there when we have needed it, when the Sunday joint has gone off or to cater for an unexpected influx of children, an oasis of calm in a culinary crisis. Yet it made its debut on the plates of Britain as recently as 26 September 1955 and even then it came about by accident.

Although in the United States, Gorton's had marketed their frozen sticks of boneless cod in 1953, Birds Eye, the company founded by the pioneer of frozen food, Clarence Birdseye, had opted instead for frozen herring sticks to capitalise on the plentiful supplies of cheap British herring.

The Herring Savoury, as it was called, went on sale in South Wales but it had too many bones for most customers. As a possible alternative, although in truth very much a second choice, Birds Eye simultaneously test-marketed frozen cod sticks in Southampton. These were snapped up by shoppers seeking something new and under the title of fish fingers, were launched at the expense of the poor old herring.

Flavoured Crisps

Careful shopping around can produce over 70 flavours of potato crisp in the UK, including Black Pepper, Chilli with Lemon and even Chocolate. Yet little more than 30 years ago, there was no choice at all. It was plain or nothing.

Crisps date back to 19th-century France but only took off in Britain in 1920 when Frank Smith began selling his wares to the public houses of Cricklewood in North-West London. At first, he provided salt cellars for flavour but these disappeared as fast as the crisps and so in 1922, Smith introduced, a little blue twist of salt.

The waxed paper bags in which the crisps were then sold were not airtight and had a shelf life of no more than a day from the time they left the large square tin in which they were delivered. Public houses tried to extend this by putting the bags into a large glass jar on the bar but even then the crisps would survive for a maximum of just three days.

Before the Second World War, crisps were mainly a middle-class product. A *Daily Telegraph* advertisement for 1931 read: 'No hiker's outfit is complete without Smiths Potato Crisps and nuts and seedless raisins. Obtainable in 2d. and 3d. packets from ham and beef shops, grocery and provision stores and village inns.'

Between 1945 and 1955 around 600 crisp manufacturers came and went. One of the few to survive started out in 1948 in a small Scottish bakery. It became Golden Wonder, the company which was to revolutionise the crisp-eating habits of the British.

In 1960 Golden Wonder introduced Ready Salted, the first crisps not to require the services of the little blue bag. That was daring enough but small fry compared to what was to follow. For in 1962 Golden Wonder brought out an entirely new flavour, Cheese and Onion, followed 12 months later by Salt 'n' Vinegar. To a country eager for change, the Cheese and Onion crisp represented an abandonment of old ideals in much the same way as the mini skirt. It was the choice of a new generation — and it was one sixties' substance you could try without ending up in court.

The new flavours were seized upon with relish, soon begetting Smokey Bacon, Bovril *et al.* Smiths were even forced to drop the little blue bag in 1965, claiming that it was too expensive to employ people to put one in each packet, but after public outcry, the salt returned nine years later in a blue sachet.

The introduction of further crisp flavours has continued apace — Tomato Sauce, Prawn Cocktail, Pickled Onion, Worcester Sauce and Pizza to name but a few. Thankfully, not all have passed the taste test and the great British public have seen fit to reject Strawberry Fool, Mince Pie, Apricot and Hedgehog.

Fluorescent Lighting

How appropriate that guests at a special dinner held in Washington, DC, on 23 November 1936 to mark the centenary of the US Patent Office, should find themselves in the presence of an exciting new invention. For making its working debut that night in the ceiling was the fluorescent light.

Developed by GEC, the fluorescent lumiline lamp, as it was called, had first been shown at the 1935 Annual Convention of the Illuminating Engineering Society in Cincinnati. The tube measured 2 ft (60 cm) in length and emitted a brilliant green light.

Following the success at the dinner, GEC and Westinghouse marketed the product commercially in the United States on 1 April 1938, the lamps coming in three sizes and seven different colours, priced at between $1.50 and $2.00. Fluorescent lighting did not appear in Britain until 1945 when it lit up the westbound platform of the Piccadilly Line at Piccadilly Circus Underground Station.

Last step in decorating— fitting the

Mazda Netaline fluorescent light

Very elegant, very inexpensive, the Mazda Netaline is also very easy to fit.

The Mazda Netaline costs only 85/-, and it's most uncomplicated—just one bracket and no extra wiring—you could fit it yourself in about twenty minutes!

It's cheap to run because the 40-watt Mazda warm-white tube gives as much light as two 100-watt ordinary bulbs, for the power consumption of one.

You can choose the colour of your Netaline from red, blue, yellow or white.

Your Netaline will poise elegantly away from the ceiling, heightening and brightening all the colours of your room without casting a single shadow!

Mazda NETALINE 85/-

(inc. P.T.) Complete with tube and 12-month guarantee

Mazda for better lighting—better living

AEI Lamp & Lighting Co. Ltd., Melton Rd., Leicester

M5034C

The Mazda Netaline lit up the world during the 1960s.

Flymo

Inspired by the invention of the hovercraft, Swedish lawnmower manufacturer Karl Dahlman set out to discover whether its principles could be adapted to his own line of business. He became fascinated by the idea of a mower which needed no wheels and could float on a cushion of air in any direction. Finally, in 1963, after months of dedicated research and experiment, Dahlman produced the world's first flying mower — or Flymo for short.

With its vertical blade and a fan which creates an air cushion under its plastic skirt, the Flymo steadily caught on, its ease of operation particularly appealing to gardeners with large undulating areas of grass. The traditional motor mowers were taken aback by the young upstart and the verdant lawns of Britain were turned into a veritable battleground as the rival camps laid their claims to superiority. The argument boiled over onto the television screens with advertisements suggesting that the motor mower was 'a lot less bovver than a hover'.

Nevertheless, Flymo has become the UK's leading manufacturer of lawnmowers, accounting for around 44 per cent of the market, as well as exporting machines to more than 50 countries.

Karl Dahlman pictured with his invention, the Flymo.

Fold-up Bicycle

The creation of the folding bicycle is a heartwarming tale of the triumph of the little man over a big organisation.

In 1958 Alex Moulton from Bradford-on-Avon, Wiltshire, developed what was the first entirely new bicycle design for over 50 years. Its tiny 16-inch (41 cm) wheels meant that it looked just like a toy bicycle but it was able to attain the same speeds as ordinary models. Also, because of its low centre of gravity and a revolutionary means of suspension, the Moulton could handle the most treacherous bumps in the road. Moulton had tested the prototypes himself on a severely pot-holed drive at his house.

By 1959 Moulton was so sure of the potential of his creation that he offered the design to leading bicycle manufacturers Raleigh who promptly rejected it, saying that the public would never adopt such an unusual machine.

Undaunted, Moulton pressed on alone, making and selling his bicycle with great success. The fold-up model was particularly popular with city gents who would park their car on the outskirts of the city, take the bicycle out of the boot and ride in to work. Quintin Hogg attracted considerable publicity by riding to the House of Commons on a Moulton.

By 1965 sales of the Moulton had reached 70 000, halting the downward trend in the popularity of cycling. To the acute embarrassment of Raleigh, the machine won numerous awards. In desperation, Raleigh launched a small-wheeled bicycle of their own but without Moulton's unique suspension system, it suffered in comparison. Eventually, in 1967, Raleigh held up their hands and admitted they had been wrong to reject Moulton's design, the then chairman of Raleigh blaming 'bad market research'. It was a costly error for when they subsequently took over Moulton's company, it cost them a great deal more than it would have in 1959.

Food Processor

Ken Wood had a vision. It was of an ever-expanding post-war market for products which enter the world as a luxury but develop into a necessity. He realised that dream in 1950 with the creation of the world's first food processor, the renowned Kenwood Chef.

Hand-operated food mixers had been around since the 19th century and Universal had brought out one of the first electric models back in 1918. But the Kenwood Chef was to transform food preparation in the home as well as in the catering industry.

It was in the 1940s that Kenneth Wood, a young Englishman involved in experimental and production work, was gripped by a powerful entrepreneurial ambition. His interest in industrial design led him to form a small company, the aim being to make electrical appliances for the home at a time when that particular business was still in its infancy as far as the UK was concerned. Accordingly, in 1947 he set up the Kenwood Manufacturing Company in a garage at Woking, Surrey.

The first product to bear the Kenwood name was an electric toaster, followed in 1948 by an electric mixing machine. The latter sold well but Wood was not complacent. He knew the post-war boom was going to create a competitive environment in the market-place and that Kenwood mixers would need to be improved and upgraded to hold their own against overseas designs.

The notion for something totally different came to Wood in a Brussels hotel. He scribbled the plans on the back of an envelope before refining his ideas on the drawing boards at the Woking factory. With a variable electronic speed control and four individual power outlets, the new concept was more than a mixing machine. It could perform a variety of functions, attachments converting it into a mixer, juice extractor, liquidiser, shredder, sieving machine, mincer, coffee mill, potato peeler, can opener and pulveriser. The Kenwood Chef could perform more jobs about the kitchen than Fanny and Johnnie Cradock put together.

It proved invaluable in commercial kitchens, finding its way into virtually all of the world's great cuisines. The Chef has been constantly updated since 1950, with over eight million having been made to date, each with a lifespan of at least 20 years. Indeed, the company's service department regularly receives letters from members of the public requesting spare parts for machines purchased in the fifties and sixties. And to underline its place in kitchen history, the Kenwood Chef has earned a place in London's Design Museum.

The changing face of the world's first food processor, the Kenwood Chef.

Football Pools

The world's largest Football Pool owes part of its success to a small boy's burning desire to own a cricket bat! The bat cost 21s. and young John Moores was told that he must save half the money himself out of his pocket money. 'A man who attempts nothing,' said his mother, 'gets nothing in this world.'

This early lesson in thrift was remembered years later in 1923 when, together with two fellow clerks from the Commercial Cable Company in Liverpool, John Moores invested £50 as his share in a spare time Football Pools venture.

Moores and his friends had been inspired by the efforts of former Coldstream Guards officer John Jervis Barnard who, in 1922, had set up Pari-Mutual Pools in a one-room office at 28 Martineau Street, Birmingham. Barnard's first coupon did not even attract enough returns to pay his postage bill but as his fortunes improved slightly and he changed the company name to Jervis Pools, the scheme came to the attention of the three young clerks. Studying a Jervis coupon, they were sure they could do better and calculated that they needed to interest 4000 punters in order to make a profit.

The snag was that running a spare-time business was against the Cable Company's rules so to keep their jobs, the men had to keep their identities a closely guarded secret. As one of the partners was known by an adopted name, they decided to call the new company by his original family name — Littlewood.

Thus with a total capital of £150, Littlewoods Pools commenced operations from a single top-floor office in Church Street, Liverpool. The beginning was far from auspicious. The 4000 copies of the coupon were printed and taken by Moores to Manchester United's ground where he hired a group of small boys to distribute them outside. Only 35 people were prepared to try their luck. The total amount of money invested was £4 7s. 6d. with a first dividend of just £2 12s. 0d. Things could hardly get worse — but they did. Of 10 000 coupons handed out at a big match at Hull, one solitary coupon was returned. History does not relate what happened to the other 9999 . . .

By the end of the season, Littlewoods Pools had incurred losses amounting to £600 and Moores' partners decided to call it a day. 'Let's face it,' argued one, 'it

4 THE LITTLEWOOD SPORTS LOG

Notes & Notions

BY F. STACEY LINTOTT ("ADJUTANT")

SCHOOLBOY IDOL.

THE centre-forward used to be the idol of every schoolboy, the hero of every football story. All goals, glitter and glamour. How times have changed. The other day a famous football manager said to me, "I want nine footballers, a goalkeeper and a centre-forward." Cynical but smart.

Some time ago, J. R. Smith, one-time famous centre-forward for Bolton Wanderers and Bury, said to me, "I have a boy who is keen on football and should make a good player. But I have forbidden him to play centre-forward. He shall stop playing rather than play there."

Of the four best centre-forwards we have in England, Glover has not played since the opening of the season, Steele has been out of the game half the season.

Drake ditto ditto. Is the fact purely coincidence?

PLAYERS WAGES.

Nearly everyone thinks that all regular first team players in the First and Second League clubs get the maximum wage, £8 a week. But they don't. Not by a jugful. Only a very few years ago, a famous club won the F.A. Cup, and, a few weeks later, offered a prominent member of the team—and probably others—£6 a week for the coming season! He held out for the maximum, and got it. But just imagine the "cheek" of the club.

THE BROKEN RULE.

There is a rule in football, quite plain, known to all. It is broken, often on many occasions, in almost every match played. Yet the referee rarely penalises the fault, and the crowd never clamours for a free kick. What is it? Answer next week.

MEMBERS OF FOOTBALL POOL PROMOTERS ASSOCIATION

LITTLEWOOD'S AGAIN SMASH ALL PREVIOUS RECORDS!

On behalf of the WORLDS LARGEST PENNY POOL . . .

SIR MICHAEL BRUCE

Presents to

MR P. WOODS
326 Dundyvan Road
Whifflet, Coatbridge
LANARKSHIRE

THE WORLD RECORD DIVIDEND OF £28,130 for 1D

For Matches played Sat Jan 22nd

And in the same pool — in the same week

4 SECOND DIVIDEND WINNERS EACH RECEIVED £3,701/7/2 FOR 1D

17 3RD DIVIDEND WINNERS EACH RECEIVED £609/12/6 FOR 1D

39 4TH DIVIDEND WINNERS EACH RECEIVED £227/15/6 FOR 1D

218 5TH DIVIDEND WINNERS EACH RECEIVED £33/19/2 FOR 1D

341 6TH DIVIDEND WINNERS EACH RECEIVED £13/0/6 FOR 1D

WHEN SIR MICHAEL BRUCE presented the cheque for the magnificent sum of £28,130, Mr. P. Woods, the fortunate winner expressed his own and Mrs. Woods' keen appreciation of the courteous and pleasant manner in which settlement had been made. The happy little presentation "ceremony" by Sir Michael had been very enjoyable, he said; adding "I wish every member of the Littlewood Happy Circle the same good fortune."

* *Sir Michael Bruce is a descendant of King Robert the Bruce, the hero of Bannockburn; the family estates at Stenhouse-Muir, Stirling, have been held since 1300. Sir Michael served with distinction in the Great War, has had a brilliant career as explorer, big game hunter, actor, and is the author of a number of Scottish historical works.*

THE LITTLEWOOD SPORTS LOG 5

HOW SEEDS MAKE OAKS

THERE'S adventure, romance, tragedy, comedy in football scouting and signing. Example: take any one club. Say Charlton,

Sam Bartram, their daring goalkeeper from Boldon (Durham), was a half-back at school. Had trials with Charlton as a *goalkeeper* and nearly missed the Athletic boat because he was off colour until the very last reserve game of the trial. Then he snone and Charlton snapped him up—quick!

Herbert Turner booked himself for an Army career, in the Welsh Guards. Enter Charlton. Now he's the Welsh international right-back and captain.

Jimmy Oakes, left-back, was all for Port Vale and his pet pigeons. Didn't like leaving them. Enter Charlton, again. Oakes makes fame in London.

John Oakes, centre-half, was seen by Anthony Seed, secured by brother Angus for Aldershot, and transferred for £650 to brother Jimmy at Charlton. Seeds make Oakes.

Donald Welsh, wing half-back, left Manchester to join the Navy, was on a draft for China and on the boat when recalled ashore. Played for Torquay United, and then to the Valley (fee £3,000).

George Robinson joined Charlton from Sunderland as an *outside*-right. Not so hot. They let him go to little Burton Town. Here he played *inside*-right and other clubs wanted him, so Charlton fetched him back. Star ever since.

And how do you think the Athletic made young Green a star? Found him in Barry. Signed him for £100 or so. Thought him fragile. Sent him to Barcelona, in Spain, to eat some sunshine, and there this centre-forward blossomed into a wing half-back. Vitamin A or something. Then War broke out. Charlton fetched him home, post haste. And so to fame.

The Littlewood Sports Log announces a record football pools winner in the 1930s.

sounded like a good idea but obviously it will never work. I vote we cut our losses and drop the whole thing.' John Moores retained his faith in the project and boldly carried on alone. Within seven years, he was a millionaire.

John was soon joined by his brother Cecil and hard work eventually began to pay dividends. Ironically, their cause was assisted by a 1926 police prosecution under the old Ready Money Betting Act. Littlewoods won the case on appeal and the resulting publicity helped enormously. In 1928 the total pool for one week reached £10 000 — another six years and it had risen to a staggering £200 000. By the time war broke out, the figure had doubled. During the 1930s the Post Office sold five times as many postal orders as usual during the football season.

But progress was not without controversy. The Baptist Union condemned the Pools industry as 'injurious to moral sense and healthy sport' while sub-postmasters demanded more money to handle the 7000 coupons a week which were passing through their hands by 1938. One sub-postmaster selflessly suggested that the government should run the Pools themselves — and spend the profits on providing a better standard of living to postal workers. And a Worthing butcher complained to the National Chamber of Trade's conference that women customers were buying cheap foreign meat 'to save money for the Pools'.

A more serious threat emerged in February 1936 with the so-called 'Pools Wars' when the Football League, who believed the Pools to be a menace and wanted to stamp them out, suspended its advanced fixture lists and only gave out details on the night before Saturday games. As well as destroying the Pools, this step would have caused chaos among supporters, not knowing where their team would be playing the following day. However, it never really materialised since the required information leaked out early from the clubs, who were secretly informed in advance who and where they would be playing, so the Pools companies carried on unhindered.

Pools wins now top £2 million. In 1979 an unemployed hairdresser from South Wales scooped £882 528 with her first-ever entry. Another woman was so overcome at winning £750 000 that she burst into tears and locked herself in the lavatory. It was some minutes before she was coaxed out of her self-imposed seclusion to meet the waiting press.

And what of John Jervis Barnard, the man who started the whole ball rolling? He continued to run Jervis Pools until 1938 when he sold out to David Cope of Cope's Pools. He never did make as much money as John Moores and Littlewoods.

Formica

It was during the American kitchen revolution of the 1950s that Formica became a household name. Manufactured in easy-to-cut sheets, Formica laminate was promoted as a worry-free product for the housewife, desirable not only for its style but also its wipe-clean, spill-proof surfaces. It became a symbol of cleanliness about the home.

Women were encouraged to buy the shade of Formica laminate most flattering to their complexion so that they could look forward to years of beauty in the kitchen. The image was of entire American families joyously gathering around mum's new Formica worktops. No longer would she have to slave away for hours trying to remove those nasty stains — it just needed an effortless wipe with the cloth. There were even reports of families bursting into song with choruses of: 'Formica, Formica, oh how we like ya.' For sanity's sake, it is to be hoped that this was just an ad man's dream.

Yet the object of this unbridled enthusiasm had been around in some shape or form since 1913. Two young engineers, Herbert A. Faber and Daniel J. O'Conor, were working at Westinghouse Electric and Manufacturing Company, Pittsburgh, Pennsylvania. Fresh out of college, they became friends in 1907 and met most weekends to discuss their vision — to come up with a material that would change people's lives. The invention of bakelite (the first totally synthetic plastic, by Dr Leo H. Baekeland in 1907) had paved the way for the production of laminates. At Westinghouse the first laminate was produced in 1910 by impregnating a heavy canvas with bakelite before O'Conor went a step further by perfecting the art of producing rigid laminate sheets.

The patent was applied for on 1 February 1913 but Faber and O'Conor, sensing they were about to realise their dream, became disillusioned with Westinghouse. They thought the company was not doing enough with the new invention and so decided to go it alone. Faber called the product Formica, indicating that it was a substitute for mica as an insulation material for electrical wiring. By then, mica was rare and expensive.

The Formica Company was set up in Faber's home town of Cincinnati in small premises rented for $60 a month. The first Formica was used to insulate parts for cars and also on early radios. At that stage, the only colour was black but when marble patterns were introduced in 1925, it found an outlet as the replacement for the metal strips on soda fountains. But the real breakthrough was the development of realwood, a laminate with a genuine wood veneer. Heat-resistant and cigarette-proof, its durability and attractive finish endeared it to café owners, canteen proprietors and kitchen table manufacturers. As the colour range expanded,

A sparkling Formica kitchen from the early 1960s.

Formica not only found its way into the kitchens of the 1950s but also into bathrooms where it was considerably cheaper than ceramic tiles.

Boosted by adverts featuring 'Formica Freddie', a small boy dressed in bow tie and braces (he was actually the son of a company employee), Formica laminate suddenly sprang up everywhere — on the interior of HMS *Queen Mary*, on the counters of Woolworth's and in the cocktail lounge of London's plush Regent Palace Hotel where 'everything possible was made of gleaming Formica, from tabletops and wall surfaces to the armrests of the couches'.

To reflect the sixties, a new range of bright colours appeared in 1964, including Signal Red, Lemon Twist, Lime and Caribbean Blue, enabling Formica to be used in works of art. With the upsurge of feminism, the accent has shifted away from housewives salivating over their new worktop. But with a range of jewellery coming out in the 1980s, Formica can still be a girl's best friend.

Fosbury Flop

Prior to the 1968 Mexico Olympics, nobody outside the United States — and not many within — had heard of Dick Fosbury. But by the end of the Olympic high jump competition, his name was on everyone's lips.

Five years earlier, Fosbury was a promising 16-year-old high jumper from Portland, Oregon, who had become frustrated with the traditional scissors technique of jumping. He reckoned he could clear greater heights by lowering his centre of gravity as the bar was crossed. So he devised a style whereby as he approached the bar in a J-shaped run, he turned his back on it at the last minute and went over head first. This backwards method was christened the 'Fosbury Flop'.

Almost immediately, his performances improved. His old scissors best of 1.62 metres was upped to 1.78 metres using the flop. Two years later, he passed the two-metre mark at high school. Selection for the Olympics was a natural progression and in the final, he found himself competing against 11 other jumpers, all of whom employed the straddle style. One by one, they dropped out and with his final attempt, Fosbury cleared 2.24 metres to take the gold medal with a new Olympic record.

From that moment, despite a warning from Fosbury's coach that imitators could end up with broken necks, the world's leading high jumpers abandoned their old techniques. Now they all use the Fosbury Flop.

Frisbee

When William Russell Frisbie started up the Frisbie Pie Company at Bridgeport, Connecticut, in 1871, he could scarcely have imagined that 100 years on his product would be responsible for a craze which swept the world.

The Frisbie bakery was situated near the University of Yale whose students enjoyed nothing more than tucking into one of the sumptuous pies and then playing a game in which they threw the empty tins to one another.

In 1948 the airworthy nature of these tins came to the attention of Los Angeles building inspector Fred Morrison who created a plastic version called Morrison's Flyin' Saucer. He later changed the name to Frisbee, amending the spelling to avoid legal difficulties. The Frisbee proved so popular among young Americans that in 1957 the wonderfully-named Wham-O Manufacturing Company of San Gabriel, California, bought the rights from Morrison.

Soon beaches and parks were crammed with youngsters demonstrating their Frisbee skills. It became a serious art, to the extent that an improved version was patented in 1967 with aerodynamic spoilers. This greatly enhanced performance and the record throw currently stands at over 600 ft (180 m). By a peculiar quirk of fate, just a year after Wham-O began mass production, the Frisbie bakery went out of business.

(above) A demonstration of the Fosbury Flop by Ralf Sonn, Germany, 1993.

(right) With a following wind, a Frisbee can be propelled over 600ft (180m).

The modern way to shop and cook...

... SHOP AT YOUR BIRDS EYE SHOP *for new, thrilling ideas for family meals on a budget — meals that give your family wonderful eating!*

STOP at your Birds Eye Shop. Stop there—shop there—for Birds Eye vegetables, fruit, fish, poultry and meats, pies and pastries. In the quick-frozen food cabinet you'll find a wonderful assortment of good things. All quick-frozen so their freshness, flavour and goodness is sealed in tight. All prepared ready to cook. No cleaning. No tiresome kitchen chores. That's all been done for you.

Yes, Birds Eye help you with your cooking—enable you to give your family better, more varied meals . . . meals that are truly wonderful eating!

The 1950s frozen food revolution changed the shopping habits of the British housewife.

Frogman's Flippers

The vulcanisation of rubber (the process of treating crude rubber with sulphur and subjecting it to intense heat) was first discovered by Goodyear and Hancock in 1844 and ultimately resulted in the mass production of many rubber products, including condoms, car tyres and Julian Clary's wardrobe.

It also changed the face of underwater diving for in 1927 Frenchman Louis de Corlieu designed the world's first pair of frogman's flippers, destined to make swimming beneath the surface much less arduous.

Frozen Food

For centuries, experts had tried to perfect the art of frozen food. Francis Bacon died of a chill after trying to stuff a chicken with snow. In the end, it was left to American biologist and fur trapper Clarence Birdseye to make the breakthrough following his observation of the freezing methods of Eskimos.

Between 1912 and 1915 young Birdseye was part of an American team conducting a survey into the fish and wildlife that existed in the frozen wastes of Labrador. He saw the natives catching fish in weather –50°F (–45°C). As soon as the fish were taken out of the water, they froze stiff in the intense cold of Canada's Arctic region. Months later, when they were thawed out, some of the fish were still alive. As he tucked into the fish and caribou which had been quick frozen by natural means, Birdseye was intrigued by how tender and fresh-tasting they were. He was by no means the first to discover the advantage of quick freezing — the Eskimos had been aware of it for hundreds of years — but he was the first to see its commercial potential.

On his return to more affable climes, Birdseye set about trying to develop an industrial process to carry out quick freezing. He found that if freezing was slow, large crystals formed which broke down the cell structure of the food, rendered it soggy and marred the taste. It took years of experiments before he finally patented the Birdseye plate froster, a device which was to become the backbone of a new industry. Fresh vegetables and foodstuffs such as fish were wedged between freezing metal plates which cooled the food from 32°F to 25°F (0°C to –3.8°C) in a few minutes, as opposed to two or three hours by the old method.

On 6 March 1930 a group of ten shopkeepers in Springfield, Massachusetts, began to sell Birdseye's frozen food. Among his early lines were peas, spinach, cherries, loganberries, raspberries and fish. American housewives had been buying frozen meat for several years but this was the first time vegetables had been available. The new range was slow to take off because the items were not only expensive but, hidden away in ice cream cabinets, were difficult for shoppers to find. Even so, by 1933 there were 516 frozen food retail outlets in the United States.

Frozen food came to Britain in 1936, pioneered by Smedley's of Wisbech whose first offering was frozen asparagus for 2s. 3d. That must have gone down a treat with the Jarrow marchers! Early British frozen produce veered towards luxury rather than necessity, possibly because at the time there were only around 3000 refrigerators in the entire country and only the wealthy could afford to buy them. It was not until the 1950s that frozen food became the food of the people.

Incidentally Clarence Birdseye, the father of the cod steak, claimed that his distinctive surname was originally written as two words. He said it derived from an English ancestor, a page in the royal court, who had been nicknamed 'Bird's Eye' by the then queen after he had shot a swooping hawk through the eye with an arrow.

Gas Chamber

Following a series of bungled executions with the electric chair, the American justice system sought a new way of carrying out death sentences. One suggestion, by Major D.A. Turner of the US Army Medical Corps, was for death by lethal gas. He declared that it was the 'quickest and most humane method of putting a human to death'. As a result, Nevada's Humane Death Bill of 1921 ruled that a condemned person should be executed in his cell while asleep and without any warning, with a dose of lethal gas.

Governor Emmet Boyle, a fierce opponent of capital punishment, signed the bill convinced that it would be declared unconstitutional as a 'cruel and unusual punishment'. But when Gee Jon was sentenced to death for the assassination of a rival Chinese gang member, Boyle was horrified to see the Nevada Supreme Court uphold the constitutionality of lethal gas. A special chamber had to be hurriedly constructed after executing Jon in his cell proved impractical and on 8 February 1924 at Nevada State Prison, Carson City, six minutes after cyanide gas was fed into the chamber, Gee Jon was dead — the first person to be executed by such means.

Within two years, Arizona, Colorado, Wyoming, North Carolina and California had all installed gas chambers. But notwithstanding the constant debates about capital punishment, the gas chamber has never been a favoured method of execution. A 1953 Gallup Poll in the United States revealed that the American public much preferred the electric chair.

Girl Guides

Presiding over a rally of Boy Scouts at Crystal Palace, Sir Robert Baden-Powell was horrified to see a small group of girls wearing woggles made from broken shoelaces.

He challenged their leader. 'And what the dickens do you think you are doing here?'

She replied: 'We want to be Girl Scouts.'

'Oh,' he said. 'No, you can't be. It's only for the boys.'

Now Baden-Powell may have been a distinguished soldier but he knew only too well that there was no enemy so dangerous as a wronged woman. So when the girls persisted, he backed down to a degree and said he would think about it. Three months later, in early 1910, he bowed to pressure (some 6000 girls had already registered themselves as Boy Scouts) and gave the go-ahead for the formation of the Girl Guide movement, the name being taken from the famous cavalry unit in the Indian Army, the Corps of Guides, who were 'distinguished for their general handiness and resourcefulness under difficulties'.

In outlining his reasons for forming the Guides, Baden-Powell, who put his sister Agnes in charge, wasted no time in once more wading into the youth of the day. He wrote of widespread decadence and of seeing 'watering-places crammed with girls over-dressed and idling'. He added: 'Girls must be partners and comrades, rather than dolls. Their influence in after-life on the actions and quality of the men is very great; they become their "Guides". They therefore need character-training quite as much as boys.'

By the summer of 1910, there were reports coming in of Guides rescuing babies from the paths of oncoming trams; of pulling drowning horses from swamps; and, in the case of the 1st Watford troop, even stepping in to play the piano at social evenings. On the debit side, concerns were expressed that Guiding would turn girls into tomboys and would lead to their rushing around with few clothes and even fewer manners. One unsavoury incident in October 1910 was a midnight raid by Guides on a Boy Scout camp. The girls were swiftly disowned.

During the First World War, the Guides' deeds were to knit socks and gloves for soldiers, look after old ladies, care for the children of Belgian refugees and try to teach them English — exactly the qualities for a future Miss World.

The movement, which now boasts nearly eight million members worldwide (the Queen was once a Guide), really did break girls' taboos since vigorous exercise had previously been strongly discouraged for fear of bringing on a haemorrhage. One letter Baden-Powell received from 'a would-be Scout' read: 'Dear Sir, if a girl is not allowed to run, or even to hurry, to swim, ride a bicycle, or raise her arms above her head, can she become a Scout?'

The answer was a resounding yes but not so successful was 12-year-old Abigail Wright. In 1991 she was barred from the Guides because she doubted the existence of God.

Thou shalt not pass. Two early Girl Guides defend their nation, their honour and their tent.

Googly

A favourite Victorian game was Twisti-Twosti, the object of which was to bounce a tennis ball on a table in such a way that your opponent, sitting opposite, could not catch it. Among those who sampled this pastime was promising young English cricketer Bernard James Tindal Bosanquet. He began to contemplate adapting the technique of Twisti-Twosti to the cricket pitch and rightly concluded that if he could make two successive balls, delivered with seemingly the same action, go in opposite directions, he would totally mystify the batsman.

Mastering the art required hours of practice and a willing partner. This he found in his young cousin Louise who was posted at one end of the family lawn to retrieve Bosanquet's experimental googlies. After further practice in the nets, he was finally ready to bowl the off-break with the leg-break action in public.

The historic occasion was the match between Middlesex and Leicestershire at Lord's in July 1900. Bowling for Middlesex, Bosanquet had been sending down his customary fast-medium when, with Leicestershire left-hander Samuel Coe on 98 not out, he suddenly tried the googly. It was not exactly a perfect demonstration but it had the desired effect, the ball soaring into the air, pitching half-way down the wicket and bouncing three times before defeating the stroke of the baffled Coe who was promptly stumped.

Called up by England for the 1902–03 tour of Australia, Bosanquet maintained that the googly was an accident so that word would not reach the Australians. The mainstay of that Australian batting line-up was the redoubtable Victor Trumper and Bosanquet refrained from trying out the googly on such an experienced batsman until their final encounter on the tour. Bosanquet later wrote: 'Trumper batting, having made about 40 in 20 minutes. Two leg-breaks were played beautifully to cover, but the next ball, delivered with a silent prayer, pitching in the same place, saw the same graceful stroke played, and struck the middle stump instead of the bat.'

The googly had claimed its most famous scalp. The Australians hastily sought out the secret and the action was mastered by their spinner Arthur Maily who worshipped Trumper to such an extent that when he bowled the great man with a googly in an inter-state fixture, he said afterwards that he felt as if he had shot a dove.

Bosanquet's invention came in for a lot of criticism. It was accused of hindering batting and bowling alike — batsmen were said to be afraid to attack spinners while bowlers were accused of spending so much time trying to work out the mechanics of the googly that they were neglecting other forms of their art.

But the googly survived the furore and remains a lethal weapon, particularly in the hands of expert practitioners such as Australia's Shane Warne. And the Australians have never forgotten who taught them the lesson in the first place — for they still refer to the googly as the 'Bosie'.

Green Shield Stamps

A myth has been perpetuated over the years that all of the beautiful people in the sixties spent their time wearing beads, flowers and open-toed sandals and preaching about love and peace. Well just as many spent their hours on a less transcendental task — licking scores of Green Shield stamps. The cameras may not have been there to capture it but who is to say that the Maharishi did not sneak into his local Green Shield gift house and exchange his 5½ books for a toaster?

You couldn't lick Green Shield stamps for making all manner of luxury goods accessible.

Trading stamps have actually been around since 1891 in the United States when they were offered at Schuster's Department Store in Milwaukee. By 1954 US stamp purchases totalled $192 million but the phenomenon had yet to take hold in the United Kingdom. A few small operations existed pre-war, before the consumer boom of the fifties encouraged Richard Tompkins to enter the market. Aware of the American 'green stamps', he deduced that if they wished to expand the ir activities to Britain, they would want to keep that name. So in an effort to forestall such a move, he kept the green and added a shield to suggest security. Thus in 1957 the Green Shield Trading Company was registered — but only after the rights had been bought from a small North London company already using the name Green Shield.

Business began in earnest in 1958 but the first mail-out to potential customers generated just three replies. The major outlets remained sceptical, Tesco boss Jack Cohen declaring: 'Trading stamps are a menace.' Instead, Tompkins concentrated on corner shops and by 1962, Green Shield stamps were available in 8000 such establishments throughout the UK.

Watching the situation carefully, the supermarkets made their move 12 months later. Fine Fare took S and H pink stamps and most of the other big chains followed suit with Pricerite and, ironically, Tesco, taking Green Shield.

Even the Beatles would have been hard pushed to match the hysteria created by the arrival of Green Shield stamps. The *Sunday Express* reported: 'In Leicester the giant Tesco store was besieged by thousands of battling housewives. Twelve women fainted. The staff were completely overwhelmed. Goods were knocked off the shelves and display stands.' In the end, the store had to be cleared and customers were made to queue and enter a dozen at a time.

The nation rejoiced at the acquisition of new golf clubs, bathroom scales and hair dryers but all good things come to an end. By the mid-1970s, petrol stations began to offer customers the choice of a price reduction or stamps. With the escalating cost of petrol caused by the oil crisis, over 70 per cent of motorists opted for the price cuts. In Britain at least, trading stamps were on the way out.

The final nail in the coffin was hammered home in 1977 when Tesco, in search of a new up-market image, dropped Green Shield. Even the lure of double stamps by rival stores was to no avail. In 1978, Green Shield linked up with sister company Argos and the former Green Shield gift houses were transformed into Argos showrooms. Green Shield finally announced the termination of stamps in October 1980 — just when I only needed to fill another 1412 books for that long awaited car.

Gro-Bag

Professional salad growers need a disease-free environment in which to cultivate the finest produce. Crops used to be grown in the greenhouse border soil but raising the same crops in the same spot year after year led to a build-up of pests and diseases which would result in severe losses. Soil had to be steam sterilised or treated with chemicals, a process which was not only very expensive but one which was not always entirely successful. Then in 1973 along came the Gro-Bag.

Launched by Fisons, the Gro-Bag quickly caught on with all gardeners great and small. Crops planted in the compost-filled bags, mainly tomatoes initially, are effectively sealed off from the contaminated soil. At the end of the crop, the bags are discarded and fresh material brought in, eliminating the need for sterilisation. Even those with nothing more than a balcony were suddenly able to grow their own salads and vegetables.

Hailed as a cultural revolution, the Gro-Bag has blossomed to the extent that annual sales currently stand at around 12 million.

A bumper crop from the trusty Gro-Bag.

Guide Dog

During the First World War, many wounded German soldiers recuperated at the Frauendorf Sanatorium near Stettin, the director of which was a Dr Gorlitz. Among his patients was a young partially paralysed German officer with whom he used to walk through the grounds as part of the soldier's therapy.

One day, Dr Gorlitz was briefly called away. In his absence, the patient tried a few steps unaided upon which the doctor's Alsatian, Excelsior, fetched the man's walking stick from the sanatorium. Dr Gorlitz returned to witness his dog leading the soldier across the lawn.

Gorlitz saw the potential of using dogs to help the war-blinded and in 1916 instigated the first recognised training of guide dogs for the blind, conducted by the Austrian War Dog Institute and the German Association for Serving Dogs.

This work came to the attention of a wealthy American, Mrs Dorothy Harrison Eustis, who, at her kennels in Switzerland, was breeding and training Alsatians to work with the customs service, the Army and the Swiss and Italian police. She visited the guide dog training centre at Potsdam in Germany and came away so impressed that she wrote an article about it for the American *Saturday Evening Post* of October 1927.

The article aroused considerable interest. A blind American, Morris Frank, was told about it and bought a copy. The 5 cents that it cost him, he said later, 'bought an article that was worth more than a million dollars to me. It changed my whole life'.

He was so excited by the piece that he contacted Mrs Eustis in Switzerland. 'I want one of those dogs,' he wrote. 'Thousands of blind people like me abhor being dependent on others. Help me and I will help them.'

Infected by his enthusiasm, Mrs Eustis trained a dog at her kennels for Morris Frank, brought him over to Switzerland to learn how to use it and then sent him back home as America's first guide dog owner.

As a result of this experience, Mrs Eustis set up a guide dog centre, L'Oeil qui Voit (The Seeing Eye), at Vevey, Switzerland, in 1928. She then devoted herself, and much of her wealth, to the guide dog movement. As news of her exploits spread, guide dog training began in Britain in Wallasey, Cheshire, in July 1931.

At that time in Britain, there were no dogs working for the police, the Army or the RAF and the public strongly disapproved of making a dog work. The early trainers ran the gauntlet of people physically trying to stop them doing their job, abusing them and declaring that what they were doing was cruel, silly and useless. It was only when the Guide Dogs for the Blind Association was formed in 1934 and people saw the obvious delight of the trainees at being able to walk freely and fast that they finally realised the importance of guide dogs in society.

Alfred Morgan and his guide dog Bella give a demonstration for MPs in London's Parliament Square in July 1936.

Hair Colourant

In 1907 Eugene Schueller, a young French chemist, invented the first synthetic hair colourants. He prepared them at night and sold them to hairdressing salons by day, an example of the drive and innovation which was to become the trademark of the company he formed in 1910, L'Oréal.

During the Roaring Twenties, women desired emancipation and short hair became the vogue. Short hair needed body and above all, colour. So, in 1929 Schueller came up with a brand new technique, Imedia Liquid, a dye manufactured from organic colouring agents and one which offered a vast range of shades. It proved particularly effective for masking grey hair.

Schueller, whose far-sightedness saw L'Oréal set up export warehouses in Italy, Holland and Austria as early as 1912, continued to experiment. He was aided by the fact that hairdressing salons multiplied at an astounding rate during the 1930s and were only too willing to try out new ideas. Among Schueller's introductions was Dop, the first mass-market shampoo, launched in 1934.

Thanks to Eugene Schueller, there are now hair colourants to cater for everyone from the little old lady wanting a blue rinse to the punk with green stripes.

Hair Dryer

Before 1920 a popular method of drying one's hair was to kneel down in front of an open fire. But with the increased interest in hairdressing came the first hair dryers in 1920.

The first models were the 'Race', made by the Racine Universal Motor Company, and the 'Cyclone', manufactured by Hamilton Beach. Both appeared almost simultaneously in Racine, Wisconsin which therefore immediately became the hair dryer capital of the world.

The hand-held 'Sol' electric dryer of 1925 was fan-driven and made of aluminium with a switch offering two levels of heat. Another electric dryer was the box-shaped 'Stebull', manufactured by the Birmingham firm of Stevens and Bullivant around 1930. An ungainly device, it was placed on a table and worked by emitting hot air through a square, gauze-protected hole, over which the user was required to drape the hair.

Since then, the hair dryer's greatest claim to fame was when Val Barlow was electrocuted in front of millions in a 1971 episode of *Coronation Street*. Such was the impact of the soap opera that sales of hair dryers suffered in the immediate aftermath amid fears that users might suffer the same fate as poor Val.

Hair Perm

It may have been a matter of some concern to the first ladies who had hair perms that the man carrying out the delicate manoeuvres on their flowing locks only became a hairdresser because his eyesight was too poor for him to be a shoemaker.

Karl Ludwig Nessler had firmly intended following in the footsteps of his German father but, forced to seek an alternative trade, opted for hairdressing, first in Switzerland and then in Paris. It was in the French capital that he learned the art of Marcel waving, the creation of Parisian coiffeur Marcel Grateau. Nessler wanted to improve upon Grateau's invention, in particular to make the 'ondulations' longer lasting, but what he really needed was human guinea pigs, willing to allow him to experiment.

In 1901 Nessler accepted a hairdressing post in London and seized the opportunity to try out his ideas on a client. However, his employer took a dim view and sacked him on the spot.

Fortunately, Nessler had made enough money to open a salon of his own. The income enabled him to continue his efforts to perfect his new machine until, on the evening of 8 October 1906, he publicly demonstrated the permanent wave for the first time to a specially invited group of hairstylists at his salon at 245 Oxford Street.

Few were impressed. For a start, the poor client had to sit for six hours with a dozen brass curlers in her hair, each of which weighed nearly two pounds, making it the equivalent of wearing 48 large potatoes on her head. And if she had enough energy left after that, she had to pay a bill of ten guineas. Small wonder then that Nessler attracted only 70 customers in his first year of business.

With the outbreak of the First World War, Nessler emigrated to the United States in order to avoid imprisonment as an alien. It turned out to be the most fortuitous move he ever made, for in 1915 the 'bobbed' hairstyle swept through America, courtesy of ballroom-dancer Irene Castle, and anyone who was anyone wanted a permanent wave.

Harley-Davidson

Elvis Presley, Muhammad Ali, Charles Lindbergh, Sylvester Stallone, Cher and Crown Prince Olaf of Norway have one thing in common — they have all owned the most famous motorcycle in the world, a Harley-Davidson. Add to that list the likes of Clark Gable, Arnold Schwarzenegger, Bob Dylan, Neil Diamond, Steve McQueen and Clint Eastwood and it quickly becomes apparent why the Harley is the machine of the stars.

The glamorous Harley-Davidson, ridden by Peter

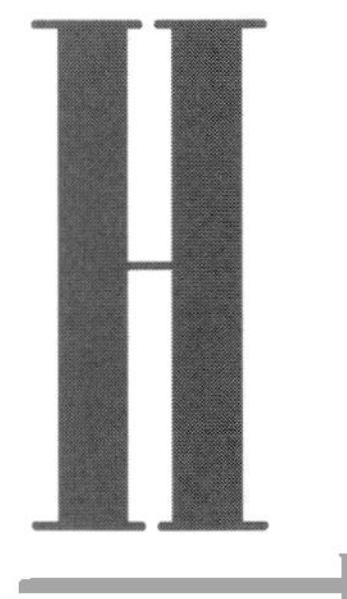

Which girl has which Toni?

(or: how to get every hairstyle in the world with one Toni or the other)

TONI makes two kinds of Home Perms. Curly Toni for curly hairstyles and the Uncurly Permanent for body hairdos. They're the basis for every hairstyle in the world.

These twelve girls show you the kind of variety you get out of a Toni perm. Are you getting that kind of variety? You will with a Toni. Have one and add a little spice to your life.

Curly Toni comes in three strengths. *Super* for hard-to-wave hair or a curly perm. *Regular* for average hair or medium waves. *Gentle* for bleached and dyed hair or a loose, loose perm. Toni gives you a no-mix neutraliser, too. No fussing. It's squeeze-bottle ready! Toni costs 8/6 and 5/6.

Uncurly Toni (called Smooth 'n Sleek) is a body perm. It gives your hair enough body to let you wear it any way you like. You get all this in one box! 24 curvers, curving lotion, styling leaflet. Costs 15 shillings. Refills 8/6 (buy one for a friend and lend her the curvers).

If you want setting instructions for these hairstyles write to: Evelyn Douglas at The Toni Hair Beauty Service, 215-222 High Holborn, London W.C.2.

2

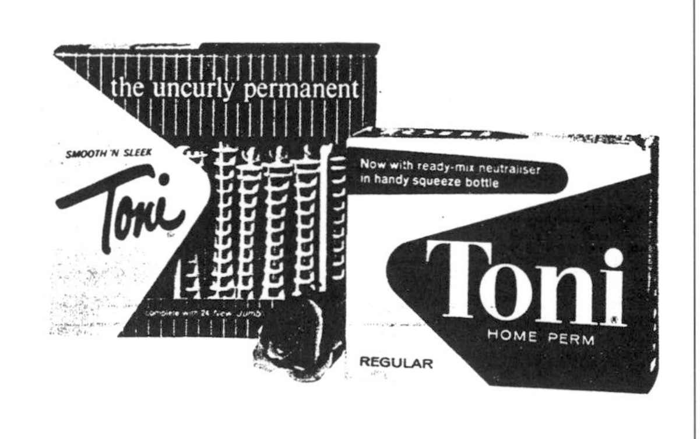

(left) A hair dryer takes centre stage in this 1930s display of electrical gadgets.

(above) No girl could afford to be without her Toni.

Fonda and Dennis Hopper in the archetypal free spirit movie *Easy Rider*, and the focal point of the 1973 production *Electra Glide in Blue* (the only film to be named after a motorcycle), began life in more humble surroundings — namely a small shed in Milwaukee, Wisconsin. There, in 1903, Arthur Davidson drew up the plans and made the machines while his pal William S. Harley did the designing. The first to emerge from the shed at the bottom of Davidson's garden was a belt-drive model with a 3 hp single-cylinder engine. In the early days, making motorcycles was little more than a hobby, to be worked on in their spare time, and by 1905, they had manufactured a total of just 11. Indeed, Harley thought it more important to acquire his engineering degree and while he was away studying, the breech was filled by the eldest Davidson brother, William.

But such was the demand that they were soon forced to move into a proper factory with nearly 20 employees. And by the end of the First World War during which US Forces had ordered 70 000 Harleys, some rigged for combat, Harley-Davidson was the world's largest motorcycle company.

At the start of the 1920s, there were 15 motorcycle manufacturers in the United States but the industry was rocked by the appearance of the mass-produced cheap car and only two companies — Harley-Davidson and Indian — survived. To overcome these hard times, Harley-Davidson generated some income by selling blueprints of current models to a Japanese business consortium. Whilst the money kept the company afloat, it also gave the Japanese an entry into the motorcycle market.

Not exactly Easy Rider. A Harley-Davidson with sidecar combination at Brooklands in 1923.

It was a move Harley-Davidson would later regret. US police departments had first ordered Harleys back in 1909 and the two had become inextricably linked, particularly the image of the city cop on the famous Electra Glide. But when the Harley factory struggled again in the 1970s, some police departments switched to Kawasakis, a decision which prompted widespread indignation. A poster of the time demanded: 'Should your police department's public image be riding on foreign motorcycles?'

Probably for the sake of law and order, it was as well that most police departments were shamed into returning to the Harley. For the Harley-Davidson is more than just another motorcycle, it is part of the great American dream.

Harpic

Next time you sit on the lavatory, ponder awhile that Harpic started out life as an explosive by-product from the First World War.

Shortly after hostilities had ceased, London heating and sanitary engineer Harry Pickup took on the job of removing waste from ammunition factories. He found that when added to water, the waste formed an acid which dissolved limescale. Sensing that this quality could be harnessed commercially, in 1920 Harry developed a laboratory cleanser from nitre cake, a commodity which was in vast supply at the time. The nitre cake proved to have as devastating an effect on germs as it had on the battlefields a few years earlier.

A 1960s Harpic advertisement emphasises the virtues of a clean S-bend.

He called his cleanser Harpic (an amalgam of his name) and the advertising and sales push were so successful that he had to move to larger premises twice in the next three years, finally settling in an old jam factory in Staple Street, Southwark.

As Harpic powder entered the domestic market, the Harpic toilet roll was produced, principally as a promotional aid, while 1927 saw the publication of the Harpic Home Book which offered a wealth of handy hints to the housewife on cleaning, cooking and of course hygiene.

In 1932 Harry Pickup decided to sell the company to Reckitt and Sons of Hull who immediately launched an advertising campaign underlining the fact that there was no need to use a brush with Harpic. A catchy slogan of the day ran: 'A little Harpic every night, keeps your lavatory clean and bright.'

A 6d. tin of Harpic was not only an essential tool in fighting germs in the smallest room, it was also a useful weapon to impress the neighbours. Advertising of the late 1930s was geared very much towards what the neighbours thought. It reinforced the housewife's desire to keep her home clean and fit for anyone to see by implying that if she did not use Harpic, however sparkling the rest of the house was, her lavatory pan would let her down.

Yet the advertising slogan most readily associated with Harpic — that it goes 'clean round the bend' — apparently never existed. A 1930s copyline said that Harpic 'cleans round the bend in the pipe where the brush cannot reach', which was modified in 1964 to 'cleans round the S-bend'. But like *Casablanca*'s 'play it again, Sam', it seems that the most celebrated line of all was nothing more than a myth.

Hearing Aid

The mechanical hearing aid could almost have been invented 'by royal appointment'. For in 1902, the year after its introduction, Queen Alexandra, who had been partially deaf since childhood, wore one so that she could follow the proceedings at the coronation of her husband Edward VII.

It was by no means the most discreet device, the batteries being housed in a 16 lb (7 kg) box, the size of a modern portable radio, situated on the person's lap or on an adjacent table, while a large telephone-style receiver was held to the ear. The receiver could be adjusted by moving a switch on its handle. Nevertheless,

As hearing aid technology progressed, models such as the Vibraphone of 1941 became markedly less obtrusive.

the queen was sufficiently impressed to present its inventor, New York electrical engineer Miller Reese Hutchinson, with a medal as a token of her gratitude.

The Acousticon, as the new implement was known, was not Hutchinson's first invention. He had previously unleashed the klaxon upon an unsuspecting world, a state of affairs which prompted his friend Mark Twain to comment: 'You invented the klaxon horn to make people deaf, so they'd have to use your acoustic device in order to make them hear again!'

For many years, the Acousticon and its successors remained so unwieldy that shouting continued to be adopted as the most frequent method of dealing with those who were hard of hearing. Then, in 1935, Londoner Edwin Stevens marketed the Amplivox, the first electric hearing aid able to be worn about the person since it weighed a comparatively light 2½ lb (1 kg). Of even greater significance was the production of the first transistor hearing aid in 1952 by the Sonotone Corporation of Elmsford, New York State.

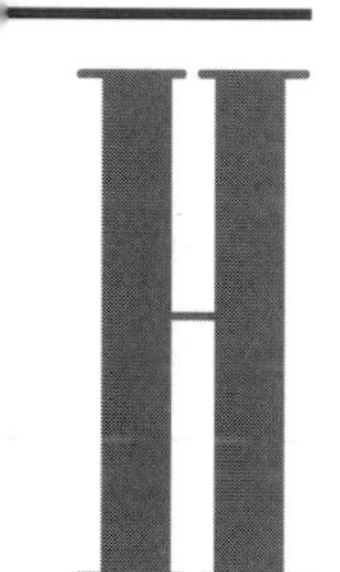

Not everyone immediately appreciated the benefits of the modern hearing aid. In 1978 a Leeds man complained to his doctor that his hearing actually improved when the aid which he had been wearing for the previous 20 years, was removed. It transpired that the mould had originally been made for the wrong ear!

Holiday Camp

Judging by the stringent list of rules and regulations and general lack of bonhomie, the only thing that was missing from the very first camp was the prefix 'concentration'.

At Dodd's Socialist Holiday Camp, Caister-on-Sea, Norfolk, an establishment founded by one J. Fletcher-Dodd in 1906, no alcohol was allowed on the premises. Bathers were expected to wear regulation costumes and 'rowdy conduct and improper language' were strictly forbidden. Indeed, any holidaymaker caught talking loudly after 11 p.m. would be thrown out of the camp!

Accommodation was under canvas and anyone failing to keep their tent spick and span was liable to a 6d. fine for each offence. Yet another rule stated that campers had to be punctual for all meals in the dining-hall to which they were summoned by the sound of a bugle.

In view of the Fletcher-Dodd regime, it was as well that a saviour was at hand — albeit nearly 30 years later. Canadian Billy Butlin had started his career as a travelling showman with one hoop-la stall in 1921. He set up a number of amusement parks, boasting the distinction of being the man to introduce dodgems to the UK when he incorporated them at Skegness in 1925. His idea for a holiday camp was born out of a wet holiday on Barry Island, South Wales, in the 1920s. He had stayed at a small boarding house and been appalled at the way in which the guests were virtually banned from the building except at meal-times. What holiday camps there were in Britain attracted only hardy young men since only they were tough enough to survive the rigorous conditions. Nothing catered for families. Recalling the friendly summer camp he had enjoyed on the shores of Lake Ontario as a young employee with a Toronto department store, Butlin set about re-creating that vibrant atmosphere but with sufficient indoor facilities to allow for the vagaries of the British weather.

Thus he paid £3000 for 40 acres of land three miles north of Skegness in Lincolnshire where he aimed to create a self-contained holiday village for families, complete with 15 000 chalet-beds, landscaped gardens and a host of sports and entertainment facilities. For the launch, Butlin booked a half-page advertisement in the *Daily Express*, offering holidays from 35s. to £3 according to season. Within a few days, he had received over 10 000 replies. The camp opened to 500 guests on Easter Saturday, 1936. The local newspaper wrote: 'Campers in this Arcadia will not be disturbed by storms of wind or rain, by shortage of drinking water, by lack of illuminations, by crude sanitary arrangements or by other inconveniences to which the average outdoor camper is subject.' On the front of the reception was a sign reading: OUR TRUE INTENT IS ALL FOR YOUR DELIGHT, a quote from *A Midsummer Night's Dream*.

There were two minor hiccups. For the first three weeks, drinking water had to be transported to the camp in lorries from Butlin's house since the workmen had been unsuccessful in drilling for water, and one party accidentally went to Sheerness in Kent instead.

Ever the showman, Butlin invited record-breaking aviator Amy Johnson as an early VIP visitor and, besides appearing in early shows himself along with his famous redcoats, soon began to book professional acts for the camp's Sunday concerts, including Elsie and Doris Waters, Ted Ray, Will Hay and Donald Peers. But Butlin once told a young Frankie Howerd who auditioned for him: 'Take it from me, son, you will never get anywhere as a funny man.'

In 1938 Butlin opened a second camp at Clacton and the following year his empire received a timely boost when Parliament passed legislation, giving a week's paid holiday a year to all industrial workers (until then only about three million Britons had enjoyed the luxury of paid holidays). Butlin's rose to the challenge with the slogan: 'Holidays with pay: Holidays with play: A week's holiday for a week's wage.'

Since Butlin could build camps faster and more cheaply than the Service departments, he was commissioned to build further camps at Filey, Ayr and Pwllheli to serve as military bases during the war. Then in 1945 he bought them back from the British government and reconverted them for the use of holiday-makers. Campers at Skegness in 1947 noted that the bedspreads still had 'HMS *Royal Arthur*' on them.

Although he liked to be known as 'Mr Happiness', there was one thing which saddened Billy Butlin — accusations of immoral goings-on at his camps. A *Sunday Pictorial* article from 1937 had stated that 'painted ladies' were often among the visitors. To repair the damage, Butlin imported the entire San Carlo Opera Company to perform Puccini's *La Bohème* at the opening of the Filey camp and later recruited the Old Vic for a season of Shakespeare. In 1947 the wholesome, fun-loving family image of Butlin's was restored for good when, after a week's stay, Labour MP Woodrow Wyatt declared: 'Illicit sex is ruled out by physical exhaustion.' For good measure, regular Sunday services were introduced, a decision which encouraged the Archbishop of York to spend a day at one of the camps. However, it is not recorded whether he took part in the knobbly knees contest . . .

An early form of transport at Butlin's.

Horse Race Starting Stalls

Starting a horse race used to be a real lottery. In the 19th century the runners set off on a given shout from the starter, the riders just hoping their mounts would be facing in the right direction at the time. It was certainly not the most efficient method, the 1830 Derby producing no fewer than 14 false starts.

At Newmarket in 1897, a starting gate of elasticated webbing was introduced for flat races but this had an unfortunate habit of catapulting jockeys out of the saddle. This equipment is still used for starting National Hunt races in Britain and, as was proved by the 1993 Grand National which was declared void after two false starts, it remains prone to disaster.

Happily, flat racing throughout the world is now started by the much fairer means of starting stalls. First seen in the United States, stalls made their UK debut at Newmarket on 8 July 1965. They have been in use ever since and, apart from the occasional unfortunate incident (Lester Piggott was once badly injured when his horse crushed him in the stalls), have ensured that the punter does not lose his money at the start — even if it is only a short reprieve.

Hot Pants

By 1970 the knee was no more. The mini skirt had, for the time being at least, raised its last eyebrow and instead ladies' legs were wrapped in yards and yards of material known as the maxi skirt. There was bound to be a backlash from men and women alike who wanted to resurrect the thigh, to create something even more shocking and outrageous than before. And so, in 1971, hot pants were born.

Popularised by British pop designer Mr Freedom, hot pants were extremely tight-fitting shorts made in a variety of materials including leather, suede, velvet, cotton and corduroy. Satin hot pants were much loved by disco queens, worn with that other quintessential seventies' fashion accessory, the platform shoe.

Predictably, the new craze (even Woolworth's stocked hot pants) upset many. Fashion guru Princess Anne commented of hot pants: 'People complain one isn't with it but honestly . . . that's the limit, the absolute limit.' And it was announced in 1971 that ladies in hot pants would only be allowed to enter the Royal Enclosure at Ascot if the 'general effect' was satisfactory.

Ageing actress Marlene Dietrich could not understand what all the fuss was about, stating bluntly: 'I wore hot pants years ago when they were called shorts.'

Hot pants perched on top of millions of legs from 1971.

As with most crazes, hot pants went out of vogue almost as quickly as they had come in, thus enabling the male blood pressure to return to normal.

Hovercraft

One of the principal requirements for any would-be inventor is a fertile imagination. Christopher Cockerell undoubtedly possessed exactly that for the way in which he managed to convert an empty tin of cat food, a coffee tin and a vacuum cleaner into that revolutionary form of transport, the hovercraft.

Cockerell had been a radio engineer for 15 years until, in 1950, he acquired an interest in a boatyard on the Norfolk Broads near Lowestoft. Four years later, he began to study the work of Sir John Thornycroft who, back in 1877, had worked on plans for a vessel that would ride over a cushion of air. But Cockerell amended the way in which air was pumped into the vessel, testing his theory with the household items. The cat-food tin was fitted inside the coffee tin and air from the vacuum cleaner was blown down the ring between them and out at the bottom. Air pressure was measured on a set of kitchen scales. The weight lifted by the thrust of air from the vacuum cleaner proved to be far greater with one can inside the other than with a single can. Cockerell deduced that a heavy craft could be supported, in close proximity to the ground, on a cushion of air produced by a thrust considerably less than the overall weight of the craft.

Buoyant, Cockerell then tried to sell his idea to industry. But aircraft companies showed little interest because it was not an aircraft and shipping firms rejected it because it was not a boat. Bloodied but unbowed, he decided to build a working model and contacted the Service ministries. After witnessing demonstrations, they promptly put it on the 'secret' list (in case it had any military value) where it languished for over a year. Finally, in April 1958, Cockerell received the backing and financial support of the National Research Development Corporation who offered him £1000 to secure the patent rights.

The job of building the world's first hovercraft (because of the vacuum cleaner experiment, it had previously been nicknamed the 'hoovercraft') was contracted to Isle of Wight aircraft firm Saunders-Roe and on 11 June 1959, the blue and silver *SR.N1* was unveiled. Thirty feet (9 m) long and weighing three and a half tons, the 'flying saucer' was hailed as a success but scientists had their doubts, calculating that such a craft would need to be several hundred yards wide in order to clear an 8-ft (2.5 m) high obstacle. Cockerell overcame this difficulty by adding a 4-ft (1 m) flexible skirt to the *SR.N1*, enabling it to handle rocky land as well as rough seas.

In 1959 to celebrate the 50th anniversary of the first cross-Channel flight by Louis Blériot, the hovercraft made its maiden Channel voyage, covering the journey from Calais to Dover in 2 hr 3 min. Later that year the Duke of Edinburgh persuaded the chief test pilot to allow him to take over the controls. HRH flew so fast that he was politely requested to slow down a little!

The first passenger service took place on 20 July 1962 across the Dee estuary between Rhyl and Wallasey. The passenger list comprised 24 humans and two mail-bags, carrying 8000 letters. Since then, hovercraft have boldly gone where no craft has gone before. In 1968 one travelled 2142 miles (3447 km) up the Amazon and Orinoco rivers, shooting fearsome rapids which even canoes had previously avoided. In West Nepal, a small hovercraft was used as a 'hovering doctor' to care for the sick, the only route to hospital being along a treacherous river, Kali Gandaki, known locally as 'the Goddess of Death'. Before the introduction of the hovercraft service, patients had to endure a 14-day trek carried on the back of a relative.

Given the magnitude of his invention, Sir Christopher Cockerell (as he was by then) surely deserved more than the £150 000 pay-off he finally received from the British government in 1971. He said afterwards: 'I had to take what I was offered. It's no big figure when you look at what was given to the inventors of radar and the jet engine in their day, but I've been living on air for some time now.'

The hovercraft — a great British invention.

Hula-hoop

Fresh from their success with the Frisbee, Richard P. Knerr and Arthur K. 'Spud' Melvin, co-owners of the Wham-O Manufacturing Company, San Gabriel, California, came up with another winning craze, the hula-hoop. Wham-O began producing the 3-ft (90 cm) polyethylene rings in May 1958 and within six months, they had sold a staggering 30 million.

Local and national contests sprang up across the United States. Around 40 rival manufacturers jumped on the bandwagon while Moscow condemned the hula-hoop as exemplifying 'the emptiness of American culture'.

By the following January, the craze with South Sea Island origins had spread to Birmingham. Eleven-year-old Gail Bradley from that city kept her hula-hoop spinning for a record 17 minutes in a contest at London's Hammersmith Palais, during the course of which she managed to turn round, kneel down and tie up her shoelace, all while keeping the hoop going. When the new pastime reached Paris, a demonstration accompanied by a country and western band brought traffic to a halt on the Champs-Elysées.

The hula-hoop was not only the prerogative of the young. Competitions were staged for toddlers and grannies alike, many women using it as part of a keep-fit routine, although medical experts warned that it was potentially dangerous to those unaccustomed to strenuous exercise. Even though the craze itself has long since passed, the hula-hoop is still around, as are the attendant competitions. As recently as 1987, Roxann Rose of Washington State set a new world record by keeping a single hula-hoop going for 90 hours.

That fifties phenomenon, the hula-hoop, is still used in fighting the flab.

Hush Puppies

As an executive with the Wolverine Shoe and Tanning Corporation, Rockford, Michigan, Victor Krause had a thing about brushed pigskin. But he had encountered a series of setbacks in trying to market shoes made from pigskin, partly because it was too soft for farm and work footwear which at the time were the company's major products. An additional handicap was that the skinning machines available were of poor quality.

The breakthrough came when, at Krause's instigation, engineers developed a machine that separated pigskin from flesh without damaging the skin or reducing the meat yield, thus appeasing both cobbler and butcher.

The doleful expression on the Hush Puppies basset hound.

Krause had a pair of shoes made up and, still wearing them, presented the idea of pigskin to the Wolverine board. Reaction was mixed but market research suggested that the new line would quickly gain a foothold.

The next consideration was a brand name. This evolved from a visit to a customer in Tennessee by the company's sales manager, Jim Muir. He asked why the small fried corn dough balls he had just enjoyed with his fish dinner were called 'Hush Puppies'. The customer replied that the fried dough was used by farmers to silence their hungry barking dogs. Muir reasoned that Hush Puppies would be an ideal name for the new comfortable casual pigskin shoes because when feet hurt, they are much like barking dogs!

In 1958 Hush Puppies were launched nationally. The timing was immaculate. With post-war affluence in America had come a rise in white-collar jobs, a move off the farms and into the cities plus a general increase in leisure time and leisure activities. And Hush Puppies shoes were the perfect leisure shoes.

The product's trademark, the sad-eyed basset hound, soon had plenty to be cheerful about. Hush Puppies became a worldwide success, arriving in the UK in 1961 at the height of the winkle-picker period. Their popularity was sealed when they were selected as off-duty wear for the 1964 British men's Olympic team.

Ice Cream Cone

The ice cream cone was invented by Italo Marcioni, an Italian immigrant to New Jersey, who was granted a patent for his special mould in December 1903. It first caught on at the 1904 St Louis World's Fair although two differing stories exist as to its precise introduction.

One tale is that Charles E. Menches, a young ice cream salesman, presented his girlfriend with an ice cream sandwich and a bunch of flowers. Since she had no vase for the flowers, the resourceful wench is said to have rolled the layers of the sandwich into the shape of a cone to act as a vase. Quite what happened to the ice cream while she did this remains unclear.

A more plausible explanation is that a Syrian waffle concessionaire named E.A. Hamwi started rolling waffles into the shape of a cone for the benefit of an ice cream vendor who occupied an adjoining booth at the Fair.

Baked from a mixture of flour, milk and sugar, the ice cream cone immediately became popular at the seaside, especially with children. The ice cream industry magazine of December 1926 pointed out: 'One of the advantages of the cone method of serving ice cream is that it does not soil the fingers, and should the contents melt owing to an extremely hot spell of weather, the cream will run into the bottom of the cone, and not, as in the case of the wafer, all over the hand and on the ground.'

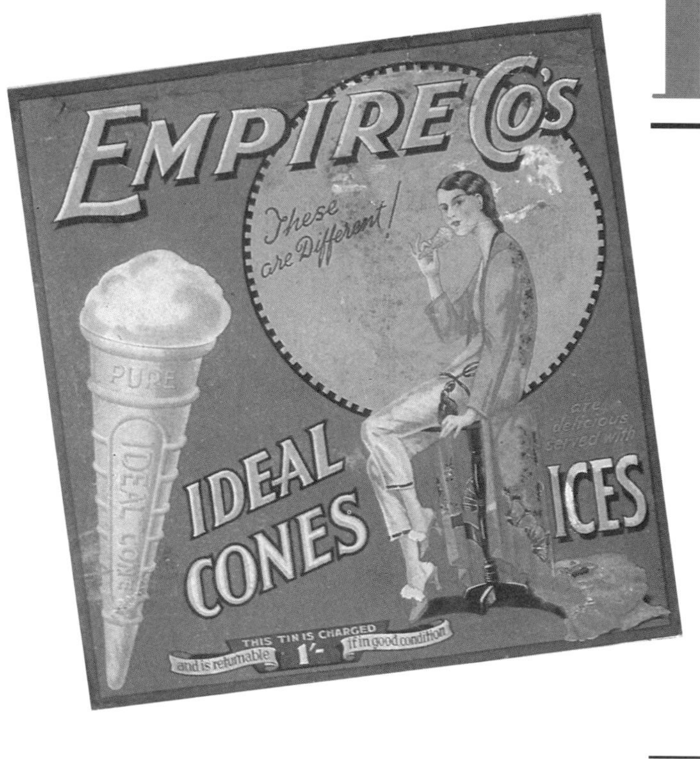

A symbol of summer — an ice cream cone from the 1930s.

An early development was that of a cone made with a non-crushable nesting ring at the top which prevented breakages and the slipping of the cone in the hand. In the 1920s British traders were reluctant to sell American cones because they thought the American cone held too much ice cream and could not be sold in the UK to show a profit. Consequently, Facchino's of Birmingham came up with the unusual boast that their cones 'hold much less ice cream than those offered by our competitors'.

The war with the wafer continued. The wafer's main advantage was its cheapness, a vital factor in 1d. ices, and in the 1930s, a tin of 1200 wafers cost just 4s. 6d. In 1935 waffles were introduced to Britain to supersede wafers, complete with the memorable advertising line: 'Have a waffle in the cinema.' But the wafer held its ground until the late 1950s when the advent of soft ice cream secured the future of the cone but sent the wafer to a soggy funeral.

Ice Lolly

For many years the ice lolly, or water ice, was a controversial, almost shadowy figure. It had first been introduced in 1923 by Californian Frank Epperson as the Epsicle (he later changed the name to Popsicle) and by 1926 reports were rife that this new refreshment line, based on fruit juices and water, was proving popular at British seaside resorts.

But frozen suckers, as they were then known in this country, enjoyed a short-lived success. The flavourings were poor (many being nothing more than frozen mineral waters or weak concentrated fruit cordials) and numerous problems occurred with manufacture — often the wrong amount of gelatine was used or there was too much sugar, leaving a concentrated pool of syrup.

Gradually the industry sorted out its act and the post-war period saw a boom in sales. However, leading manufacturers were concerned about 'back-room spivs' who were trying to cash in and who had jumped on the tricycle. Concerns were voiced that ice lollies were being made in unhealthy premises, a situation which caused the Chief Sanitary Inspector for Ayrshire to speak in melodramatic terms of the 'ice lolly trade which flared up during the year (1951) like an epidemic and flashed over the countryside, as some novelty-hunting genius discovered a new sweetmeat possessing an irresistible appeal for youngsters'.

Although an outbreak of food poisoning in 1954 led to worries about the lead content in ice lollies, a 2d. Snowdrop and its contemporaries soon exercised a grip on the nation. In that same year, Norman Wisdom, described as 'Britain's Greatest Star', was to be seen extolling the virtues of a Topsy.

With health scares a thing of the past, the ice lolly has confirmed its status as the most refreshing way to spend 50p on a hot day. And what could be more thirst-quenching than the 12 346 lb (5600 kg) ice lolly constructed by a Dutch café and bar owner at Oostkapelle in 1992? It must have had one hell of a stick.

Identikit

One of the major handicaps the police often suffered in the ongoing fight against crime was the inability of witnesses to provide an accurate description of suspects. Hugh C. McDonald, a detective with the Los Angeles Identification Bureau, believed the answer lay in the compilation of a photographic likeness of the wanted person which could then be circulated internally and, if necessary, to the media. To effect his scheme, some 50 000 photographs were cut up and reduced to 500 master foils with a jigsaw-like kit of 130 hairlines, 102 pairs of eyes, 52 chins, 40 lips and 37 noses plus assorted beards, moustaches, eyebrows, spectacles, hats and scars. The theory was that every person's facial characteristics would be there somewhere.

The identikit system, as it became known, was first used in February 1959 by Sheriff Peter Pitchess of Los Angeles County Police in the hunt for a man who held up a liquor store. An identikit was distributed locally, prompting the naming of a suspect who duly confessed.

Alerted to this new breakthrough, Scotland Yard brought the identikit to Britain and in 1961, it led to the conviction of the murderer of Mrs Elsie Batten who had been stabbed to death in the antique shop where she worked off London's Charing Cross Road. Det. Sgt Ray Dagg had been on an identikit course and after interviewing two witnesses, was able to build up a description of a man of Indian appearance, seen behaving suspiciously in the area. The resultant identikit picture was sent out to all police forces and the media, and four days later PC Cole, on duty in Soho, spotted a man who bore an uncanny resemblance to the circulated picture. The suspect, Edwin Bush, was arrested and taken to Bow Street police station. After finally admitting the murder, he was found guilty and executed.

Instant Coffee

Nestlé invented instant coffee in 1938, after a massive surplus between the two world wars left growers with an awful lot of coffee in Brazil. The Swiss-based company devised Nescafé in response to a plea from the Brazilian government who were faced with an excess of a crop too bulky to store — a crop which was the country's biggest export earner.

The Brazilians made their request in 1930 but it was another eight years before Nestlé felt able to launch the product. There were many obstacles to be overcome,

(left) Ice lollies had become more adventurous by the 1960s.

Packaging has improved since the old brown tins of Nescafé.

including that of making the powder soluble so that it did not form a deposit at the bottom of the cup. Also, the container had to be airtight, filled under a vacuum. Indeed, rival manufacturers had previously attempted to introduce instant coffee but, quite simply, the results were undrinkable.

Finally, Nescafé was ready. It was sold on the Continent first, hitting the streets of Britain in 1939. Not everyone was enthusiastic. One of Nestlé's top salesmen was said to have remarked: 'It will never sell — the British only drink tea.'

The almost immediate outbreak of war with its consequent ban on advertising could well have proved him right but for the arrival in Britain of vast quantities of American servicemen who developed something of a taste for the new coffee.

Even so, it was not until hostilities had ceased that Nescafé really took off, allied to the introduction of a genuine 100 per cent instant coffee in 1954, the Nestlé researchers having discovered how to do without the stabilising carbohydrates which were prevalent in the prototype. Staid tea drinkers had used the old Nescafé mainly as a flavouring for hot milk but by the mid-1950s, the social world of espresso coffee bars had opened up a new consumer — the teenager.

Nescafé became synonymous with the coffee bars and by 1961, it was repackaged from tins into the famous brown jar. Four years later came Gold Blend, Britain's first freeze-dried coffee. It was originally launched only in the south but demand was so great that retailers in Scotland were reported to be 'bootlegging' supplies over the border.

Backed by plentiful television advertising (the Gold Blend couple became one of the most talked-about TV partnerships and even spawned a paperback novel), Nescafé has confirmed its place as market leader. Nearly 100 million cups of coffee a day are drunk in Britain — and 40 per cent of those are made with Nescafé.

Jeep

Seeking a new military general-purpose vehicle, the US Army invited 135 American motor manufacturers to compete for the contract to build a quarter-ton, four-wheel drive, light truck. But the 75-day deadline imposed for the delivery of prototypes was so tight that only three bothered to respond.

First off the mark were the Bantam Car Company of Butler, Pennsylvania. Their vehicle was designed by Karl K. Pabst in just five days and built in 49. However, the Army adopted the longer view and decided that despite the fact that Bantam had the best overall design, they did not possess the production capacity to meet the anticipated output. Instead, the contract was awarded to Willys-Overland Motors.

Between 1941 and 1945 some 600 000 Jeeps were built with peak production at the busiest factory reaching one every 80 seconds. The Jeep took its name from GP (general-purpose) although it was also christened Blitzbuggy, Jitterbug, Iron Pony and the evocative Panzer Killer.

At the end of the war, 'civilian' Jeeps went on sale in the US but not in Britain. However, the plentiful supply of surplus Army Jeeps was quickly snapped up by eager British farmers. One was bought by Maurice Wilks, chief engineer of the Rover Company, for use on his estate in Anglesey, North Wales. Wilks soon spotted the potential of the vehicle for peacetime operations and in 1948, his company introduced a modification of the Jeep called the Land Rover.

Jukebox (preselective)

The jukebox dates back to 1889 when a hand-operated Edison was introduced to the Palais Royal Saloon, San Francisco. However, with no choice of recordings, the listener was forced to endure whichever cylinder happened to be in the machine. It was another 16 years before the preselective model made its bow. Called the Multiphone and invented by John C. Dunton of Grand Rapids, Michigan, it stood 7 ft (2 m) high with a glass-fronted cabinet and a hand-cranked rotary selector which offered a choice of 24 cylinder recordings. The cylinders were numbered, matching up with a list which gave the titles.

In 1906 the John Gabel Company brought out the Automatic Entertainer, one of the first to use discs instead of cylinders, and by 1927, the arrival of radio having increased the demand for music, the first all-electric model had appeared. The same year saw the J.P. Seeburg Company market the Melatone but it demonstrated an undesirable habit of destroying records and all 100 had to be recalled.

Until 1939 the machines were known by their individual names but the issue of *Time* magazine dated 27 November reported that: 'Glenn Miller attributes his crescendo to the "juke-box" which retails recorded music at 5 cents a shot in bars, restaurants and roadside dance joints.' This was the first occasion the term had appeared in print, having travelled up from the deep south where blacks used the word 'juke', meaning to dance.

At that time it was estimated that there were 225 000 jukeboxes in the United States. The majority were made in the new translucent plastic, replacing the furniture-like wooden ones. In addition, the Automated Musical Instruments Company (AMI) had just brought out the first wall jukebox, the Mighty Midget. Jukebox production was banned by the US government during the war along with other coin-operated machines but made up for lost time in the immediate aftermath. The Wurlitzer 1015 alone sold 56 000 models in 1946.

The rock 'n' roll years merely served to improve the status of the jukebox with Elvis Presley's 'Hound Dog' and 'Don't Be Cruel', earning the accolade of being the all-time most-played jukebox records in the United States.

'Jean, shall we put on some David Whitfield?'
— 'Oh, Norma, don't you think that's a bit racy?'

Karaoke Machine

Perhaps not altogether surprisingly, the Japanese seem perfectly happy for the British to lay claim to inventing that scourge of pub and club, the karaoke machine. It has always been generally accepted that karaoke (which means 'empty orchestra') was first introduced by the Japanese in 1976 but Cheshire electrical salesman Roy Brooke says that he invented the principle a year earlier.

The venue for this melodious milestone was the White Horse public house at Disley, an establishment where Friday night was traditionally sing-song night around the piano. When the pianist was unavoidably detained elsewhere one evening, rather than disappoint the assembled throng, Brooke stepped in with a spot of hasty improvisation.

He said: 'I put together a little box of tricks to play the backing tracks to favourite songs. It was basically just a cassette deck and an amplifier but it worked well. I called it Roy's Singalong Machine but I suppose it was in fact the first karaoke machine.

'I sold a few to acts at Manchester clubs who used them for backing tracks instead of employing bands. Then about a year later I began to read about the Japanese enjoying karaoke. As with a lot of things, we originated the idea in this country but development was slow.'

For better or worse, the karaoke machine has enabled the humblest individual to be a star for three minutes. Shop assistants convince themselves that they could be the next Madonna — if only they could get away from the laxatives counter — while railway station booking clerks, fortified by a half of lager and lime, try to show that they can swivel their hips and thrust their pelvis just like Tom Jones.

Roy Brooke sees no end to karaoke. 'People like to sing when they are happy and sing when they are sad. It is just a natural human desire and it's the same in Tokyo as in Disley.' One thing puzzles him though. 'Everybody seems to want to sing "My Way" but I can't stand it.'

Karting

Back in August 1956, Art Ingels was an employee of the Kurtis Kraft Company of Glendale, California, where he was engaged in the manufacture of the famous Indianopolis 500 racing cars. As a sideline, he decided to fix some of the spare tubing to a 2½ hp lawnmower engine and create the world's first go-kart.

That first kart was an extremely basic affair. There was just one pedal — the accelerator — while braking was achieved by means of a simple lever connected to a pivoting plate allowing it to press on the right hand rear tyre. Ingels tested his creation around car parks and the craze quickly caught on with his friends who started building their own karts and using any patch of spare ground to stage race meetings, a situation which did not always endear them to local residents or the police.

Ingels tried to interest the Kurtis Kraft management but without success, so he left the company, joined forces with Lou Borelli and began making the Caretta kart.

Still desperate for a permanent track, the newly formed Go-Kart Club of America finally managed to persuade officials of the Eastland Shopping Centre in West Covina to allow the huge car park to be raced on twice a month. Thus the world's first organised kart race took place in the Eastland car park in December 1957. The venue proved so popular that long tailbacks resulted on the San Bernardino freeway as drivers paused to gain a glimpse of the action. The ensuing chaos meant that the karters were soon once again forced to move on.

Meanwhile Sgt Micky Flynn, an American airman stationed at Burtonwood in Cheshire, had read about the new breed of mini racers in an American motor sport journal. He promptly ordered five karts. They arrived in September 1958 and were initially raced around various American Air Force bases, notably Lakenheath in Suffolk. Karting had come to Britain.

The sport, which has its own World Championships, is now an accepted training ground for the Grand Prix stars of tomorrow. Nigel Mansell, Alain Prost, Ayrton Senna, Ricardo Patrese — they all started out driving karts. It can safely be said that karting has come a long way from those original flying lawnmowers.

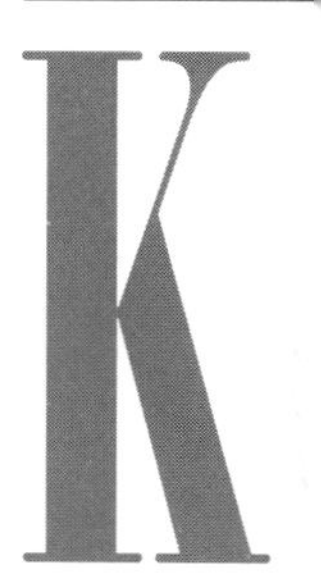

Kentucky Fried Chicken (KFC)

In the 1930s former ferry-boat captain Colonel Harland D. Sanders ran a filling station in Corbin, Kentucky. Always on the lookout for fresh ideas, he opened up a fried chicken restaurant on the premises as a sideline to selling petrol.

There was nothing new about fried chicken but Sanders' coating contained a distinctive combination of 11 herbs and spices which tickled the taste-buds of his customers. Despite the unfavourable business climate of the time, his enterprise boomed until the early fifties when a new highway bypassed his filling station.

The colonel sold out at a loss but a chance encounter with fellow restaurateur Leon W. (Pete) Harman was to

Colonel Sanders, the founder of Kentucky Fried Chicken.

K

revitalise his fortunes. The pair first met at a food seminar in Chicago and shortly afterwards Sanders visited Harman on his way to a Church convention in Australia. Harman, who ran a hamburger restaurant in Salt Lake City, said he was looking for a speciality dish to add to his menu whereupon Sanders immediately offered to cook dinner that night, treating his host to the best fried chicken he had ever tasted. Harman wasted no time in acquiring the recipe and adding it to his menu. On the window of his restaurant, he painted the words 'Kentucky Fried Chicken'.

The chicken was such a success that Harman expanded to another restaurant in 1952. He invited Sanders to the official opening, billing him as the 'Kentucky Colonel'. Harman also encouraged Sanders to sell the rights to Kentucky Fried Chicken nationally on a franchise basis and so in 1954, at the ripe old age of 65, Sanders toured America, trying to interest restaurant-owners in his product. Within ten years there were 838 Kentucky Fried Chicken franchises in the US, with a $37 million turnover. The concept came to Britain in 1965 with the opening of a store in Preston.

Recently abbreviated to KFC, the Colonel's secret recipe can now be tasted in over 8700 outlets in 64 countries.

Kiwi Fruit

To the greengrocers of the world, there was no such thing as the Kiwi fruit until 1959. But it had existed in a previous life as the Chinese gooseberry.

As its name implies, the gooseberry originated in the Far East before being cultivated in Europe from 1900. But the only nation to see its potential was New Zealand where it arrived in 1906, thanks to a Mr James McGregor who transported the seed from China. He passed it on to Alex Allison who is credited with being the first person to grow the Chinese gooseberry in New Zealand.

The vines grown from that seed fruited in 1910 but even then, nobody considered growing it commercially for another 30 years. Then production began around the Bay of Plenty and as the green fruit increased in popularity, farmers began to plant up their orchards. Eventually it was decided to aim for the export market and New Zealanders renamed the fruit as their own, after their national bird.

Kodak Brownie

'The dollar camera is at last a fact. Of course, there have been pin-hole affairs, with a groove in the back to hold a glass plate, which have sold for almost nothing — and were worth it, but the Brownie is the first really practical instrument at the price.'

So announced the Eastman Kodak Company of Rochester, New York, in February 1900 at the trade launch of the camera line which, for the next 60 years, was to be the most famous in the world.

The dollar camera was the dream of Kodak founder George Eastman, a former banker. He wanted to market a children's camera which would retail at the lowest possible price, realising that the profit from film sales was more important than that from camera sales. Although designed by Eastman's chief designer, Frank Brownell, the new camera was not named in his honour. Instead, it took its name from the Brownies, little elfin-like creatures who featured in the stories of Canadian writer and illustrator Palmer Cox, and whose friendly efficiency reflected the image Eastman desired.

That first Brownie box camera (for which an extra 15 cents bought a six-exposure film cartridge) was made of heavy jute board, reinforced with wood, and covered with neatly creased black imitation leather. But its construction was somewhat flimsy and before going on sale to the public, certain modifications were made.

Eastman opted for saturation advertising in children's magazines, emphasising the fact that the Brownie could be 'Operated by Any School Boy or Girl'. An early campaign depicted 'The Boy With a Brownie', showing a youngster with such 'boyish' items as a kite or a fishing rod and, of course, a Brownie camera.

The Brownie was an instant success, its cheapness and simplicity inspiring a succession of imitators. But the Brownie saw them all off, constantly updating the range while maintaining the basic premise of being easy to operate. The popular 127 model was introduced in 1953, costing $4.75, and by the time the Brownie gave way to the Instamatic in the 1960s, nearly 70 different styles and sizes of Kodak Brownie had been produced in America alone. It had become a national treasure.

One of the first Kodak Brownie cameras from 1900.

Launderette

As a romantic meeting place, few spots would appear to have less potential than one where you sit and watch the gradual sanitation of each other's dirty underwear. Yet the launderette has been the setting for many a 'briefs encounter', possibly because there is nothing much else to do there than talk to the person next to you. After all, when you've seen one pair of soapy socks, you've seen them all.

The very first launderette was the Washeteria, opened at Fort Worth, Texas, by one J.F. Cantrell in 1934. It had four electric washing machines which were paid for by the hour, customers being obliged to provide their own soap. It was another 11 years, however, before the self-service laundry came into existence, the basis of the launderette we know and love today.

Most of the apartments of forties' New York were not large enough to house a washing machine and so the basements served as laundry rooms, the machines therein being fitted with a mechanism to accept a 5- or 10-cent coin. Early in 1945, an apartment block owner in Upper Manhattan noticed empty shop premises on the corner adjacent to his block. He reasoned that if he could transfer his basement laundry to that corner shop, he could convert his basement to living accommodation. So that spring, the vacant shop became a self-service laundry, called a 'Laundromat'.

To the owner's amazement, the laundromat not only attracted residents from his block but from the whole neighbourhood. Going there became a social event and soon the concept had spread across the city.

Towards the end of 1946 Glaswegian Wilfred Russell-Neil, an executive with Bendix Home Appliances Ltd, visited America to study laundromats. He came away impressed and set about opening similar establishments in middle-class areas of Britain. He christened them 'launderettes' and the first, in London's Queensway opposite Whiteley's department store, was opened by actress Jean Kent on Thursday 9 May 1949. By the Saturday, there were queues. Customers were delighted with the price of 2s. 6d. per load although some more sensitive souls suggested putting lace curtains at the windows so that they could not be seen doing their dirty washing in public!

The march of the launderette continued unabated. Rival firms began setting up virtually next door to existing sites, leading to the so-called 'launderette war' of the early 1960s. At the same time, attendants were dispensed with and Britain went over to the American system of coin-ops.

In 1985 this great 20th century innovation received its finest accolade when having a film named after it, *My Beautiful Launderette.*

L

The largest Lego construction in the world of Indian chief Sitting Bull at Legoland Park, Billund, Denmark.

L

Lego

The story of Lego is a Danish fairytale that would do justice to Hans Christian Andersen. For it has been calculated that nearly 300 million children in 115 countries have played with Lego bricks — an invention which can be traced back to a humble Danish carpenter.

It was 1916 when 25-year-old Ole Kirk Christiansen set up business in his home town of Billund, making stepladders and ironing boards. By 1932 he and his few employees had precious little custom and so in desperation, he decided to start manufacturing wooden toys. Two years later, he named his toys Lego from the Danish words 'leg godt' meaning 'play well'. One of the best-selling Lego lines of the 1930s was a hand-painted wooden duck on wheels before the production of plastic toys began in 1947, resulting from the installation at Billund of the first injection moulding machine in Denmark. Babies' rattles were followed in 1949 by plastic Automatic Binding Bricks, a forerunner of the Lego bricks, but these were sold only in Denmark. The hollow bricks had studs on top and could be built on top of each other — but without much clutching power. And even when the moulds were modified, the bricks still did not sell particularly well.

There was, nevertheless, a definite demand within the Danish toy trade for something offering a strong idea and system. Examining its own merchandise, Lego decided that the building brick was the only product in the existing range which could be developed into a system and mass-produced.

In 1955 the Lego brick was launched but the key to future success came three years later when the innovative stud-and-tube coupling system was invented by Godtfred Kirk Christiansen, son of the founder. This ensured excellent clutching power, thereby vastly increasing the number of possible building combinations. Lego has never looked back.

While over a million visitors pour into Legoland Park each year and enthusiasts build 65 ft (20 m) towers of 300 000 coloured bricks, Lego was put to a more practical use by Devon veterinary surgeon John Parkinson. When a 70-year-old tortoise was savaged by a cat and had to have a front leg amputated, the vet replaced it with a pair of Lego wheels taken from his son's toy set. The new artificial limb was stuck to the underside of the tortoise who was promptly christened 'Wheely'. The animal's owner said: 'Wheely is coping quite well but has difficulty turning. He may need a different type of wheel fitting to help him corner.'

Long-playing Record

The earliest attempt at producing a long-playing record was made by the Neophone Company of London who, in 1904, issued discs of celluloid and cardboard laminate which, playing between eight and ten minutes, could contain an entire overture without the listener having to turn over. However, not only were the new discs inordinately expensive, costing 10s. 6d. as opposed to the ordinary 12-inch disc which cost 1s., they were also noisy and cumbersome with an alarming tendency to curl up if left in a sunny spot. Thus, few tears were shed when production ceased within two years.

The idea lay dormant for 25 years until revitalised by the American company RCA-Victor. They selected a playing speed of 33⅓ rpm and, by doubling the number of grooves per inch, were able to offer sides playing up to around 14 minutes, prompting the boast that their Stokowski-Philadelphia Orchestra recording of Beethoven's Fifth Symphony was 'the longest movement of a symphony without interruption'. But the quality of the recordings were inferior to the average 78. One US critic wrote: 'The recording is conspicuously lacking in color, brilliancy and character; it is thin, flabby, faded and lustreless; the music is all there, but it is pale and weak and lacks the life of the original . . . We would prefer to put up with the nuisance of frequent record-changing and listen to the standard discs.'

A major drawback was that to play 33⅓, the listener needed a two-speed turntable and that meant buying an expensive RCA-Victor radio-phonograph costing anything between $247.50 and $995. Faced with widespread public apathy, RCA were forced to concede defeat and plans for further releases were scrapped.

The breakthrough finally came in June 1948 when Columbia invited journalists to hear 'a revolutionary new product'. Their system, perfected by Peter Goldmark, involved the creation of microgrooves, some 300 in all, to give a playing time of up to 23 minutes per side. The discs were made of vinylite, a non-breakable plastic, and the sound quality was enhanced by the development of lightweight pickups. Columbia called them LPs, the first recordings being Mendelsohn's Violin Concerto, *South Pacific* and Tchaikovsky's Fourth Symphony. Naturally, a few teething troubles manifested themselves — sustained notes tended to waver slightly while loud passages sometimes made a faint and untimely appearance ahead of the beat, a phenomenon termed 'pre-echo'.

Ironically, RCA-Victor despised the LP, principally because they wanted to introduce their own 45 rpm records. But by 1950 they were forced to accept its arrival and promptly sacked all their executives who had opposed it.

Decca brought the LP to the attention of the British public in 1950, selling 12-inch discs for 39s. 6d. Among early offerings on the new medium were Mantovani, Edmundo Ros and Vera Lynn. Some diehards, including Compton Mackenzie (editor of *The Gramophone*), deplored the demise of the 78, but soon had to admit that the LP was here to stay — at least until the compact disc came along.

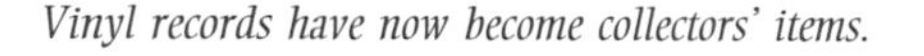

Vinyl records have now become collectors' items.

Lucozade

Worried by his daughter's jaundice, William Walker Hunter, a Newcastle upon Tyne chemist, sought to produce a palatable, easily digestible glucose drink to aid her recovery. He perfected the potion in the shop of W.W. Owen & Son, of which he was proprietor, and the product became known as Lucozade after its chief constituent.

Hunter's formula was prepared in 1927 and was in such demand that 11 years later local sales were superseded by national distribution when he was bought out by Beecham.

Lucozade retained its popularity until the 1970s when sales started to plummet. The decline was only halted in 1983 by the introduction of television commercials featuring Olympic decathlon champion Daley Thompson. Suddenly Lucozade seemed the way to sporting excellence and between 1985 and 1988, sales doubled. Lucozade itself was on the road to recovery.

Lucozade: 'So energising and palatable.' It may not have been catchy but it was effective.

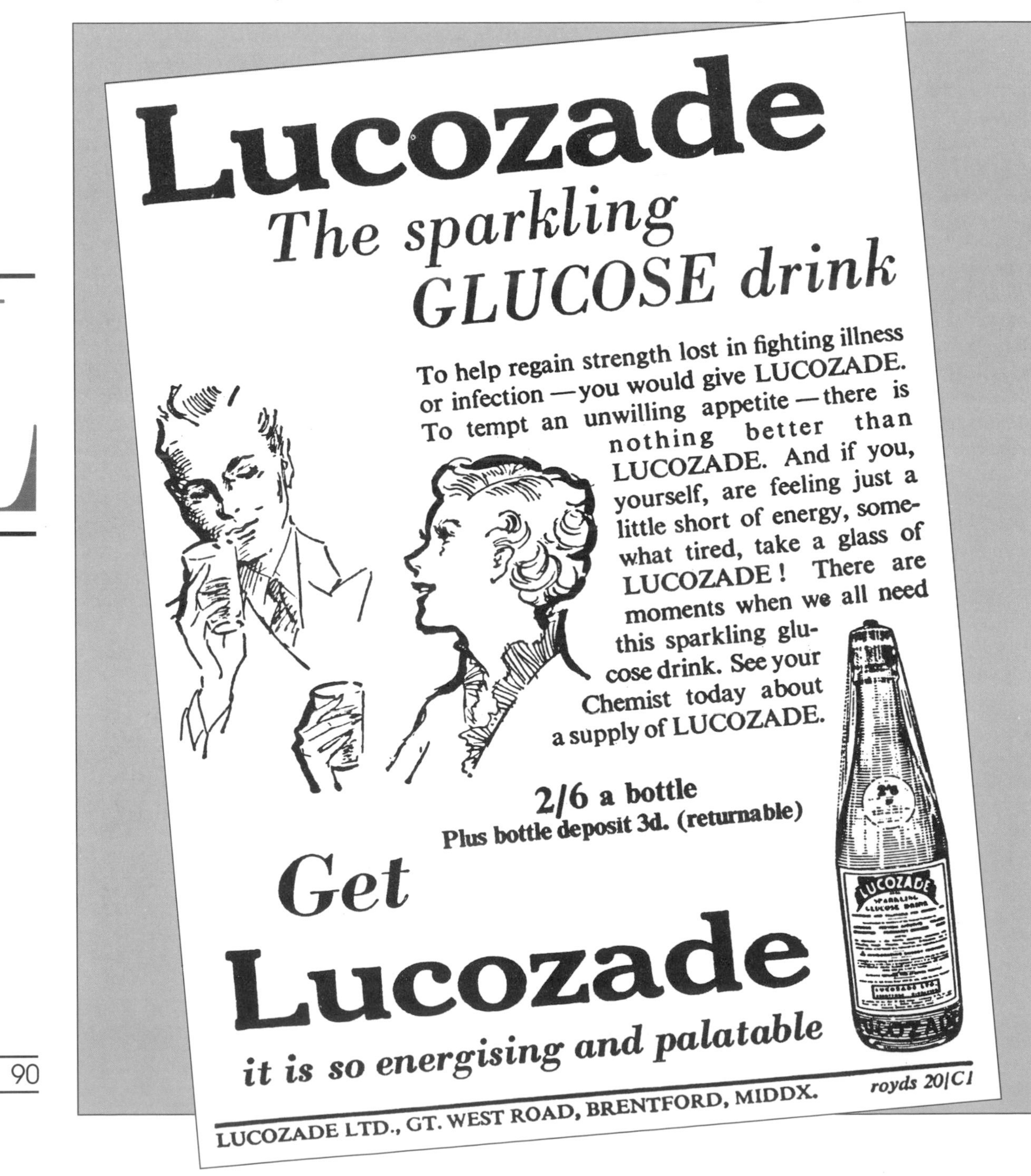

Luncheon Vouchers

As might be expected, the concept for Luncheon Vouchers was thought up over lunch. London businessman John Hack was dining with some friends in 1954 when he noticed people paying for their meals with slips of paper. Being curious, he asked the waiter about this and was told that the restaurant had arrangements with various companies whereby their employees could use these printed slips to settle the bill. The slips were then returned to the respective company who subsequently paid the restaurant.

Obviously, this involved a considerable amount of work for any company who wished to subsidise staff lunches. There was the matter of having vouchers printed, making the necessary arrangements with two or three restaurants, checking and counting the vouchers on their return and finally settling the account. John Hack decided to start a company which would do all the work for a service charge and on 1 January 1955, Luncheon Vouchers Ltd began trading.

The original intention was to extract a service charge from both client and caterer. But whilst a few caterers were keen to accept luncheon vouchers, they flatly refused to pay the five per cent service fee and so the idea of charging them was dropped. Denominations of vouchers ranged from 1s. to 5s.

Progress was slow at first because the larger catering companies refused to join the scheme and since these concerns owned the restaurants at which staff preferred to eat, clients, too, were reluctant to join. This stalemate was resolved in 1956 when nine of the biggest companies (including J. Lyons, Forte, Express Dairy and A.B.C.) formed a consortium and bought out Luncheon Vouchers Ltd.

The wage freeze of the 1970s proved a real boon to Luncheon Vouchers but business started to decline in the eighties and in 1985 the company was acquired by Ticket Restaurant, a division of the French group Accor. It is ironic that Ticket Restaurant had only started up after a French visitor to London in the early sixties had been so impressed by Luncheon Vouchers that he had decided to export the system to France.

Lycra

One of the fashion sensations of the past decade, Lycra has in fact been around since 1958. It was invented by the American company Du Pont who had been conducting research aimed at finding methods of producing a fibre which would possess the elastic qualities of rubber but at the same time be a true textile. They came up with a synthetic polyurethane fibre which, weight for weight, was three times more powerful than rubber elastic. In the experimental stages, it was referred to as Fibre K but the trade name Lycra was announced in October 1959.

Lycra was the first of a succession of spandex fibres which were stronger and longer-lasting than rubber and which could be covered with silk, cotton or wool to provide a stretchable lightweight yarn. Its earliest commercial use was in underwear. In December 1960, Warner Bros. advertised their first garment 'in the new Lycra fabric', a step-in girdle known as 'Little Godiva'. They followed this in 1961 with their appropriately named 'Birthday Suit', a close-fitting Lycra garment, the forerunner of body stockings and the 'nude look'. It weighed just 3 ounces (85 g) but cost 8½ guineas. Berlei began to incorporate Lycra in bras and by the start of 1962 it was reported that 'Spandex fibres are currently bringing about a revolution in the foundation garment industry'.

Due to its excellent figure control and the fact that it resisted perspiration, oils and lotions, Lycra also became much in demand for swimwear. In June 1965, *Vogue* magazine promoted Lycra as a second skin, eulogising: 'When it's dried in the sun, it's a sinuous velvety black, and when it's soaked with water, it glistens like a seal on the rocks.' As far as Lycra was concerned, this was the seal of approval.

In the 1960s, a 3s. Luncheon Voucher could be a passport to a square meal.

L

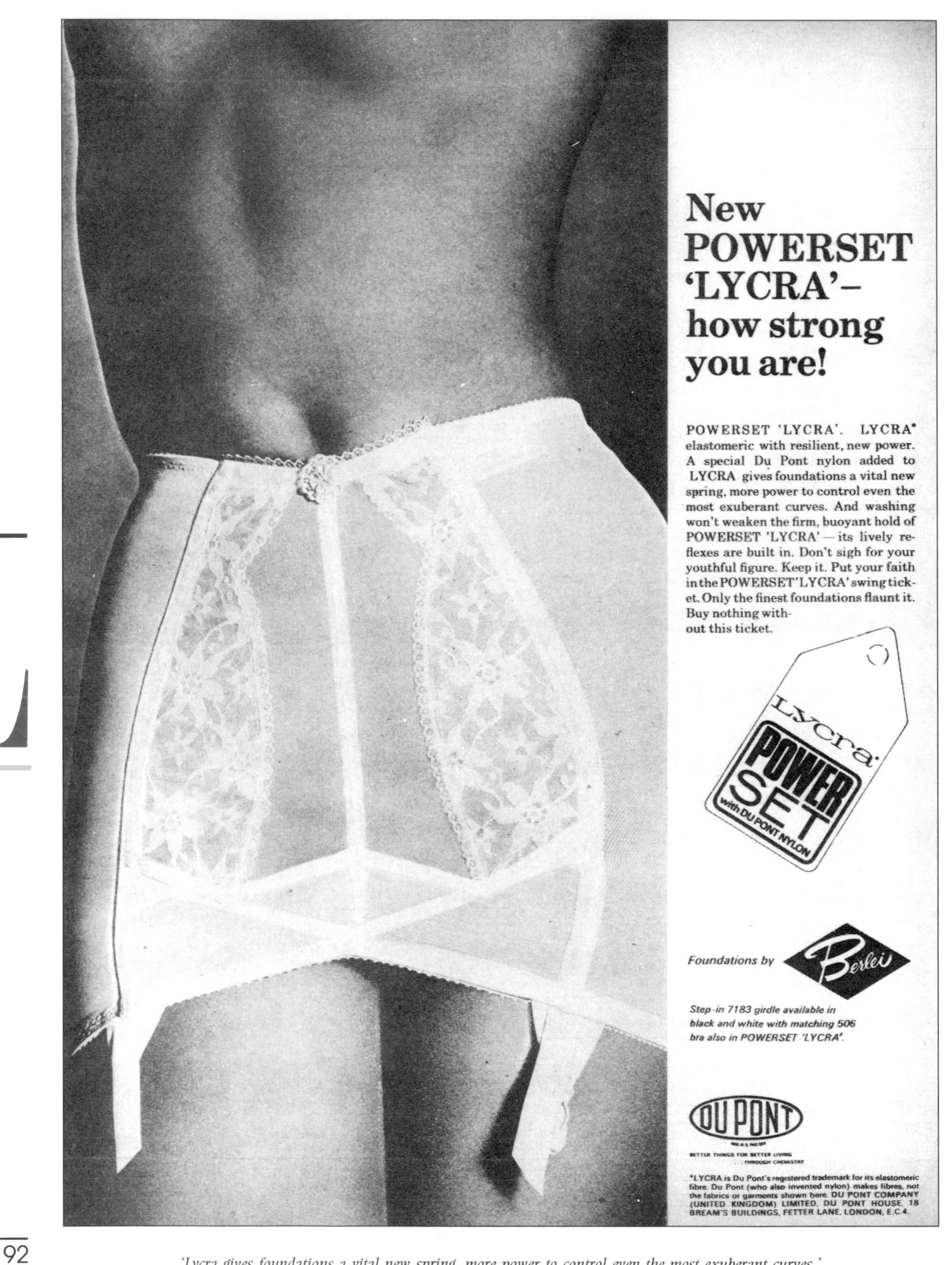

'Lycra gives foundations a vital new spring, more power to control even the most exuberant curves.'

Marigold Rubber Gloves

Once upon a time, the lady of the house had hard, rough skin on her hands from all those hours of washing floors, dishes and clothes. Then, along came rubber gloves to protect those precious palms and ensure that the hardest-working cleaning lady could have hands like Marie Helvin.

It was the same technique of dipping in liquid latex which perfected the introduction of Durex, that enabled the London Rubber Company to launch rubber gloves in 1952. Many of the early products were aimed at surgical or industrial use but in 1961, LRC brought out Marigold household gloves.

With raised patterned palms and fingers to give additional wet grip on the most accident-prone crockery and flock lining for extra comfort, Marigolds, in their joyous yellow, have become a cherished item in any girl's wardrobe. But it is so difficult to find a matching handbag . . .

What woman could resist a pair of suedette lined rubber gloves?

Marmite

In the 1930s the trademark Marmite reached the lofty heights of inclusion in *The Oxford Dictionary of Modern English.* The makers wrote to the editors, defining Marmite as: 'An extract from fresh brewers' yeast, rich in vitamin B complex. Used for culinary purposes, e.g. for making soups etc., and also medicinally (Trade Name).'

'Marmite Is Good' enthuses an advertisement from the 1930s.

This illustrates just what a versatile little substance Marmite yeast extract is. For whilst today we tend to think of its culinary prowess, Marmite has been known to cure a wide range of ailments. Indeed, a special booklet was produced for the medical profession in the early 1950s extolling the remedial virtues of Marmite. Its high vitamin B content meant that it was considered efficacious for those with such diverse disorders as diabetes, gastric ulcers, rheumatism and nervous and mental complaints.

Of course, Marmite yeast extract has had a long history of providing an ideal source of nourishment for children. The Marmite Food Extract Company was formed in 1902 at Burton-on-Trent, the product taking its name from the French for cooking pot which has always been represented pictorially on the label of the jar. Generations of infants have been raised on Marmite by way of its use in child welfare centres and nurseries throughout the world. In 1940s Nigeria it achieved spectacular results in curing retrobulbar neuritis, a disease responsible for the progressive blindness of large numbers of children.

There was even a suggestion in 1930s women's magazines that Marmite could act as a marriage guidance counsellor. A character called Ma Marmite, the Claire Rayner of her day, declared: 'If every married woman could make really good hash, there'd be fewer hashes made of marriage. That's why I say — always have a jar of Marmite at hand.' A further indication of the importance of Marmite to the nation came during the Second World War when the public were urged, '*Please* go easy with the Marmite.'

To return to its medical benefits, Marmite was once prescribed in the Eastern tropics where burning feet and beriberi were prevalent while the Medical Research Council's 1951 report on Deficiency Diseases in Japanese Prison Camps stated that Marmite yeast extract had proved effective in the treatment of scrotal dermatitis. The report did not, however, indicate whether the Marmite was meant to be taken orally or applied to the affected parts but presumably the patients were the original 'Marmite soldiers' . . .

Mars Bar

When four British skiers were stranded for six days after a fierce blizzard on Russia's Mount Elbrus in 1993, they stayed alive by eating Mars Bars.

When Dorset diabetic Jess Yates felt himself slipping into a coma, he waved a Mars Bar wrapper under the nose of his pet dog Guinness and said 'fetch'. The dog responded and the sugar content of the Mars Bar brought Jess round and saved his life.

And when broadcaster David Dimbleby faced a marathon session as anchorman for the BBC's General Election coverage, he kept going on a steady diet of Mars Bars.

Elizabeth Taylor, Joan Collins, Paul Gascoigne — they have all declared themselves avid devourers of the Mars Bar — not to mention intrepid explorer Sir Ranulph Fiennes, who claims to eat four in a session, or Marianne Faithfull . . .

British Rail trains travelling in remote areas of Scotland carry Mars Bars in their emergency packs in case they are cut off by snow while Mars was adopted as the official snack food at both the 1990 World Cup in Italy and the Barcelona Olympics.

In some quarters, it is even used as an economic guide. The *Financial Times* has described the Mars Bar as 'a currency for our time' because it contains staple commodities including cocoa, milk, vegetable fats, solids and sugar. The *FT* said that Mars was a more reliable 'currency' than gold which is prone to speculation. And

A stiff upper lip sings the praises of the Mars Bar.

a young sculptor at Cheltenham and Gloucester College of Higher Education managed to turn it into an art form by designing a giant chocolate tongue made from 150 Mars Bars.

The architect of this confectionery institution was American Forrest E. Mars, himself the son of a sweet manufacturer. In 1932 Forrest Mars crossed the Atlantic with the recipe for the Mars Bar and set up business in a small rented factory in Slough. Beginning with just a dozen employees, he sold the first Mars Bars, each made by hand, locally for 2d. each.

At the time, block chocolate was very much in vogue and so the Mars, with its nougat and caramel and covered in thick milk chocolate, was refreshingly different. Demand was so great for the new product that by the end of that first year, the workforce of Mars Confections Ltd had increased to 100.

Boosted by the introductions of Milky Way (1935) and Maltesers (1936), the company expanded further and although sweets were rationed during the Second World War, the Mars Bar was considered an essential part of supplies for American G.I.s. In 1991 it was exported to the Soviet Union for the first time where, in the face of lengthy queues, numbers were restricted to four per person.

The old slogan of 'A Mars a Day Helps You Work, Rest and Play' has been supplemented by 'There's More to Mars'. The recipe, too, has changed slightly but its success continues unabated, even encompassing Mars ice cream. Some three million Mars Bars are made every day at Slough (the now highly automated process takes two hours from raw materials to finished product) and a staggering 2.7 million bars are eaten in Britain per day.

However, not everybody profits from a Mars Bar. In August 1979 racehorse No Bombs snatched a Mars Bar from his stable boy on the way to Ascot races and won by eight lengths. But the horse was subsequently disqualified after a routine dope test revealed traces of caffeine and theobromine, two mild stimulants naturally present in cocoa beans, which are guaranteed to make anyone run faster. It emerged that the Mars Bar was to blame. The horse's trainer, Peter Easterby, lamented: 'That's the most expensive Mars Bar ever — it cost £4064 in prize money.'

McDonald's

Terms such as 'Big Mac' and 'Chicken McNugget' are now as much a part of our language as afternoon tea or fish and chips. At the last count, there were over 13 000 McDonald's restaurants operating in some 60 countries. It is estimated that a branch of McDonald's is opened somewhere in the world every 14½ hours and

The McDonald brothers with the first restaurant to bear their name, in Des Plaines, Illinois.

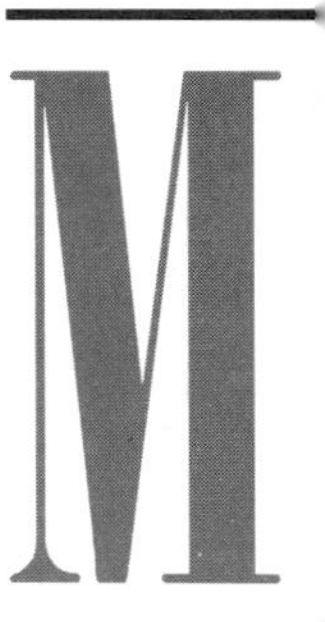

that 145 McDonald's hamburgers are consumed worldwide every second. There is even a McDonald's at the North Pole, a floating McDonald's on a steamer in St Louis and when, in 1990, a 900-seater McDonald's opened in Moscow, 20 000 curious Muscovites queued up to sample this latest western phenomenon.

Yet the McDonald's success story started out in 1937 at a tiny drive-in restaurant (in truth it was little more than a hut), built with borrowed wood near Pasadena. And what's more, there was not a hamburger in sight!

Richard McDonald and his older brother Maurice (known to all as Dick and Mac) had intended pursuing a career in Hollywood. They landed jobs as scene shifters, often on silent one-reelers featuring boss-eyed slapstick comedian Ben Turpin, before buying their own cinema to capitalise on the expanding movie industry. But they struggled financially and after four years switched their attentions to a different growth area — the drive-in restaurant. That first Pasadena venture saw Dick and Mac cooking hotdogs (not hamburgers), mixing milk shakes and waiting on customers perched on a dozen canopy-covered stools. Meanwhile, three employees served patrons in their cars.

Business boomed and in 1940 the McDonalds opened a self-service outlet in San Bernardino. Their fame and fortune spread throughout Southern California but they showed little interest in expanding further. Then, in July 1954, came the chance encounter that was to make McDonald's a household name throughout the world.

Ray Kroc, a 52-year-old entrepreneur, held the exclusive US rights to the Multimixer milkshake machine, a contraption capable of whipping up five shakes at a time. He was fascinated to discover that one restaurant in San Bernardino had no fewer than eight of the machines and so decided to pay a visit to this trail-blazing establishment. The sign outside said 'McDonald's Hamburgers' and promised 'Speedee Service'. Kroc sat in his car and watched in wonderment as the crew of young people in clean, white uniforms raced around to get the place ready for the day's business. And from the moment the little octagonal-shaped hamburger stand opened, trade was non-stop.

For two days Kroc just sat and observed, pausing only to approve the food on offer. On the evening of the second day, he introduced himself to the brothers and persuaded them to let him sell their franchises throughout the rest of the United States. On 15 April 1955 Kroc opened his first McDonald's in Des Plaines, Illinois. That day's takings were $332 which, at 15 cents a hamburger, was pretty good going. The new company's motto was Quality, Service, Cleanliness and Value.

In 1961 Kroc bought all rights to the McDonald's concept from the brothers for 2.7 million dollars. Two years later Ronald McDonald replaced the old mascot, Speedee, as Kroc's investment began to look like the bargain of the century.

The rest, as they say, is history. In September 1990 McDonald's was able to announce the serving of its 80 billionth hamburger.

Meccano

It is somehow incongruous that the man responsible for the invention of one of the century's most celebrated constructional toys had no formal training in either engineering or mechanics. Indeed he worked as a book-keeper with a meat-importing business. But what Frank Hornby lacked in diplomas, he made up for in ingenuity and was able to make toys out of sheet metal for his sons.

He specialised in railway accessories such as bridges and trucks but felt that the one drawback was that his models did not have interchangeable parts. On a train journey one day, he came up with the solution — to use thin strips of copper with perforated holes, the strips being fastened together with nuts and bolts. The idea would make Frank Hornby a millionaire.

Excited by the potential of his discovery, Hornby filed a patent in 1901, the specification describing it as 'Improvements in Toy or Educational Devices for Children and Young People'. He soon named his system 'Mechanics Made Easy' but struggled to interest manufacturers until finding an ally in the Liverpool firm of Philip, Son and Nephew. One of the first creations was a gantry crane with working trolley but sales were slow, mainly because sets cost 7s. 6d., half the weekly wage of a labourer.

Throughout these early years, Hornby kept his day job and without the financial support of his meat-importer boss, David Hugh Elliott, would surely have gone to the wall. By 1906 Hornby's enterprise was reaping rewards, albeit a modest annual profit of around £80, but it was sufficient for him to take the bold step of leaving Elliott's employ the following year. At the same time, instead of farming out the manufacture to various companies, Hornby decided to make the product himself. He also opted for a new name — Meccano — reasoning that its Latin air would appeal to overseas buyers.

The Meccano Manual first appeared in 1908, the cover showing a boy and a girl, both with bright orange hair. Soon the girl was ousted. More ammunition for Mrs Pankhurst!

Hornby was a shrewd businessman, quick to spot a market opening. As early as 1910 he latched on to the potential of aviation by bringing out a Meccano aeroplane, based on the Wright brothers' biplane, and the following year, to mark the coronation of George V, he dubbed the system 'Royal Meccano'.

Well-scrubbed children illustrate the merits of Meccano.

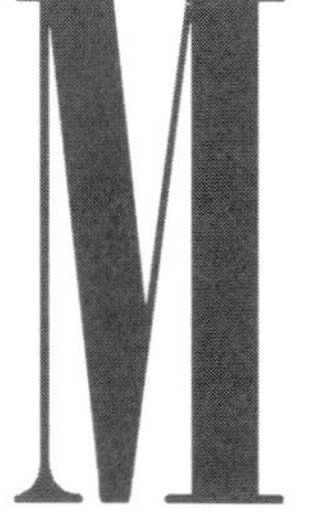

At the end of the First World War, Meccano literature was being printed in 15 different languages to cater for the rapid expansion in overseas sales. Visualising himself as a moral guardian as well as a toy-maker, Hornby formed The Meccano Guild, the aims of which were 'to foster clean-mindedness, truthfulness, ambition and initiative in boys'. All the boys used to illustrate the Guild had the regulation short back and sides haircut.

By the time the Second World War came around, Meccano was available in colour and boys could battle it out with authentic tanks, battleships and planes. There were even plans for a decontamination lorry to counter mustard-gas — a macabre plaything for children — but these were scuppered by the British government's decision to suspend the production of metal toys during hostilities.

The toy industry is more transient than most. As the Cabbage Patch Dolls and others will testify, one year's sensation is the following year's jumble sale. Meccano had enjoyed a remarkable run but by the late 1970s, the signs were ominous. Finally, on 30 November 1979, while a giant Meccano dinosaur was being built for an exhibition in Manchester, the famous factory in Binns Road, Liverpool, was closed down. Meccano itself was in danger of becoming something of a dinosaur. But the name lives on with production continuing in France.

Microwave Oven

First impressions are said to be all-important, in which case it is remarkable that the microwave oven ever entered production. The principle of microwave cooking had been discovered by Percy Spencer, a physics engineer with the American radar equipment company, Raytheon, but before his work could be taken any further, he needed to convince the Raytheon board of its merits. So to demonstrate the cooking powers, he placed an unpierced egg in front of a series of microwaves while the various board members looked on in eager anticipation. The experiment was proved in the most dramatic fashion when the egg exploded over the watching directors. Fortunately for Spencer, the fact that they were left with egg on their faces did not blinker their judgement. The microwave oven was given the green light.

Spencer's invention almost came about by accident. His principal task in the Second World War was to make the magnetrons used in radar systems. These detected planes and ships by beaming out microwaves and recording the reflections which bounced back. Spencer had noticed that the magnetrons gave off as much heat as a large light bulb and had frequently used them to warm his hands on bitterly cold days. But it was not until he discovered a melted sweet in his pocket and realised the cause that the possibility occurred to him of cooking food with microwaves.

His first experiment involved a bag of popcorn which proceeded to become exceedingly animated in the presence of the microwaves. He then moved on to greater things and hung a pork chop on a string in front of microwaves. It cooked. By now he was ready to try the egg routine with the directors.

Spencer patented his idea in 1953 and within a couple of years Raytheon had produced the first microwave oven, the Radareye. However, it was bulky and expensive and its use was restricted to hotel kitchens. Indeed it was not until 1967 that the first domestic microwave oven appeared on the market and Percy Spencer's extreme measures really began to pay off.

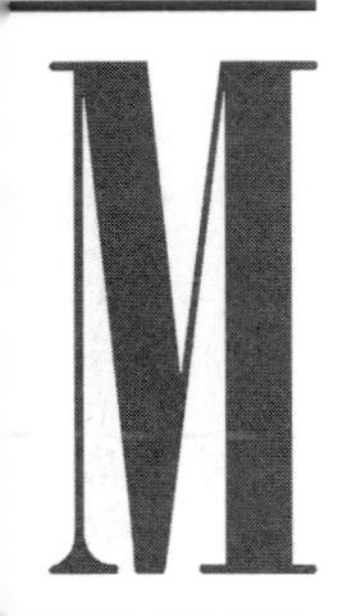

Mini Car

'Remember the impact this little car had in 1959. The surprise of everyone at a responsible lot like BMC putting their famous Austin and Morris labels on a comic creation whose engine faced the wrong way; had tiny wheels, no drive-shaft down the middle and rubber springs.'

That was how five years on, *Motor* magazine recalled the widespread bewilderment which had greeted the Mini, the car whose sales would exceed five million and become a symbol of the sixties, driven by everyone from the Aga Khan to Twiggy.

The Mini story really begins in 1956 when the Suez crisis, which saw Egypt's President Nasser cut the oil pipeline feeding the west, fuelled the demand for small cars with good mileage per gallon. First to emerge was that funny little creation the bubble car, a vehicle which had a comfort level and acceleration later matched only by the spacehopper. Leonard Lord, chairman of the British Motor Corporation, detested bubble cars and determined to replace them with a small car. Designer Alec Issigonis was instructed to drop everything and produce a smaller version of the popular Morris Minor. The result was the Mini, although in its early stages of development it was referred to as the Austin Newmarket since it was aimed at a new market and because at the time BMC liked to name cars after places — witness the Somerset, Westminster and Cambridge.

The Mini was formally launched on 26 August 1959. The newspaper advertisements that day ran: 'You've never seen a small car like this before. Front-wheel drive. Fully independent suspension. Up to 50 mpg. Over 70 mph. And that's only the beginning . . . Ten feet long, but roomier inside than many an £800 saloon.' Priced at £496 19s. 2d. (including purchase tax) and with a spartan interior, the Mini was slow to take off. Motorists mistrusted it because it was so cheap, the situation worsening during that first winter by a technical fault which caused water leaks and rotting carpets. A senior BMC executive confessed that the Mini had 'quivered on the brink of failure'.

The turning point came when the Mini was adopted by trendy middle-class Londoners who saw it as the solution to their parking problems. Lord Snowdon bought one. He had a wind-up window fitted on the driver's side but kept the standard production sliding window on Princess Margaret's side because it blew her hair about less. Suddenly everyone wanted their Mini to be different. Peter Sellers had wickerwork panels added to the doors of his. He later had one specially built with an opening tailgate 'so that Harry Secombe could come along'. When a 20-ft (6 m) long Mini was displayed in a Piccadilly showroom as a publicity gimmick for Christmas 1964, seven people rang to place orders!

Firmly established as a fashion accessory, the reputation of the Mini was further enhanced when its creator, Alec Issigonis, took the Queen on a test drive in Windsor Great Park. Sales rocketed again when Paddy Hopkirk won the gruelling Monte Carlo Rally in 1964. The Mini had earned a place in our hearts and motoring magazines were left to reflect on how absurd those early doubts seemed now.

Mini Skirt

The outrage which greeted the arrival of the mini skirt in some quarters was nothing new. As far back as 1925, the Archbishop of Naples had blamed the Amalfi earthquake of that year on the scandalously short new skirts being worn.

Although the mini skirt was held responsible for many things in the sixties — moral decadence, a slump in textile manufacturers' profits because less material was sold, plus an increase in road accidents through male drivers' eyes wandering to take in the sights — it was at least spared the blame for any natural disasters. There were two prime movers in the introduction of the mini — French couturier André Courrèges and Britain's Mary Quant. Courrèges' avant-garde, space age designs appeared in 1964 but the person who introduced the mini

(right) In 1959, BMC unveiled its exciting new creation, the Mini.

M

to the girl in the street was Quant. In fact, she had been raising hemlines in her boutique Bazaar since the late 1950s.

'I liked the big skirts that were in vogue at the time,' she said, 'but I wanted something less restricting and easier to dance in. The short tunic dresses and the mini skirt sprung from that and Chelsea girls had the legs to wear them.'

The mini made its impact in 1965. The initial reaction of many girls was that they would never wear one but as familiarity bred content, even older women began to shorten their skirts a little each year. Meanwhile, young girls who invariably teamed the new fashion with skinny-ribbed sweaters, coloured tights or white PVC boots, wore skirts as short as nine inches above the knee, the garments in question being dubbed 'pelmets', a cynical but accurate assessment. When the sixties' sensation reached New York, it stopped the traffic on Broadway, the city's Mayor, John Lindsay, declaring of the mini: 'It will enable young girls to run faster, and because of it, they may have to!'

The changing trends flummoxed dry cleaners and customs officials alike. The former were forced to start charging by the inch while customs men had to completely revise their regulations. Until then, the length determined whether a dress was a woman's (liable to ten per cent purchase tax) or a child's which was tax-free. But skirts became so short that officials were finding difficulty differentiating between the two. So, from 1 January 1966 new rules stated that a dress would be taxed according to bust size, too, anything over 32 inches (81 cm) being classed as a woman's.

Personified by models such as Twiggy and Jean Shrimpton, the mini became popular from Australia to Alaska. It was even deemed acceptable at Royal Ascot and in 1966 Mary Quant received the OBE for her services to fashion exports, fittingly going to Buckingham Palace in a mini skirt.

By 1968 the hippie revolution was under way with the accent on nonconformity. Girls followed the hippie ideal of 'doing your own thing' and *Vogue* magazine announced: 'The length of your skirt is how you feel this moment.' Sensing that the mini was on its last legs, fashion designers introduced the midi skirt but, after experiencing the mini, many women thought it made them look too old. American magazines called the midi 'instant age'. It never really caught on and by 1970 had been passed over in favour of the even longer maxi.

When the time came to conduct the autopsy on the mini, the verdict was death by natural causes. For whilst it was said that the Pill bred the mini, it was something as simple yet unpredictable as the severe winter of 1969 which eventually killed it off.

The mini skirt created such a stir that in 1966 moral guardians banned it from all halls in the London borough of Merton.

Mixed Bathing

At the turn of the century, ladies wishing to partake of the waters at British seaside resorts had to change in large garden shed-like bathing machines on wheels which were then wheeled to the water's edge so that the occupant could discreetly disappear beneath the waves, safe from prying eyes. Not that there was much chance of embarrassment since the bathing costumes of the time were made from unflattering materials such as corduroy and serge, and anyway, bathing-huts for men and women were strictly segregated.

But then, in 1903, the genteel Sussex town of Bexhill, a resort not exactly renowned for trend-setting, boldly became the first to allow mixed bathing. Others remained stoical in the face of such wanton disregard for public morals. A Broadstairs by-law of 1906 proclaimed: 'No female over eight years shall bathe from any machine except within the bounds marked for females. Bathing dresses must extend from the neck to the knees.'

Those resorts which considered themselves to be among the more select continued to try to appease their Sabbath-loving residents by discouraging weekend trippers. Brass bands were not permitted to play on Sundays and piers remained firmly shut in case unsavoury visiting types should endeavour to purchase saucy postcards. Bournemouth banned all Sunday trains until 1914 while Eastbourne forbade gardeners to dig their allotments on Sundays. It is easy to see how that would be a corruptive influence.

One small leap for womankind. Out of the bathing machine and into the sea.

Monopoly

Few have exercised such questionable judgement as the executive with US games manufacturers Parker Brothers who initially rejected Monopoly as having '52 fundamental playing errors'. Bearing in mind that Monopoly has since sold nearly 100 million sets, it was fortunate that his company were given a second chance.

The origins of Monopoly lay in the Landlord's Game devised by Mrs Elizabeth Phillips of Virginia in 1924, a board game centred around a theory of taxation, hardly a topic to guarantee a fun-packed evening around the fire. But Clarence B. Darrow, an unemployed heating engineer from Philadelphia, saw something in it and began to amend it as an antidote to the Depression of the 1930s.

For his first efforts, Darrow used materials which were easy to come by — an oilcloth for a playing surface, discarded scraps of wood for houses and hotels. In earlier, more prosperous days, one of the Darrow family's favourite holiday haunts had been Atlantic City and so this was the town from which he chose his street names.

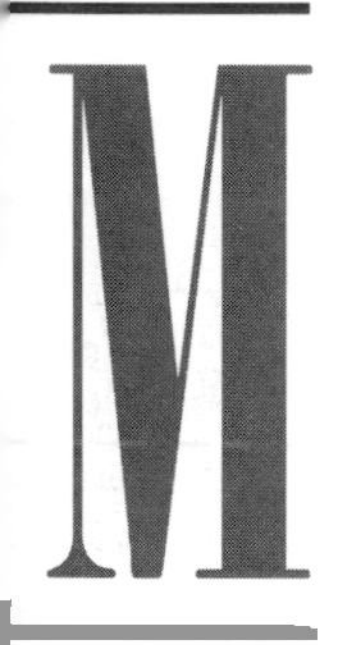

Word soon spread about the merits of Monopoly, as Darrow called his new game, but Massachusetts-based Parker Brothers turned him down flat. Convinced they were wrong, Darrow had 5000 copies made up by a local box manufacturer and converted the basement of his home into business premises. At $10 a time during a recession, Monopoly still sold like the proverbial hot cakes, as a result of which Parker Brothers reviewed their position and took over production in October 1935. Even they were hard-pressed to meet the Christmas demand.

The following summer, Parker Brothers received their first overseas enquiry for Monopoly. It came from Victor Watson, the then managing director of John Waddington Ltd, whose son, Norman Watson, had been 'enthralled and captivated' by the game. Granted a licence to manufacture Monopoly, Waddingtons proceeded to anglicise the names of the properties and railway stations. Victor Watson's London secretary was told to choose names from the capital and she graded them according to property values from Old Kent Road to Mayfair. The game has since been translated into 19 languages. In most cases, the property locations take the name of local real estate — Mayfair becomes Broadwalk in the American version, Rue de la Paix in French and Paseo del Prado in Spanish. The Russian version is set in Moscow, the Japanese in Tokyo, the Greek in Athens. Currency is also usually local. In 1975 twice as much Monopoly money was printed in the United States as real money.

Besides World Championships, Monopoly has been played in just about every conceivable setting — in a moving elevator, in a bathtub, on a ceiling, even underwater when in 1983, 350 divers from the Buffalo Dive Club played in relays for 45 days. The largest game took place in April 1967 at Juniata College, Pennsylvania. The playing board was laid out on an area greater than a city block, using campus streets and sidewalks. The dice were large foam rubber cubes and players were informed of their moves by cycling messengers equipped with walkie-talkies. In London, the real streets have been used with teams moving from one location to another according to the throw of the dice, using whatever means of transport available — bus, Underground, or on foot.

As for Charles Darrow, Monopoly transformed him from bleak unemployment to multimillionaire status. Atlantic City erected a commemorative plaque in his honour and when the city fathers tried to change two of his original street names in 1972, there was such a huge public outcry that they had no option but to back down. Baltic and Mediterranean Avenues lived on, as they do on the Monopoly board.

Motel

The rapid increase in the number of motor cars in the United States during the 1920s brought about the need for roadside hotels where weary travellers could park their vehicles and rest for the night. The first such establishment was designed by Arthur Heinman who decided to call it a motel. Thus on 12 December 1925, Hamilton Hotels opened the world's first motel — the simply-named Motel Inn at San Luis Obispo, California. It had accommodation for 160 guests, each chalet having a bathroom, a telephone and a garage, and flashing lights alternated the letters H and M before ...otel.

In common with the drive-in movie, the motel was largely confined to America at first, not reaching the UK in any significant numbers until the 1960s. Arguably the most famous British motel was the fictional Crossroads Motel, setting for the long-running television soap opera. Unfortunately, the everyday occurrences — bodies in the swimming pool, kidnapping, attempted murder and international terrorism — were enough to put anyone off motels for life.

Almost as bizarre was the horse motel opened at Marshfield, Missouri, in 1967, charging $5 a night for lodging, rising to $7 with feed and care. Pity the chalet maid.

(right) Monopoly: a best-seller for nearly 60 years.

MONOPOLY
PATENT NO. 3796-36.
THE NEW GAME
AND THE
RAGE OF AMERICA
MILLIONS NOW PLAYING IT
MADE BY JOHN WADDINGTON LTD.
MAKERS OF LEXICON,
OBTAINABLE FROM ALL STATIONERS, STORES & TOY DEALERS.

M

Motor Mower

Over the closing years of the 19th century, various British minds were concentrated on inventing a powered lawn-mower. Mr Kirkham's curious combination lawn-mower-tricycle was followed by James Sumner's steam-powered mower, a monstrous cumbersome machine which would not have looked out of place in a Moscow May Day parade. Ultimately, it was the ingenuity and determination of James Edward Ransome, from the Ipswich firm which bore his name, that took grass cutting technology into the 20th century.

W.J. Stephenson-Peach had designed the first petrol-driven mower in 1896 but it was Ransome who developed the idea and took out a patent in 1902. Ransomes, Sims & Jefferies Ltd commenced manufacture immediately, one of the first machines being used by Cadbury Bros. of Bournville, for their sports ground. The new motor mower quickly proved superior to any steam models, confirmed when King Edward VII invited a demonstration of the Ransomes machine on the lawns of Buckingham Palace and afterwards expressed his approval.

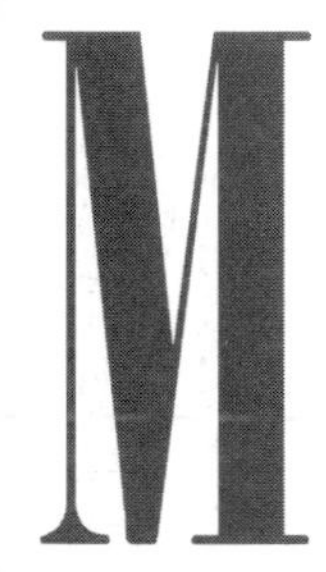

A further glowing testimony came from cricket legend W.G. Grace who said that the Ransomes motor mower 'used on the London County Cricket Ground at the Crystal Palace last season, did very well'. He added: 'Every cricket ground should have motor mowers and rollers as, early in the season, whenever the ground is soft, you can get on with the motor machine when it would be impossible for a horse machine to be used without doing harm to the ground.'

Three petrol-driven mowers appeared in Ransomes' 1906 catalogue, ranging in price from £75 to £150. The smallest was described as 'a simple and compact machine, which an intelligent gardener can soon learn to manage and will be found capable of getting over a large amount of work in a day, as it travels as fast as a man walks and no time need be lost'.

In the years leading up to the Great War, Ransomes produced 80 machines each year, despatched to cut a swath on such far-flung territories as the lawns of Government House, Calcutta, and the tracks of the Victoria Racing Club in Melbourne. In addition, cricketers in Rio de Janeiro, golfers in Port of Spain and tennis players in Brussels all enjoyed the benefits of the revolutionary Ransomes motor mower.

A Ransomes motor mower of 1911 at the home of golf, 'The Royal and Ancient' at St Andrews, Scotland.

One man and his broom. Only another 50 or so miles to sweep before the M1 is finally ready for opening.

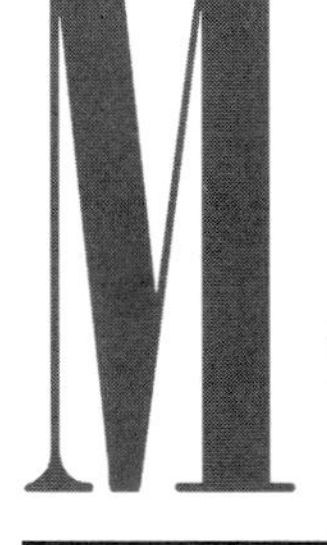

Motorway

The idea for a motorway in the UK dates back to 1906 when a Parliamentary Bill suggested the construction of a road between London and Brighton, the specification for which was equivalent to the official definition of a motorway. The Bill was not proceeded with nor was another private member's Bill in 1923 for a 226-mile (364 km) toll motorway to be built in sections between London and Liverpool. The first section was to be between Coventry and Salford and it was thought that motorway-building would provide much-needed work for the unemployed. However, the Commercial Motor Users' Association objected to the plan.

In the meantime, Germany had stepped in with the world's first motorway, the 6-mile (9.8 km) Avus autobahn west of Berlin, completed in 1921 in time for the first post-war Berlin Motor Show. Four years later, the Italians built their first autostrada near Milan and in 1929, work started on a second autobahn, between Cologne and Bonn. Unlike Avus, this lacked a central reservation between the carriageways and the ensuing spate of serious accidents alarmed public opinion, not only in Germany but in other countries who were contemplating a motorway-construction programme. Plans for further autobahns met with fierce local protests until in 1933 Hitler rode roughshod over them all and announced the building of many more autobahns.

The motorway eventually made it to Britain in December 1958 when the Prime Minister, the Rt. Hon. Harold Macmillan, opened the 8-mile (12 km) long Preston by-pass. Alas, it had to be closed barely six weeks later, heavy rain followed by a sharp frost causing the surface to become dangerously uneven. The areas in question were relaid and extra drains installed, and work is expected to be completed any day now . . .

Multi-storey Car Park

Strange as it may seem, that modern eyesore, the multi-storey car park, first appeared as long ago as 1901 when the City and Suburban Electric Carriage Company opened a seven-floor building at Denman Street, near London's Piccadilly Circus, for the benefit of owners of vehicles supplied by the company. With a total floor space of 19 000 sq ft (1765 sq m), it was dubbed the largest garage in the world. A remarkable feature was an electric elevator capable of lifting a three-ton lorry to the top storey.

The Piccadilly experience failed to encourage similar edifices. The first multi-storey in the United States, at Cambridge, Massachusetts, did not rise up until 1928 and modern building in the UK only began with the car park at Fairfax Street, Bristol, in 1958, that city being selected for its appalling traffic congestion. Since then, multi-storeys have become so popular that motorists can be seen driving around them for hours — just in the hope of finding a space on the ground floor.

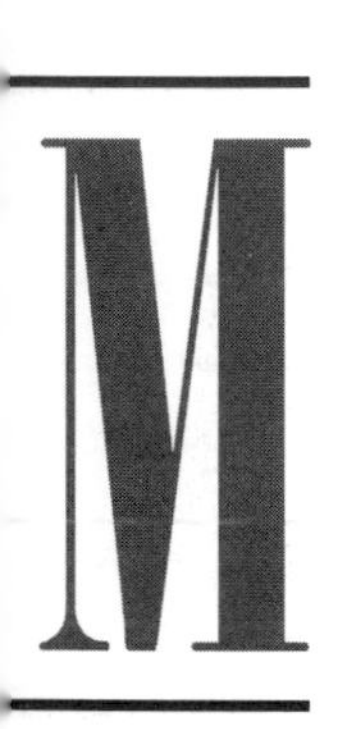

A 24-storey building in New York devoted entirely to the garaging of motor-cars, 1929.

Neon Lighting

A familiar sight in cities across the world where it can brighten up the drabbest facade, neon lighting first came to prominence in Paris over 80 years ago. It was nurtured by French physicist Georges Claude and made its debut at the city's motor show held at the Grand Palais in December 1910.

Advertising agency Paz et Silva saw potential in using the red lighting for illuminated signs and soon LE PALACE COIFFEUR, the first neon sign, was erected above a barber shop on boulevard Montmartre. By 1914 there were in the region of 150 neon signs scattered throughout Paris in a wide variety of colours.

In 1913, London's West End Cinema achieved the distinction of being the first British firm to have its name in neon and 11 years later, the neon advertising sign came to Piccadilly Circus, proclaiming, ANY TIME IS ARMY CLUB TIME to promote the brand of cigarettes of that name. But that was small fry compared to the sign for Marlboro cigarettes which lit up Kowloon in 1986. It measured 210 ft by 55 ft (64 × 16.7 m) and contained 35 000 ft (10 668 m) of neon tubing.

The world's largest neon sign at Las Vegas.

Non-stick Saucepan

The birth of that essential modern commodity, the non-stick saucepan, came about not by one accident, but two.

The first chance discovery came about in 1938. Dr Roy Plunkett of the American company Du Pont was working on refrigerants when he stumbled across a polymer called polytetrafluoroethylene (PTFE), later given the slightly catchier trade name of Teflon.

Du Pont began producing Teflon commercially ten years later but it took another fortuitous encounter before it was realised that its properties would be suitable for use on kitchenware. In 1954, French fishing-rod manufacturer Marc Grégoire was working on new production techniques when he found a process which would enable a Teflon coating to be applied to metal. It occurred to him that the non-stick nature of Teflon would be ideal for kitchen utensils and the following year he founded the Tefal company to make frying pans and saucepans.

The interior surface of an aluminium vessel is roughened and a primer coat of PTFE sprayed on it and fired at a temperature of around 390°F (200°C). Extra coats are added for high-quality cookware. Non-stick coatings have also been applied to ovens.

It was in the sixties that non-stick cookware really began to find its niche in domestic kitchens, large-scale production in the United States commencing in 1962. Teflon was introduced to the UK five years later. Now, thanks to Messrs Plunkett and Grégoire, scraping the remains of the fried egg off the frying pan is a thing of the past.

Nudist Camp

During the early years of the century, the idealist theory was advanced that naturism was beneficial to the mind as well as the body. An American, Bernard Macfadden, advocated nudity for children as part of the process of purity in the home while the Germans discovered that their children, undernourished during the First World War, benefited enormously from exposure to sunlight. It followed therefore that the sun's rays would improve the quality of healthy adult bodies.

Germany had in fact boasted a naturist resort since 1903 (Der Freilichtpark at Klingberg) but it was the 1920s which saw an outbreak of nudity across the land. The world's first official nudist camp, Frei-Sonnenland at Motzener See, was opened in 1920.

Some Britons took a keen interest in the German movement, believing that repressions would disappear once the human body could be taken for granted. In 1922 H.D. Byngham formed a group called the English Gymnosophist Society for those interested in nude life culture. The society, which consisted mainly of men, put its ideas into practice in 1924 on a site at Wickford, Essex, which belonged to one of its members.

A number of other British nudist camps started up in the twenties, mainly in the south where it was anticipated that the sun would shine more, and usually in country houses close enough to suburban London to be accessible by car. To discourage voyeurs, applicants were accepted only if single or with the permission of a spouse or fiancé.

Although the new societies attracted applicants from all age groups, press and public opinion would not be swayed. And with the typically miserable British weather putting a dampener on proceedings most summers, naturism began to lose its impetus. A compromise of sorts was proposed by Gymnosophy Society member N.F. Barford who suggested that sunbathing in minimum clothing could serve as a step towards nudity. This was frowned on at first by members as something of a 'sell-out' but a rare summer heatwave in 1928 encouraged

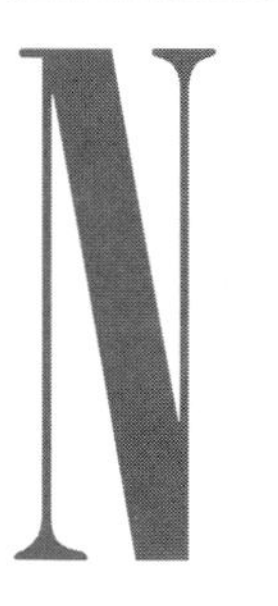

public tolerance, the Dean of St Paul's pronouncing: 'The new freedom of the body which is sweeping Europe is a splendid omen of increasing health.'

In this climate, Barford launched his Sun Bathing Society, the aims of which were to promote the practice of active sun and air bathing among families and young children, using the new scanty bathing costumes. At the same time, the society allowed those who wished to progress from bathing costumes to nudity to do so.

Public opposition may have been weakening but there were still isolated incidents. When a land-owner at Hendon allowed young unemployed people to use shacks on his property for sunbathing in 1930, the preceding publicity resulted in the bathers, some of them nude, being attacked by a mob of 200 trespassers. Ironically, the subsequent sympathy for the sun-worshippers brought about an increase in membership.

Despite the formation of the Central Council for British Naturism in 1964, nudism remains less acceptable in the UK than in France or Germany. Private resorts have existed since the opening of Woodside on the Isle of Wight in 1933 but it was not until 1978 that a few public beaches, notably one at Brighton, were designated for naturists.

Budding film-makers discover there's more to nudism than meets the eye.

Nylon Stockings

In 1927 when Dr Wallace Hume Carothers, a research chemist with Du Pont, commenced his study of polymerisation, he could scarcely have imagined that the result would be a product which would grace the legs of women the world over.

The task of Carothers and his team was not even to create a specific product but to examine how and why tiny molecules join up and form large ones. However, by 1930 Carothers had found that a fibre of extreme tensile strength could be drawn from a mass of polymers. Over the next five years, he perfected the technique of producing the fibre, the chemical name for which, polyhexamethyleneadipamide, was shortened to nylon. The 'nyl' was said to stand for New York and London, presumably where Du Pont hoped to market it.

In addition to its strength and elasticity, nylon appeared resistant to grease and dirt. Initially, the invention remained an industrial secret until in 1938 Du Pont formally announced the discovery of the world's first man-made fibre. Sadly, by then Carothers, who suffered from severe depression, had killed himself.

Du Pont's commercial manufacture of nylon began with toothbrush bristles but it was the showing of the first-ever nylon stockings at the 1938 New York World Fair which really aroused interest in the new fibre. The

N

Sheer ecstasy. A post-war shop assistant demonstrates the new line in nylon stockings.

company began to realise that the $27 million it had spent on all those years of research would pay off.

The first batch of nylon stockings was offered for sale to Du Pont employees at its experimental station in Wilmington, Delaware, in February 1939 and the following month public sales started at a few stores in Wilmington. Launched nationally, the new stockings immediately found favour with American women despite the fact that in dry weather nylon generated so much static electricity that ladies often found themselves undressing in a shower of sparks. In those early days, nylon also had a nasty habit of yellowing after a while.

British women were denied the luxury of nylon stockings. There was a war on and for the next five years, all available nylon was needed for parachutes and tarpaulins. With silk stockings also unobtainable owing to the ban on Japanese silk thread, ladies were forced to improvise. One ingenious, though somewhat impractical measure, was to plaster wet sand on the legs and have a friend draw a black line up the back to simulate a seam. Then there was Cyclax Stockingless Cream, described in advertisements as 'the cosmeticians' most astounding gift to the style minded world. For here in a dainty jar, is all the slim beauty of the sheerest ankle clinging hose'. Four shades were available at 5s. 6d. a jar.

Of course, some nylon stockings did reach Britain during the war (it must have been some ladder!), courtesy of American servicemen who used them to win the hearts and bodies of local girls. The bargaining power of a pair of nylons produced many a war baby.

Even after 1945, nylon stockings remained in short supply in the UK for a number of years so that women were unable to experience the 'nude leg' look provided by new sheer, seamless stockings. Much of the nylon output was earmarked by the government for the export drive needed to revitalise Britain's trade. In 1950 hosiery manufacturers Kayser Bonder admitted: 'It will be many years yet before the home market can be satisfied and the price reduced.' Prices had been kept up by the cost of installing new machinery and this led to the creation of a black market in nylon stockings. In April 1950 when the transatlantic liner *Franconia* docked at Liverpool, customs men boarded the ship and found it 'stuffed with nylons' tucked in first-class cabins as well as behind the ship's inner hull. The smuggled goods had an estimated black market value of over £80 000.

Odor-Eaters

Man created the wheel, he can create fire but until 1975 he could not combat foot odour.

Then, to cure a problem facing over 90 million Americans, Dr Buddy Lapidus of foot care specialists Combe Inc. came up with a solution far longer lasting than the sprays, powders and lotions previously on the market. It involved the use of charcoal, already in use in sewage plants, hospitals and other areas where purification of liquids or gases was required, and probably best known for its use in cigarette filters.

Dr Lapidus decided to incorporate charcoal into a latex insole worn inside the shoe, the charcoal being used to absorb the harmful odours. It took months of experiment but by 1972, he had perfected the product and Odor-Eaters were marketed three years later. The makers claimed that the amount of activated charcoal contained in each pair of Odor-Eaters was equal to that in 3500 charcoal cigarette filters and that the actual absorption area available in one pair was larger than a football pitch.

Results were impressive. A Florida podiatrist tested a panel of his own patients complaining of severe foot odour and excessive perspiration. Over an eight-week period, 85 per cent reported a marked improvement in their feet. As a bonus, many people said that they found walking more comfortable with Odor-Eaters fitted in their shoes.

In these frenetic, high-pressure days, Odor-Eaters are an oasis of calm. Smelly feet have gone the same way as the Penny Farthing, the Beehive hairdo and jamboree bags.

Old Age Pension

On 1 January 1909 a wave of euphoria surged through the senior citizens of the United Kingdom. Chancellor of the Exchequer Lloyd George had introduced a non-contributory old age pension scheme in his 1908 budget, a measure which finally freed the elderly from the humiliation of the Poor Law. The amounts themselves were not exactly generous — 5s. a week to persons over 70 on an income of less than £21 a year and 7s. 6d. for married couples — but it was manna from heaven to those who qualified (anyone with a known criminal record was not allowed to claim).

On that first day of payment, tears of gratitude would roll down the cheeks of pensioners as they went to the Post Office to collect their money. As they picked up the cash, they would say to the girl behind the counter: 'God bless that Lloyd George . . . and God bless you, miss!' Post Office staff were rewarded with garden produce and in Walworth, South London, an old lady offered the postmaster two rashers of bacon for helping her fill in the forms.

In cartoons, Lloyd George was depicted as the 'Philanthropic Highwayman', robbing the rich to pay the poor. With his customary flair for imagery, Lloyd George himself saw the Pension Act and the National Insurance Act of 1911 'descending like breezes from the hills of my native land . . . and clearing the gloom away until the rays of God's sun have pierced the narrowest window'.

However, not everyone welcomed the free hand-outs. The Lord Provost of Glasgow told a savings-bank meeting that the pensions would encourage the thriftless and destroy the pride and independence of the Scottish people.

Ovaltine

There was a time when the most important item in any sportsman's training equipment was his mug of Ovaltine.

In 1927 after breaking the record for swimming the English Channel, Georges Michel stated: 'During my training I used Ovaltine and learnt to appreciate its exceptional qualities. During the crossing I did not experience any of the stomach trouble which had previously troubled me. I was in a position to finish the crossing in a relatively fresh condition, and I ascribe this to the fact that Ovaltine gave me strength and endurance.'

The following year, motorcycling ace J.J. Hall weighed in with his praise: 'I have obtained 104 World's Records at Brooklands Track. Many of my runs have lasted for as long as 8 to 12 hours, and I have to be exceedingly careful in my choice of beverages during the periodical stops. I found Ovaltine infinitely superior to anything else I have tried.'

So what are the origins of this remarkable powder which, according to its early advertising, 'Builds up

A WARMING, comforting cup of 'Ovaltine' is a delicious prelude to the night's duty. Its concentrated nourishment—derived from Nature's finest foods—strengthens, energises and sustains.

When duty is done and opportunity comes for rest, you will find 'Ovaltine' a soothing influence and a great help in quickly inducing sleep. Moreover, the special nutritive properties of 'Ovaltine' assist in making your sleep fully restorative and revitalising.

By day or night, whenever there is work to be done, strength to maintain and energy to conserve, make 'Ovaltine' your constant stand-by. It will do much to reinforce your resistance against the chills and ills of wintry weather, and to keep up your fitness-for-service.

'Ovaltine' is easily and quickly prepared. If milk is not available, water can be used, as 'Ovaltine' itself contains milk. 'Ovaltine' also has the advantage of being naturally sweet so that there is no need to add sugar.

Brain, Nerve and Body'? It was invented by Dr George Wander, an assistant at the University of Berne in Switzerland, who, after studying the value of a new malt soup for infants, set up a laboratory to manufacture barley malt in concentrated form. The result was a dark malt extract which quickly gained popularity when tested at Berne's University Hospital. Successive products based on the use of malt extract culminated in 1904 with the launch of Ovomaltine (the 'ovo' denoting the egg content). But five years later, when the Wander company applied to register the Ovomaltine trade mark in the UK, it was wrongly transcribed by a ministry clerk as 'Ovaltine'. The name stuck.

Quite apart from providing 'internal central heating' and ensuring a peaceful night's sleep, Ovaltine's greatest contribution to the welfare of Europe began in 1935 on Radio Luxembourg. It was the formation of the Ovaltineys, a children's club whose lively radio shows, under the watchful eye of musical director Clarence Wright, were a mainstay of Sunday's night's listening. The League of Ovaltineys had its own secret code as well as a strict rule book which encouraged members (there were five million by 1939) to observe high moral principles with particular regard to their consideration for others. Among the young Ovaltineys was latter-day television entertainer Leslie Crowther.

Pacamac

Some great inventions have unfortunate side effects. The motor car had the traffic jam, the tyre had the puncture, plastic had the pacamac.

The development of plastics in the 20th century has produced many exciting offshoots in the world of fashion. The pacamac was not one of them. This lightweight garment, which came in shades of dark grey, light grey or grey, was much coveted in the fifties and early sixties because it could be rolled into a tight ball when not in use. If it had remained in that position permanently, it would have offended nobody but, at the merest hint of rain, parents insisted that it be unfurled and worn in full view of passers-by. As a fashion statement, it was incoherent.

For the demise of the grey pacamac, we have to thank Peter Cook and Dudley Moore who wore them in their television series *Not Only . . . But Also* when philosophising about the world from a park bench. What the makers probably thought would be a fine advertisement for their product, had the opposite effect, it becoming an object of ridicule. Thereafter, plastic was put to better use.

(left) A cup of Ovaltine kept the home fires burning during the Second World War.

Paper Clip

When discussing the major innovators of the century, one name is repeatedly overlooked — that of Johann Vaaler, inventor of the paper clip. This forgotten hero may not have created the most glamorous article but few items have enjoyed such widespread use in everyday life. Over two billion paper clips are manufactured annually in the UK.

Vaaler, a Norwegian, patented the paper clip in Germany in 1900 and its basic design has remained unchanged ever since. Happily, his fellow countrymen have remembered Vaaler's pioneering spirit and in October 1989 an iron paper clip measuring 23 ft (7 m) and weighing 1328 lb (602 kg) was made in Norway and unveiled near Oslo in his honour.

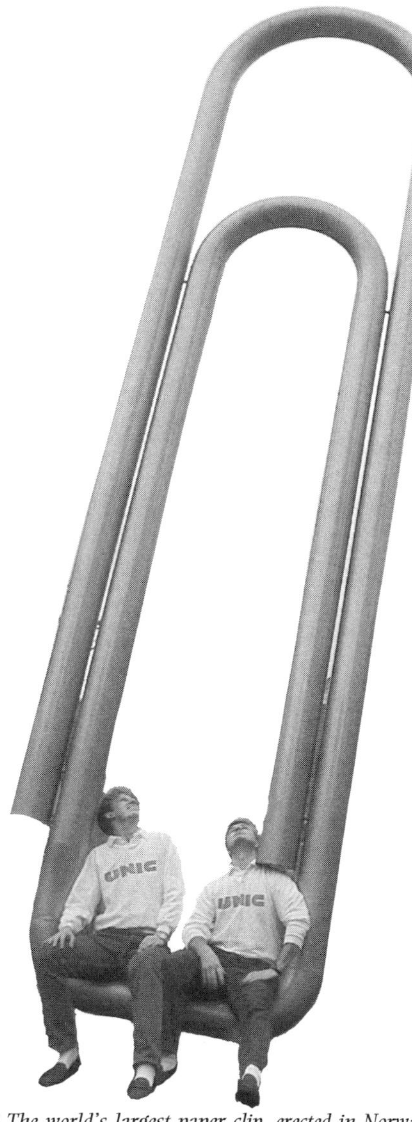

(above) The world's largest paper clip, erected in Norway in honour of Johann Vaaler.

New-type handkerchief
checks the spread of Colds!

use

KLEENEX

THE *Tissue* HANDKERCHIEF

in place of germ-carrying handkerchiefs

...no washing! no self-infection!

No more passing on your colds to the whole family now! For unhygienic germ-filled handkerchiefs are out—and Kleenex is in! Kleenex checks the spread of colds. You use each tissue once only and destroy it—germs and all! You don't keep reinfecting yourself either. Colds go quicker, and Kleenex avoids all possibility of raw red noses. You can use 30 Kleenex tissues for the average cost of laundering two handkerchiefs. Get the Kleenex habit today!

Women everywhere also find Kleenex invaluable for removing Cold Cream and to apply Cosmetics.

6D. 1/- 2/3

At all Chemists and Stores. In handy pull-out boxes.

wide, forty fe
rocks and oily
water; when
face pressed
held her in
stories in h
and, with
humour,
When Pa
and Eva
carrying
singing
from "The
and Jilly w
And then
lights and
it was Jere
pulled them
them, bring
cedure.
Then, qu
Ian was st
in his ar
her for
them. Tl
Ian's ste
exhausted
the scrubb
the blow-l
knelt down
"Tell me
softly, "do
like you sa
rescued Jill
He saw
the clear
tired head
"Won't
my very
ing his
out there
Pamela's
"Yes,
exclaimed
back to fet
he saw int
stock of En

Ask Th

Write to he
Fleetway H
E.C.4, enclo
envel

SUFFERS AC

I am a sho
feet all day lon
to harden the sc
perspiring, ankl

BATHE you
water, t
half a
bath salts.
Dry your
the soles a
spirit. Th
soles and r
In the mc
ice (you can
chemist's) in
between the
little talcum
The "ice"
should keep

Paper Tissue

In 1872 John Kimberly and Charles Clark teamed up with two other local investors to build a small paper mill in the vast forests of Neenah, Wisconsin, to produce newsprint. Realising the potential of the surrounding forests, they diversified to produce high quality paper and soon owned and operated nine mills. To further a philosophy of innovation, Kimberly-Clark established a research and development team, and at the start of the First World War, company chemists created an entirely new paper product — cellulose wadding. We know it today as soft paper tissue.

The cellulose wadding had been developed to meet the vital need for medical dressings during the war, being used as a substitute for cotton wool. It was more absorbent than cotton wool, soft but strong, and before long, American nurses were making sanitary towels from it. In 1920 Kimberly-Clark marketed these sanitary towels under the name of Kotex.

Seeking additional applications for the new material, in 1924, Kimberly-Clark brought out Celluwipes, up-market make-up removers. Sales were slow until the company began to take note of customers' letters which reported that the tissues were perfect for nose-blowing. So they were relaunched, first as Kleenex-'Kerchiefs and then as Kleenex. Today the Kleenex trademark is registered in over 130 countries to cover a wide variety of disposable products including toilet tissue, kitchen towels and, of course, facial tissue.

Parking Meter

Having expressed their disquiet about lax parking restrictions, the businessmen of Oklahoma City set up a special traffic committee in 1933 to look into ways of clamping down on errant vehicles. The chairman of the committee was Carlton C. Magee, editor of the local newspaper. His solution was to devise the world's first parking meter.

Magee was quick to spot the potential of his idea and formed the Dual Parking Meter Company. The first 150 Park-O-Meters came into operation in the business area of Oklahoma City in July 1935. Twenty-foot (6 m) spaces were painted on the pavement and a nickel-in-the-slot meter installed at each space.

It was over 20 years before parking meters came to haunt British motorists. On 10 July 1958, 625 meters, installed in the north-west Mayfair area of London,

Initially designed as make-up removers, Kleenex paper tissues only became popular when relaunched for blowing noses.

entered service. The charge was 6d. for one hour; 1s. for two hours; with an excess payment of 10s. for up to an additional two hours and a £2 fine for any waiting time exceeding four hours. Drivers were wary of the threatening new objects and many spaces remained vacant all day. A number of motorists complained about the lack of any refund for unused time while commercial travellers objected to having to pay over the odds for a short stay.

The increased use of meters and speed limits in Britain by Transport Minister Ernest Marples, gave rise to what was (semi) jokingly called Marples' Law: 'If it moves, stop it; if it stops, fine it.'

Parking meters on parade.

Perrier Water

To recuperate after a serious motor car accident, Englishman St John Harmsworth, brother of newspaper magnates Lord Northcliffe and Lord Rothermere, visited the French spa town of Vergeze in 1903. There he was introduced by his doctor, Louis Perrier, to the local spring, Les Bouillons ('the bubbling waters'), said to have been discovered by Hannibal around 218 BC.

Harmsworth was intrigued to see water gurgling from the ground full of natural bubbles and was interested to hear the locals referring to its health-giving properties. Recognising the commercial possibilities of marketing this special water, he decided to purchase the spring and bottle it.

He named the water after Dr Perrier and moulded the now famous green Perrier bottle on the Indian clubs he had been using to strengthen his arms and back following his car accident.

A man of vision, Harmsworth acknowledged a market for Perrier among Englishmen abroad. Civil servants and the Army, posted to countries in the British Empire where water was in short supply or too contaminated to drink, welcomed a water that was safe, enjoyable and which could be mixed with whisky! Similarly, when the English abroad returned home on leave, they expected to find Perrier readily available. This helped develop an exclusive market for the brand and in the 1920s it could be found in London's finest hotels and restaurants. Harmsworth described Perrier as 'The Champagne of Table Waters' and when he died in 1933, the Perrier Source at Vergeze was producing over 18 million bottles a year, of which over eight million were exported. Curiously, for many years it was better known among the higher echelons of London, Delhi and Singapore than it was in Paris.

The company was sold back to the French in 1948 but continued to hold an appeal for the distinguished Englishman. Even James Bond drank it. Today Perrier is sold in nearly 150 countries, including the United States, Australia and Japan. As its advertisements say, it has become 'Eau So Successful'.

An early advertisement for Perrier water.

P

Perspex

Baths, vehicle number plates, light fittings, helicopter canopies, advertising signs, sun beds — they have all been made from that most versatile of plastics, Perspex, a product created 60 years ago by ICI.

It was in the early 1930s that ICI's John Crawford conducted research aimed at finding a laminated safety glass interlayer to replace cellulose nitrate which tended to yellow in sunlight. Working independently, in the course of a general study of polymers, Rowland Hill of British Dyestuffs Corporation prepared the polymer of methyl methacrylate which turned out to be unexpectedly hard and tough with a relatively high softening point. Crawford knew this was the product he had been looking for and perfected a process of making it in sheet form on a larger scale. On 16 November 1934 the name 'Perspex', from Latin 'to see through', was registered as the trademark for ICI's new light acrylic sheet.

Commercial production began in 1936 in a constant temperature of 104°F (40°C). The operators were weighed each Friday to check for any loss of weight. To demonstrate the strength of their invention, a sheet of Perspex was used as a partition in an ICI office. Visitors were conducted into this inner sanctum and a heavy ashtray was hurled against it. Everyone was suitably impressed by the fact that the Perspex withstood the assault — until one day a visitor was shown into the wrong room and the ashtray was thrown at an ordinary sheet of glass!

The resistance and weatherproofing qualities of Perspex made it ideal for fighter aircraft cockpit covers, the demand increasing dramatically with the outbreak of war. So vital was the role of Perspex that the Ministry of Supply insisted on manufacture being spread over several sites to minimise the risks from enemy air attack. At the height of combat, 5000 tons of Perspex were sold a year.

The immediate post-war period created a variety of unusual markets for Perspex, including beehives where it was claimed to add to honey yield, produce more prolific queens and provide a home in which enlightened bees would work for at least two hours longer than their sisters in dark hives. At the other end of the scale, Perspex formed the canopy at the entrance to the annexe at Westminster Abbey, specially constructed for the coronation of Queen Elizabeth II in 1953. Sculpture, furniture and fashion all adopted Perspex in the sixties but of its multitude of uses over the years, perhaps the most bizarre was in a 1967 hi-tech production of Shakespeare's *As You Like It* at London's National Theatre where 100 Perspex tubes, some as long as 23 ft (7 m), played the Forest of Arden.

Post-war cocktail glasses and tray in Perspex.

Photobooth

We go into a photobooth fearing the worst. For we know that no matter how composed we try to be, the resultant photograph will invariably depict us as some kind of manic gargoyle. That is, unless the seat collapses at the vital moment in which case we are not in the picture at all.

The man to blame is Hungarian Anatol Marco Josepho who invented the photobooth in 1924. British production commenced four years later, in those days the money being handed to an attendant. Indeed mechanisation did not arrive until 1968 when the attendant was ousted by a coin slot. In the same year, colour photographs became available so that our blushes of embarrassment showed up better.

Photocopier

Toiling in an Oklahoma City land-claim office, George C. Beidler became exasperated at the amount of time consumed in retyping or copying by hand legal documents which needed duplicating. He decided to search for a swifter, alternative method and began to experiment with a dry-plate camera. In 1903 he conceived the world's first photocopier, marketed four years later as the Rectigraph by the Rectigraph Company of Rochester, New York.

Welcome though Beidler's invention may have been, it did not attract widespread attention. It remained painfully slow and most offices preferred the equally unsatisfactory method of typing onto a wax stencil. The lack of suitable equipment came to the attention of American patent lawyer Chester Carlson whose work constantly necessitated copying patents. In 1938 he conducted a series of tests in his kitchen, based on the principle of static electricity. These involved the use of blocks of sulphur, the stench from which rapidly made dinner-parties a rarity in the Carlson residence.

After all that effort, Carlson struggled to find a research institute interested in developing his idea. Eventually he struck lucky and in the late 1940s, the first electro-static copier came onto the market in the shape of the Haloid 1385. But manually operated and taking several minutes to make each copy, it was impractical for office work.

It was not until 1959, 21 years after first dreaming up the concept of an office copier, that Carlson's vision became reality with the introduction of the huge Xerox 914 (Haloid having changed its name to Xerox). This machine was automatic, operating at the push of a button, and produced seven copies a minute. An American advert for the 914 featured a fictional secretary called Miss Jones saying: 'I can't type, I don't take dictation, I can't file. My boss calls me indispensable. I push the button on the Xerox 914.' Thousands of secretaries have since modelled themselves on Miss Jones.

Pinball Machine

The need for an inexpensive form of entertainment during the Depression of the early 1930s created a market in America for the pinball machine. Its predecessor was the popular 19th-century parlour game, bagatelle, and in 1930 young Chicago businessman David Gottlieb bought the rights to manufacture a coin-operated bagatelle game called bingo.

Playing bingo encouraged Gottlieb to conceive a machine of his own and later that year he introduced Baffle Ball in which the scoring holes were small pockets surrounded by a ring of nails or pins — hence the name 'pinball'. It was a pretty basic affair — no bumpers, flippers or luminous scores, indeed no electricity at all. The only sound was that of the small steel marbles hitting the nails. And although a stand was available, Baffle Ball was designed to be played on a counter.

Despite its limitations, Gottlieb sold over 50 000 games in 1931 at $17.50 each. The pinball boom had begun. That same year, Raymond Maloney, one of Gottlieb's distributors, formed his own company which he named Bally to reflect the popularity of his game Ballyhoo. New manufacturers brought in new ideas. Rock-Ola made a pinball game called Jigsaw with a hidden puzzle, revealed only when the balls landed in the correct holes.

Pinball wizards try to get the knack.

Besides electricity, the most important innovation of the early years was the introduction of the tilt mechanism by Harry Williams in 1934 which prevented players cheating by lifting the machines. It was originally known as a stool pigeon, any jolt of the apparatus causing a small steel ball to fall off its pedestal and land on a metal ring, thereby completing an electrical circuit and ending the game. Prior to Williams' invention, manufacturers had tried various ways of stopping players tipping the machines. Some weighed the games down with sandbags, others inserted sharp nails beneath the table to discourage players from banging on the base.

Improved technology saw the arrival of bumpers (1936) and flippers (1947) while the range of pinball subjects has gone on to encompass everyone from the Rolling Stones to Superman, Muhammad Ali to James Bond, the Pink Panther to Dolly Parton. There was even a patriotic wartime game called Smack The Japs. The 1970s rock opera *Tommy* featured a pinball wizard, a role also played by Brooke Shields in the 1978 movie *Tilt*. Poor old bagatelle never enjoyed such status. But would The Who have had such a hit with something entitled 'Bagatelle Expert'?

Piped Music

London's Ideal Home Exhibition has been responsible for many exciting innovations as well as a few forgettable ones. Into the latter category comes piped music, introduced at Olympia by Western Electric in March 1923. Nevertheless, demand grew, particularly in factories where employers concluded that brightening up the working environment would improve productivity. One of the first British companies to install piped music were ICI who fed heavy brass bands into the noisy machinery room and more melodious sounds into the quieter management offices.

Nowadays, on the end of a phone, in lifts, in shops, muzak (as it has become known) is all around. It is a particular favourite of Chinese and Indian restaurants. Perhaps our abhorrence of this phenomenon stems from the announcement, 'Meanwhile here is some music', suggesting that the playing of a meaningless ditty is somehow adequate compensation for the loss of one's favourite television programme.

Plasticine

Very much a creative artist, William Harbutt had resigned from the post of headmaster at Bath School of Art because his ideas were decreed too radical, and was teaching the subject locally when he came up with his most progressive idea yet.

Recognising that the clay traditionally used for modelling was too heavy for accurate representation, Harbutt set about creating a new material, enlisting the services of an old soldier whose basement he commandeered for the task. To obtain the required consistency and remove excess water, a heavy garden roller was pushed back and forth over the mixture. The grey substance was then allowed to dry out for several weeks.

More pliable than the old clay, Harbutt's invention proved so popular with his own children that he started to consider its potential as a plaything. His family thought up the name Plasticine and production of a three-colour pack (red, blue and yellow), called 'The Complete Modeller', began in May 1900 at a disused flour mill at Bathampton.

Together with his daughter Olive, Harbutt toured Britain in an effort to interest retailers in his product. It was a slow process but Plasticine eventually grew in popularity. By a quirk of fate, one of its earliest assignments was not as a toy but in its originally intended capacity as a modelling medium. For during the First World War, Plasticine's chief modeller, Albert Blanchard, was commissioned by the British Army to make a scale model of the countryside around Vimy Ridge, scene of heavy fighting. In classrooms throughout the world, Plasticine now serves more peaceful purposes.

Pocket Calculator

Self-taught in electronics, Londoner Clive Sinclair started his own business at the age of 22 when he borrowed £50 to set up the firm of Sinclair Radionics which sold repaired radios by mail order.

Sinclair's inventive mind then turned to grander schemes. He said: 'I thought there was a need for a small calculator, and designed the whole thing from start to the actual production in nine months.'

His pocket calculator measured just 6 inches (15 cm) in length and was some 20 times smaller than the most compact model then available. Selling it directly through mail order in order to keep the price down to £79, Sinclair was initially 'overwhelmed with orders' in 1972 and his design won a number of international awards.

Overseas competitors were quickly alerted. The Americans undercut his prices while the Japanese perfected a new improved silicon chip. Suddenly, Sinclair realised he could not compete, his profits plummeted and his pioneering calculator was withdrawn. The Japanese were left to corner the market.

Plasticine has been used in everything from army models to animated films.

P

Polaroid

As a student at Harvard University, Edwin Land developed an interest in the properties of polarised light. He became so involved with his work on polarisation that he never graduated and instead in 1937 he set up the Polaroid Corporation at Cambridge, Massachusetts, to follow through his ideas.

During the Second World War, he turned his energies towards adapting light polarisers for military purposes such as gunsights and rangefinders. His new kind of polarising filter reduced sun glare and served in the manufacture of spectacles, binoculars, prisms and other optical instruments. But it was his young daughter's impatience which brought about his most famous invention.

So desperate was she to see a photograph her father had taken, not in the next few days, but 'now', that Dr Land gave thought to the concept of instant photography. The process had actually been partly developed by Agfa back in 1928 but the patent was never commercialised and became obsolete when Land perfected the art in 1947.

The Polaroid Land Camera was duly marketed in Boston in November of the following year. The first instant camera, the Model 95, promised 'finished pictures in a minute', producing a sepia-toned monochromatic image in just 60 seconds. Meanwhile, Kodak showed little interest in Dr Land's invention and by the time they did in the 1970s, it was too late.

During the fifties, Polaroid cameras became less bulky and the film was soon giving a precise black and white image rather than a brown and white one. Instant photography became more accessible to the general public with the arrival of the popular Swinger camera in the 1960s and sales were further stimulated by the introduction of Polaroid colour films in 1963.

Today, Polaroids are invaluable in many walks of life from film and television make-up supervisors wishing to ensure continuity, to police scene-of-crime experts needing to photograph footprints. Or they can simply be used to capture those magic moments — just as Dr Land's daughter had always intended.

Only two of the huge 20 × 24 Polaroid Land cameras, the largest of all Polaroids, are working in the world today — in Boston, Massachusetts, and Offenbach, Germany.

Polo Mints

Each week around 100 million Polo Mints are consumed in the United Kingdom alone. Annual sales exceed 275 million tubes and it has been calculated that if all the Polo Mints produced every two hours were stacked on top of each other, they would form a 6-mile (9.6 km) tall tower, higher than Mount Everest and considerably more difficult to climb.

Polo Mints are actually highly compressed rings of sugar and glucose, flavoured with peppermint oil. Each one is formed under enormous pressure, roughly equivalent to two elephants jumping on it.

The famous 'mint with the hole' has been part of our lives since 1948 although it did have a predecessor in the form of Navy Mints which, along with Navy Fruits and Navy Scotch, were billed as the 'sweet with the hole'. Polo quickly established itself as the mint market leader with the public enjoying the refreshing quality provided by the hole as well as relishing the opportunity to poke their tongues through it. For some, a Polo became as much a plaything as a sweet.

For many years, the mint, which has remained largely unchanged since its inception (the packaging had its first major overhaul as recently as 1991), was advertised on television with the theme 'People Like Polo' to indicate its wide range of appeal. But recently Nestlé Rowntree have returned to emphasising the uniqueness of the product — the hole.

There is no doubt about the world's most expensive Polo. In 1993, the company ran a competition offering 100 prizes of £1000 for lucky purchasers who bought specially marked Polos. Ten-year-old Devon schoolboy Henry Jefferies spotted the distinctive marking on his Polo as he popped it into his mouth. But he was so amazed that he gulped and promptly swallowed it, thus saying goodbye to a mint.

The Polo mint has remained largely unchanged since its inception in 1948.

P

Polyfilla

The man who simplified those horrendous do-it-yourself jobs about the house was Dr Saloman Neumann, a Czech who studied chemistry and arrived in England in 1933 with a Doctorate of Technical Science.

After trying assorted careers, he approached businessman Norman Shand Kydd with a process which he had already patented and installed in German wallpaper factories. He was immediately appointed a consultant to Shand Kydd's company to advise on chemical problems of all kinds.

During the war, Neumann served as a boffin and afterwards was able to proceed with his idea for a new wallpaper paste, based on water-soluble cellulose. He had settled on a great public need, for the average home decorator was incapable of putting up wallpaper without leaving unsightly marks caused by the paste seeping through onto the pattern. The advantage of Dr Neumann's new paste was that it could simply be wiped clean. No mess, no stains.

Samples were produced in 1953 and tested by decorators. Their response was enthusiastic, as a result of which Polycell (named by Dr Neumann himself) went into production on a second-hand machine in the corner of a garage at the Shand Kydd works in North London.

When it went on sale the following year, Polycell was seized upon by hitherto reluctant domestic decorators. Meanwhile, fired by his success, Dr Neumann had diagnosed another decorating need. To the amateur, filling holes and cracks in plaster in such a way as to produce a long-lasting smooth surface, was a real headache. The doctor had the cure and in 1956, Polyfilla cellulose plaster and wood filler was introduced.

Polypeel wallpaper stripper, Polyclens brush cleaner and Polystrippa paint remover followed in quick succession but it is Polyfilla which has proved particularly indispensable. However, a worrying tale emerged recently of its illicit use in the practice of conker 'doping'. It seems that in major championships, contestants have been known to cut their conker in half and cram it with Polyfilla in order to make it more resilient. Some people will stop at nothing.

Polyfilla covers a multitude of sins.

Polythene

Working at the company's Northwich, Cheshire, laboratories in March 1933, ICI chemist R.O. Gibson reacted the gas ethylene with benzaldehyde at a temperature of 338°F (170°C), an experiment which caused the formation of a 'white waxy solid' in the reaction container. This polymer of ethylene was christened polythene.

Tests on the new product revealed it to be tough, easily moulded and water-repellent, its first practical use being as an insulating material in a mile length of submarine cable laid between the Isle of Wight and the English mainland. Impressed by trials, ICI commissioned a commercial plant with an annual capacity of 200 tons which came into operation on 1 September 1939, the day Germany invaded Poland. It was inevitable, therefore, that polythene would initially become part of the war effort. Besides insulating cables, it was also used on radar components.

Like humans, some materials fail to adapt to civvy street. In the early stages, polythene was thought of as just a specialist chemical but from the moment the first polythene washing-up bowls appeared in 1948, it became apparent that it possessed much broader scope. Soon it was being used in toys, bags, cosmetics bottles and many other items in home and industry.

Pop Music Chart

The growth of popular music and the increasing competitiveness of record companies led to the publication of the first music chart in New York's *Billboard* magazine on 4 January 1936. There was no all-embracing chart, simply a list of the ten sheet music best-sellers of the three major companies, Columbia, RCA-Victor and Brunswick. The respective chart-toppers were 'Stop, Look and Listen' by Joe Venuti and his Orchestra; 'The Music Goes Round' by Tommy Dorsey and his Orchestra; and 'Quicker Than You Can Say' by Ozzie Nelson and his Orchestra.

An overall chart finally emerged on 20 July 1940 when *Billboard* showed 'I'll Never Smile Again' by Tommy Dorsey and his Orchestra at number one. Five years later, *Billboard* issued the first album chart, topped by the King Cole Trio featuring Nat 'King' Cole.

The first UK Top Ten was published by the *New Musical Express* on 14 November 1952. The top five read:

1. 'Here in My Heart' — Al Martino
2. 'You Belong to Me' — Jo Stafford
3. 'Somewhere Along the Way' — Nat 'King' Cole
4. 'Isle of Innisfree' — Bing Crosby
5. 'Feet Up' — Guy Mitchell

Al Martino remained at the top for nine weeks, fighting off the dual threat of Vera Lynn (who had three songs in the chart) and Max Bygraves, lurking at number 11 with 'Cowpuncher's Cantata'. Elvis was a world away.

Pop Video

As television took a growing interest in pop music through the 1960s, acts found that scheduled TV appearances often clashed with concert dates. So, some of the leading groups — such as the Beatles and the Rolling Stones — made short films to be inserted in the TV programmes. The majority were fairly unimaginative, merely showing the performers in concert, miming badly, but a few displayed a certain flair for the unusual. The Who dressed as burglars to promote 'Happy Jack', the Kinks donned the guise of undertakers for 'Dead End Street' and, most memorable of all, the Rolling Stones appeared as women for 'Have You Seen Your Mother Baby Standing in the Shadow?' Charlie Watts has never looked better.

THE NEW MUSICAL EXPRESS

Editorial and Advertisement Offices:
5, DENMARK STREET,
LONDON, W.C.2.
PHONE: TEMPLE BAR [illegible]/2.
EDITOR: RAY SONIN.
Assistant-Editor: JACK BAVERSTOCK.
Advertisement Manager:
PERCY C. DICKINS.

Announcing the first

RECORD HIT PARADE

FOR the first time in the history of the British popular music business, an authentic weekly survey of the best-selling "pop" records has been devised and instituted.

We are proud to have been able to launch this Record Hit Parade, which we know will be of the greatest interest and benefit to all our readers.

It would not have been possible to organise this without the willing co-operation of the largest gramophone record retailers, in all parts of the country, who are supplying us weekly with details of their biggest selling discs.

We express our great appreciation of their assistance.

(For Week ending November 8, 1952)

1. HERE IN MY HEART. Al Martino (Capitol).
2. YOU BELONG TO ME. Jo Stafford (Columbia).
3. SOMEWHERE ALONG THE WAY. Nat Cole (Capitol).
4. ISLE OF INNISFREE. Bing Crosby (Brunswick).
5. FEET UP. Guy Mitchell (Columbia).
6. HALF AS MUCH. Rosemary Clooney (Columbia).
7. FORGET-ME-NOT. Vera Lynn (Decca).
7. HIGH NOON. Frankie Laine (Columbia).
8. SUGAR BUSH. Doris Day/F. Laine (Columbia).
8. BLUE TANGO. Ray Martin (Columbia).
9. HOMING WALTZ. Vera Lynn (Decca).
10. AUF WIEDERSEHN. Vera Lynn (Decca).
11. COWPUNCHER'S CANTATA. Max Bygraves (HMV)
11. BECAUSE YOU'RE MINE. Mario Lanza (HMV)
12. WALKIN' MY BABY BACK HOME. Johnnie Ray (Columbia)

Reproduction in whole or part is strictly forbidden unless specific permission is obtained. Copyright by the "New Musical Express," 1952.

BAILEY AND BELLSON TO WED NEXT WEEK

SINGING star Pearl Bailey, the coloured girl currently delighting London's night-lifers in cabaret at the Colony Restaurant with her entrancing blues vocals, has fixed the date [illegible] to Duke Ellington's

The first UK Top Ten, published by the New Musical Express in November 1952.

But the first acknowledged pop video was not seen until 1975. To assist with the promotion of Queen's 'Bohemian Rhapsody', EMI commissioned director Bruce Gowers to make a video to accompany the single. The result, which reportedly cost £3000, was hailed as a visual masterpiece and its weekly appearance on the BBC's *Top of the Pops* undoubtedly strengthened sales and helped the single to remain at number one for nine weeks, the longest stay at the top since Slim Whitman had been there for 11 weeks in 1955 with 'Rose Marie'.

In the wake of this triumph, Gowers joined forces with another film-maker, Jon Roseman, to advise record companies of the importance of videos. Over the next three years, Roseman worked with Elton John, Genesis and Rod Stewart and the video became an accepted promotional aid for every single. Sadly, it sometimes seems more important than the song.

Post-it Note

The Post-it Note was a classic example of a product waiting for a use.

Back in 1970, Spencer Silver was a research chemist with the American 3M Corporation working on adhesive technology. His brief was to create the strongest glue on the market but by some extraordinary mischance he developed one that had absolutely none of the qualities he was looking for. Far from being extremely powerful, it appeared reluctant to stick to anything for long. It was very much a temporary glue — one that stuck momentarily and then came away again. However, it did have two interesting properties which Silver had never previously encountered — it could be reused and it left no residue on the material to which it was applied.

Nobody at 3M expressed any enthusiasm for Silver's glue but he remained convinced that somewhere there was a market for it. For the next ten years, he toiled away in vain. The nearest he came to a practical idea was a bulletin board coated with his glue but the concept attracted the minimum of interest. People preferred tacks.

Just when all seemed lost, a saviour arrived in the shape of Arthur Fry, a colleague of Silver's. Fry sang in a church choir. Every Sunday, he would carefully mark his hymn-book with slips of paper and every Sunday, the slips would fall out. Remembering Silver's 'useless' adhesive, Fry applied it to the paper strips and found that they now made fine markers which did not tumble out when he opened the book. Nor did they soil the pages.

Fry had finally found a use for Silver's invention and the following year, 1981, 3M marketed small blank notes with Silver's glue along one edge, calling them Post-it Notes. The product that for ten years seemed good for nothing now serves a host of different functions, from city offices to rural Switzerland where postmen wanting to let recipients know quickly that a special parcel is awaiting them at the post office, simply stick a Post-it Note with the appropriate message to the customer's letter box and continue with their round.

Premium Bond

In his budget of 17 April 1956, the then Chancellor of the Exchequer, Harold Macmillan, announced a new £1 Premium Bond, offering tax-free prizes of up to £1000. Describing it as 'something completely new for the saver in Great Britain', he added: 'This is not a pool or a lottery where you spend your money. The investor in the bond I propose is saving his money.'

Inevitably some were ready to pour scorn on the scheme, denouncing it as 'state sponsored gambling and moral slackness'. The opposition called it a 'squalid raffle' and a number of churchmen believed it would encourage gambling.

Nevertheless, the first bonds went on sale on 1 November 1956 at a high-profile launch. The Chancellor was escorted to Trafalgar Square by the redoubtable Dagenham Girl Pipers for the start of the campaign at a special temporary post office. And at the Royal Exchange, the Lord Mayor of London bought the first Premium Bond. At the close of business on that opening day, some £5 million worth of bonds had been sold. By the end of the month it was £50 million, equivalent to a staggering £608.3 million at today's values.

The first prize of £1000 (the jackpot is now £250 000) was drawn on 1 June 1957 by ERNIE. Although the machine was started by government minister Ernest Marples, it took its name from its function — Electronic Random Number Indicator Equipment. The first ERNIE was built by the Post Office Research Department. He has had two successors (marks II and III) and such is his fame that coach parties travel to visit him at his home near Blackpool where grateful winners sometimes kiss him and frustrated losers have been known to kick him. His only known relative is a similar model named ELSIE who lives in New Zealand.

Since 1957, ERNIE has given out over £2.5 billion in prizes. Some of the winners have appeared none too grateful at first. One bondholder refused to answer the door to the visiting officer, who happened to call on Hallowe'en, because he was convinced it was children playing 'trick or treat'. A £100 000 winner, who was of no fixed abode, carried around his worldly goods in three shopping bags. When the visiting officer took him to the bank to open an account, he calmly asked the manager to lend him £100 until the prize money came through.

(above) A participant jumps for joy at the prospect of winning £1000 on the Premium Bonds.

And an elderly lady, on hearing that she had won £250 000, asked: 'Couldn't you just make it £10 000? I don't really need a quarter of a million pounds.'

Another winner was a doctor at a maternity clinic. In order to arrange an appointment, the female visiting officer phoned her at work. The doctor thought she was a patient having pregnancy problems. On meeting, both were relieved to find that this was not the case!

Processed Cheese

At the age of 16, James Lewis Kraft travelled from Canada to Chicago to seek his fortune. He settled into a series of retail jobs, including the delivery of eggs to hotels and shops and working in a grocery store, before landing a post as a delivery boy for a cheese manufacturer. From that moment, young Kraft vowed to dedicate his life to cheese.

In 1903 he decided to utilise his knowledge of the retail trade, renting a horse and wagon and each day purchasing a stock of cheese from a wholesale warehouse to resell to small stores. With the expansion of his business, he was joined by four of his brothers to form J.L. Kraft & Bros Co. in 1909.

Since the cheese did not keep well and tended not to be uniform in texture or flavour, Kraft began to experiment. He aimed to produce a cheese which would last longer, maintain a uniform quality, have a taste that would appeal to the American palate and be packaged without any waste. It seemed a tall order but after years of research, Kraft successfully managed to grind, blend and pasteurise cheese to create a product which had all of the above characteristics. In 1915 his company started to manufacture the 'process cheese' in tins and a year later, Kraft was granted a patent for this method.

Kraft sold $5000 worth of the new cheese in the first year of production and 300 times that amount over the following 12 months. In 1917 his cheese was supplied in tins to the US government for the armed forces.

As the popularity of Kraft's cheese spread, further advances were made in the processing methods. In 1921 Kraft introduced five-pound loaves of pasteurised processed cheese, wrapped in foil and packaged in wooden boxes. The more compact Dairylea Cheese Spread arrived on the scene in 1950.

(right) An early tin of Kraft processed cheese.

Radio Luxembourg

'For years, I didn't realise Luxembourg was a place. I thought it was just a couple of rooms with DJs in it.' So says Cliff Richard, one of the millions who used to tune in to 'The Station of the Stars', 'Fab 208', Radio Luxembourg.

Cliff was not entirely misguided in his beliefs for, while the station's base was the palatial Villa Louvigny in the Grand Duchy of Luxembourg, a number of the programmes were recorded from the less exalted surroundings of a studio in London's Hertford Street.

Radio Luxembourg came on air on 3 December 1933 with Stephen Williams as its first disc jockey. It quickly won a large audience on Sunday nights because BBC radio steadfastly maintained its commitment to religious programmes on the Sabbath. Ironically, Williams was the son of a clergyman.

During the war, the Germans took over the commercial station and transmitted Lord Haw Haw's propaganda but normal service resumed with disc jockeys such as Pete Murray, Jimmy Savile, and later Noel Edmonds, David 'Kid' Jensen and Tony Prince ('Your Royal Ruler'). Also in the line-up during the 1950s was David Jacobs who hosted the honeymoon show, sponsored by Fyffes bananas. Many of these famous voices were listened to under the bedclothes and with the constant knowledge that the weak transmitter signal would invariably mean a fade-out during each record.

But the most celebrated voice of all belonged to one Horace Batchelor, inventor of the *In For A Draw Method* on the football pools' treble chance. Each Sunday evening, following his introductory 'Good evening, friends, this is Horace Batchelor at the microphone', he would invite listeners to write to him at 'PO Box number 6, Keynsham, that's K-E-Y-N-S-H-A-M, Keynsham, Bristol.' Batchelor, who claimed to have won over 1000 first dividends for himself and many more for his clients, ran his operation from a house on Bath Road which he called 'In For A Lodge'. The house number was 321 which coincidentally was the then points value for draws, aways and homes on the pools.

Horace Batchelor died in 1981 and was therefore not around for the final rites of Radio Luxembourg. For in December 1991 the station, hit by dwindling audiences, was finally taken off the airwaves.

Rawlplug

A minor maintenance problem in the British Museum led to the invention of the humble Rawlplug in 1919. The museum needed electrical fittings to be fixed to the walls unobtrusively and without damaging the masonry but this was no easy task under the traditional practice of chiselling a hole, plugging it with wood and then screwing the fitting into the wood. Fortunately, John J. Rawlings, a Kensington building contractor, solved the problem by inventing a fibre plug, made of jute bonded with animal blood. He called it the Rawlplug.

The Rawlplug Company Ltd embarked on production in a tiny Kensington mews with just one small machine. However, demand for Rawlplugs became so great that within a year the company had been forced to take over a factory at Lewisham. Much of the early success could be attributed to blanket advertising, including the taking of the entire front page of the *Daily Mail* on one occasion, a move which caused something of a sensation within the building trade.

Today the Rawlplug stands as a testimony to the ingenuity of one man. It is a worldwide success story, a name as synonymous with masonry fixings as Singer is for sewing machines and Hoover for vacuum cleaners.

Reader's Digest

The story of *Reader's Digest* began in 1909 after DeWitt Wallace left his student course at a Presbyterian college in Minnesota and took a job in a bank. He read widely, religiously keeping a card index of the highlights of the various articles.

Wallace first turned his pastime to profit in 1916 with a booklet called *Getting the Most Out of Farming*, a compelling condensation of government pamphlets on agriculture! Then lying awake one night in a hayfield bunkhouse during a summer job in Montana, he suddenly had the idea that what worked for farmers might well work for a wider readership.

Later, while recovering in France after being wounded in the war, he practised condensing articles from general-interest magazines. As soon as he was discharged from the army in 1919, he spent six months in Minneapolis Public Library, searching through old and current magazines, and reducing a selection of the best articles he found within. In 1920 he compiled 31 of his longhand précis into a sample, pocket-sized magazine and had several hundred copies printed.

Wallace tried to interest publishers in his prototype but they all turned it down. To add to his woes, Wallace was made redundant from his job in the publicity department of Westinghouse Electric but prior to his departure, a colleague suggested selling *Reader's Digest* by direct mail. Wallace duly wrote to professional

In the world of advertising, even Rawlplugs can be associated with merriment.

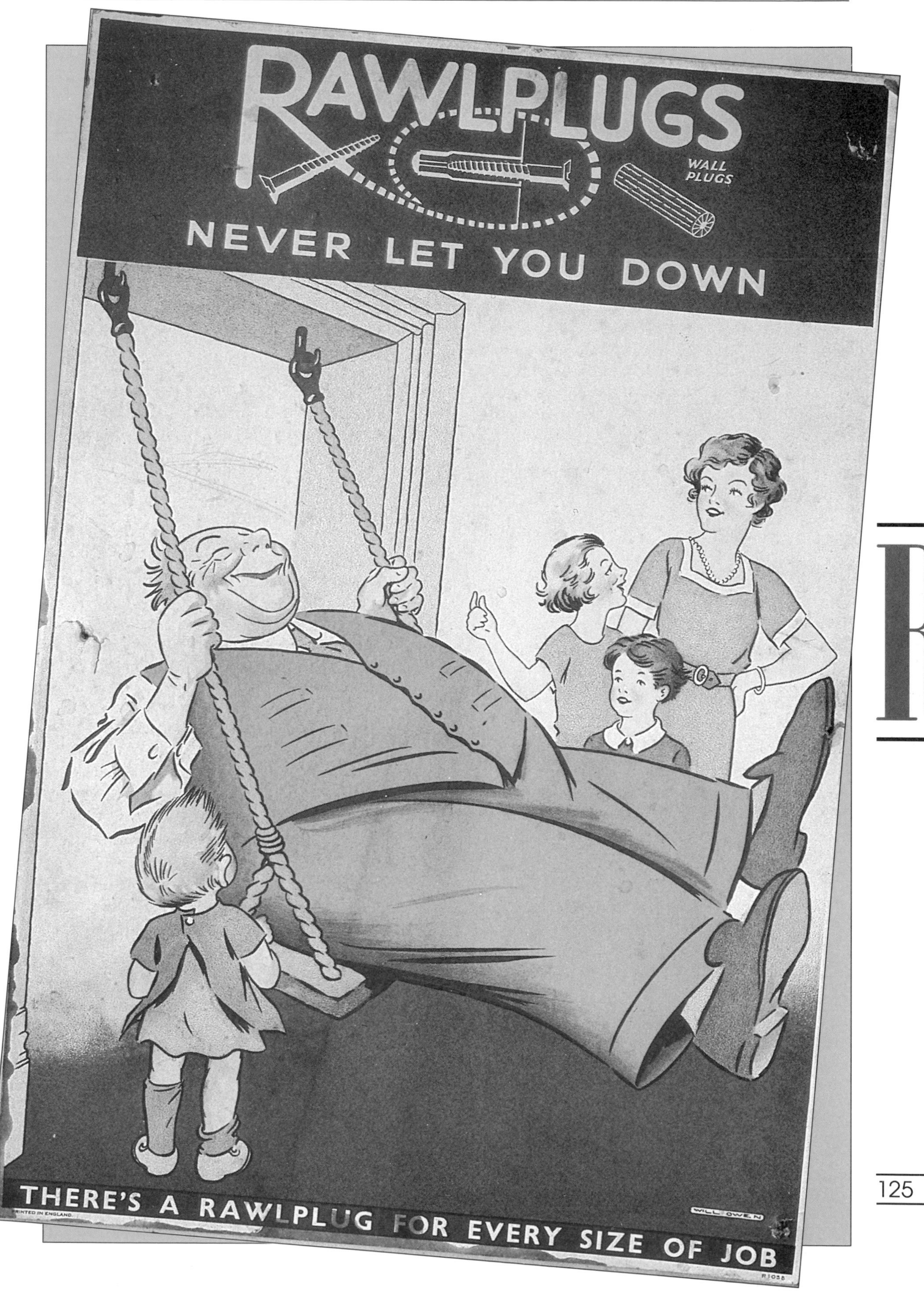
RAWLPLUGS
WALL PLUGS
NEVER LET YOU DOWN
THERE'S A RAWLPLUG FOR EVERY SIZE OF JOB
WILL OWEN

R

people, charging a $3 subscription for 12 issues, the money to be refunded if the first edition did not meet with the customer's approval. He posted the last of the circular letters before going on honeymoon and returned to find 1500 replies. With the advance subscription money and the help of a loan, Wallace and his new wife set up shop below a speakeasy in New York's Greenwich Village. The first issue of *Reader's Digest* was mailed out in February 1922, opening with an article entitled 'How To Keep Young Mentally' and with the motto 'to inform, educate, entertain and inspire'.

The immediate success of the magazine enabled the business to move to Pleasantville, 30 miles north of New York, where it was run from a disused pony shed. *Reader's Digest* is still based at Pleasantville and, despite selling 28 million copies worldwide in 17 languages, has remained true to DeWitt Wallace's ideals. For example, Wallace campaigned vigorously against smoking, as a result of which the magazine has refused all cigarette advertising since 1970. So next time you learn that you have won a *Reader's Digest* mystery prize, it is unlikely to be a box of cigars.

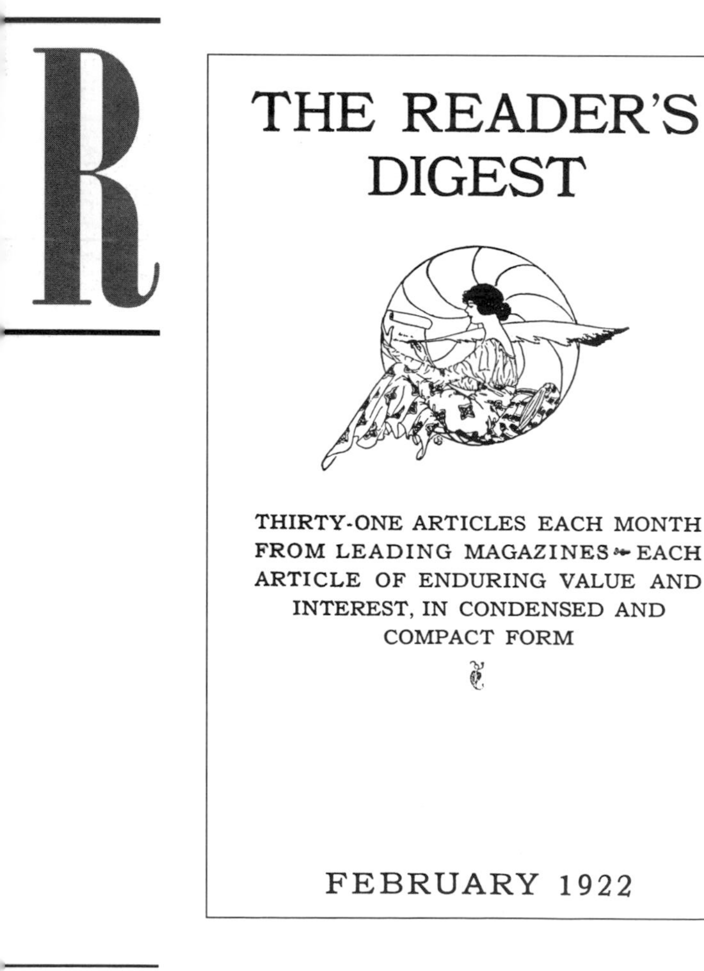
THE READER'S DIGEST

THIRTY-ONE ARTICLES EACH MONTH FROM LEADING MAGAZINES EACH ARTICLE OF ENDURING VALUE AND INTEREST, IN CONDENSED AND COMPACT FORM

FEBRUARY 1922

The first mailed-out issue of Reader's Digest.

Red Telephone Kiosk

Many felt that the heart had been ripped out of Britain with the removal of the red telephone kiosk in the 1980s. For some 50 years it had been a symbol of the nation's stability, readily visible in an emergency, as well as an invaluable tool for overseas film-makers wishing to depict Britain at a glance without having to resort to originality.

Britain's first telephone kiosks were anything but red and came in a variety of shapes and sizes. One in Blackburn, Lancashire, was fitted with a table and seats which, unfortunately, served as a shelter for various destitute types. Most Post Office kiosks were wooden except in dockland areas where they were made of galvanised iron, since it was thought likely that a docker who lost his 2d. might attempt to kick the door down. A kiosk in London's Holborn boasted a high domed roof and an attendant while a short-lived scheme of 1912 saw the provision of doodling pads in a bid to eliminate graffiti.

The first standard design appeared in 1921. Called the K1, it was made of concrete, apart from a red wooden door, and was topped by a curious ornamental spear protruding from the roof, the overall effect being not unlike that of Dr Who's TARDIS. The K1 was unpopular — particularly with the Ministry of Transport who called it a hazard to traffic — and so a competition was staged to come up with a new design. The winning submission was that of Sir Giles Gilbert Scott, esteemed architect of Liverpool Cathedral. His K2 was built of cast iron with a teak door and a concrete base. It made its debut in London in 1926, although a number of provincial authorities preferred to retain the cheaper K1. Some K2s were modified to include stamp machines and a letterbox but the noise from the machines made it impossible to conduct a telephone conversation and anyway the stamps had a habit of congealing in wet weather. This Vermilion Giant, as it was known, also proved unpopular with drivers since its bulk obscured pavements and pedestrians. Not surprisingly, it was swiftly phased out.

The familiar red telephone box was designed by Sir Giles in 1935 to commemorate the silver jubilee of King George V. Appropriately named the Jubilee Kiosk, it was a foot shorter than the K2 and the first to incorporate 'Button B', a press of which supposedly returned one's money. It hit the streets in 1936 but aroused considerable ill-feeling among rural communities who thought that red would be a veritable blot on the landscape. After the war, a concession was made to some beauty spots who were allowed to paint their kiosks dark grey, provided the glazing bars were red.

Such status did the red telephone box acquire that when the GPO proposed painting it yellow in the 1970s, public outcry caused the plan to be abandoned. Alas the rising tide of vandalism eventually proved its downfall and it steadily began to disappear when British Telecom was created in 1984.

Rather like James Dean and Marilyn Monroe, the red telephone kiosk has become more popular than ever since its death. Much prized by collectors, a number have been shipped to the United States while owners have put their kiosks to a wide variety of uses, transforming them into aquariums, shower cubicles, garden sheds, even a lavatory. And a kiosk in Huddersfield was converted into a bar by a hotel who promptly dubbed it the smallest public bar in Britain.

That much-loved structure, the red telephone kiosk.

Refrigerator

As with so many household items, the development of the electric motor at the start of the century paved the way for the domestic refrigerator.

The first, the Domelre (short for Domestic Electric Refrigerator), went on sale in Chicago in 1913. The motor drove a compressor which produced compressed air to reduce the temperature of the insulated cabinet. However, the Domelre and subsequent models, such as the Kelvinator made in Detroit in 1914, were noisy, expensive (costing around $900), inefficient and decidedly pungent since they often used sulphur dioxide as a refrigerant. Added to which the cooling mechanism was so cumbersome that it had to be placed on top of the refrigerator, outside the food compartment. In the circumstances, it was little surprise that many households preferred cheaper wooden insulated chests, filled daily with ice.

In 1922 Baltzar von Platen and Carl Munters, two young engineering students from the Royal Institute of Technology in Stockholm, presented a study which aroused a great deal of interest — a cooling machine which converted heat to cold by absorption. It could be driven by electricity, gas or kerosene. Called the 'D-fridge', it was marketed by Swedish company Electrolux in 1925.

The Kelvinator of the same year saw the cooler descend to the cabinet itself while the first air-cooled refrigerators appeared in 1931. But despite the reduction in noise level and price (down to $170 by 1935) and increased efficiency, they remained too large for many kitchens. Consequently they were viewed in Britain, at least, as an unnecessary luxury. Frigidaire, who marketed the first UK model in 1924, later reflected: 'The hard sell was probably essential in a Britain which regarded ice only as an inconvenience of winter-time and cool drinks as an American mistake.'

The other factor which, of course, hindered British progress was the lack of a reliable electricity supply until after the Second World War. Until 1945 it was a privilege of the middle classes to have electricity. The working classes had gas because it was cheaper. There was also an attitude which prevailed among those in authority at the time that working-class folk, especially women, were too stupid and irresponsible to be trusted with electricity. Presumably it was OK for them to gas themselves.

The domestic refrigerator opened the door to healthy eating.

Rubik Cube

One of the most irritating and frustrating little gadgets of the seventies was the Rubik Cube, the torturous invention of Professor Erno Rubik, a Hungarian lecturer in architectural design. It was a large cube composed of 27 small cubes, the outward-facing surfaces of which were each a different colour. The object was to arrange the cubes in such a way that the colours were the same on each side.

Marketed by New York's Ideal Toy Company in 1979, the Cube made Rubik a multi-millionaire. Worldwide sales exceeded 100 million.

While mere mortals fidgeted and floundered, higher minds were recruited to solve the riddle and soon reports came in of individuals successfully completing the Rubik Cube in a matter of seconds. Once its infallibility had been destroyed, the Cube lost its appeal. The inventor tried again with the fiendish Rubik's Clock in 1988 but it failed to engender the same enthusiasm.

(right) Looking more like a lawn mower, the Wilkinson safety razor of 1904.

Safety Razor

What's in a name? If King Camp Gillette sounds an unlikely inventor for a masculine product, what future would the safety razor have had if it had been named after his associate William Nickerson?

Born in Wisconsin in 1855, Gillette came from a family of inventors. Searching for an idea of his own, he was advised by William Painter, father of the disposable crown cork, to think of 'something which will be used once and thrown away. Then the customer will come back for more'.

Gillette went through the alphabet in vain until one morning in 1895, while shaving in the mirror at his home in Brookline, Massachusetts, he realised that the only part of his cut-throat razor used for the actual process of shaving, was the edge. So he considered producing a keen edge without the unnecessary steel backing, a disposable blade which could be thrown away when blunt without the tiresome chore of sharpening.

There followed a period of frustration for Gillette. His plans looked fine on paper but steel makers told him that it was impossible to produce a blade that was fine, flat, sharp and cheap. Then, in 1901, William Nickerson, the sole employee of Gillette's Boston-based American Safety Razor Company, earned his wages by perfecting the machinery required to manufacture such blades. His first efforts resulted in crooked and crumpled blades but before long, he was able to produce splendid double-edged blades shaped like a hoe.

The safety razor finally went on sale in 1903. The blade was fixed inside a guard so that only the very edge was exposed to the skin. It was thus much less dangerous than the old cut-throat and with the declining popularity of beards, Gillette anticipated healthy sales. For that first year, he was to be sorely disappointed. Only 51 safety razors were sold throughout the United States, exhausting just 168 blades. The following year Gillette sold 90 000 razors, using 12½ million blades!

Neither the man nor his company ever looked back. By 1905 sales had reached 250 000 and in 1917 the US government placed an order for 3½ million razors and 36 million blades to supply the entire armed forces. It was therefore with some justification that on the eve of his death in 1932, Gillette boasted that he had done more than any other person before him 'to change the face of mankind'.

Scotch Tape

To most of us, the sticky reel of cellophane tape that we use for a multitude of jobs about the home is known as 'sellotape'. Yet the first product, invented some years before its rival 'Sellotape', was 'Scotch' tape. It is simply that the generic term has tended to obscure the true origins.

'Scotch' tape was the brainchild of Richard G. Drew who, after strumming the banjo full-time in a dance band, joined the 3M company at St Paul, Minnesota, as a laboratory assistant. One of 3M's latest introductions had been a waterproof abrasive paper for use in the car industry and young Drew was sent out to ask auto paint shops to test the product.

One morning in 1923, he walked into such an establishment and heard 'the choicest profanity I'd ever known'. The fashion at the time was for two-tone cars and the painters were cursing what happened when they masked a car for two-tone paint application with glued-together newspapers. The paint on a new Packard had just been damaged when the paper was ripped off. Drew immediately promised the shop boss that he would provide a solution.

It took two years of experimenting before Drew came up with an adhesive masking tape. To make it easier to put on and remove, 3M initially applied adhesive only to the edges of the tape. Having trouble with the adhesion and suspecting that this was really a method of saving money, one irate car body painter told the 3M salesman: 'Take this tape back to your stingy Scotch bosses and tell them to put more adhesive on it.' Even if the tape did not stick, the name did.

Inspired by the success of his masking tape, Drew was eager to solve another pressing customer problem, that of a St Paul firm which had an order for insulating several hundred railroad refrigerator cars. In trying to fulfil the order, the company learned that the insulation slabs would have to be wrapped and sealed to protect them from moisture. The firm asked 3M to help solve this packaging dilemma.

Drew laboured long and hard but could find nothing which was sufficiently watertight until a fellow researcher considered packaging 3M's masking tape in the new moistureproof cellophane (recently introduced by Du Pont) to protect the rolls from heat, cold, dryness and damp. He showed Drew the cellophane. Drew looked at it and thought: 'Why couldn't that stuff be coated with adhesive and used as a sealing tape for the insulation slabs? It's moistureproof.'

In June 1929 he ordered 100 yards of cellophane for experiments. When it arrived, he cut the cellophane into 6-inch (15 cm) widths so that it could be pulled through the laboratory coating equipment. But cellophane did not act like any other backing which 3M had used. It curled near heat and split in the process of coating by machine. Also, it was difficult to apply the adhesive evenly — some areas had bare spots while others were too thickly coated. At the end of each day, piles of spoiled cellophane stood several feet high on either side of the experimental coating machine. It needed a lorry to cart away the daily waste.

However, 3M persevered and the production difficulties were overcome, a primer coat being applied to the cellophane to ensure that the adhesive held evenly. Finally, on 8 September 1930, a roll of 'Scotch' cellophane tape was sent to a prospective client. Two weeks later, the firm told 3M: 'Your gum will adhere to glass or practically any surface. It needs no moistening or smearing and is so easily applied that it should be an ideal means of sealing moistureproof packages for cakes, cookies etc. You should have no hesitancy in equipping yourself to put this product on the market economically.'

The new product was marketed during the first year of the Depression. Fears that the timing was inopportune proved groundless as the American public, forced into thrift and thus to repair rather than throw away, discovered that the cellophane tape was ideal for mending torn pages of books, fixing toys and even small rips in clothing. Farmers found it handy for patching cracked turkey eggs; secretaries discovered it would hold down torn fingernails; and housewives used it for pinning cheese on mousetraps and taping cracked plaster to the ceiling.

Although everyone clamoured for the new tape, there were still teething problems. The shelf life was shortened by humidity, heat or cold and salesmen had to warn customers to keep it away from radiators and windows. Nor was there any easy way of unwinding it from the roll — that is until 3M's John Borden designed a dispenser with a built-in cutter blade.

So, Drew had begun development of a product line which was to become indispensable — and, thanks to Borden, dispensable — in homes, offices and factories throughout the world. Just to add to the confusion about the name, in Australia 'Scotch' tape used to be known as Durex which proved mightily embarrassing for visitors to England and alarming for British tourists Down Under . . .

Scrabble

The Queen Mother likes it. So do Richard Nixon, Joan Collins and Michael Jackson. Beirut hostages John McCarthy and Terry Waite made a set from a cardboard box to pass time; BBC television news reporter Kate Adie enjoyed a game with the Allied troops on the front line

Scrabble — one of the Queen Mother's favourite games.

during the Gulf War; and when British mountaineer Chris Bonington and his party scaled the south face of Annapurna, they often spent their free evenings playing it.

The object of such devotion is Scrabble, the world's most popular word game, and one which, like Monopoly, was born out of the mass unemployment caused by the Depression that infected America in the early thirties.

Alfred Butts had lost his job as a New York architect when, in 1931, with time on his hands, he pursued his passion for word games by developing a new one which he called 'Lexico'. He played it constantly with his family and friends, regularly improving it and changing its name, first to 'Alph' (a play on his own name) and then to 'Criss Cross Words'. However, he singularly failed to make any commercial progress.

Then, in 1939, Butts met up with James Brunot, a retired government social worker, and for the next ten years they worked together on a number of ideas. Butts showed him the word game and in 1948, having been turned down by manufacturers as too dull to sell, it was made by Brunot and his wife in the living room of their house in Newtown, Connecticut. Brunot called the game 'Scrabble' and marketed it in 1949, turning out 200 sets a week via his cottage industry.

The omens were not good when the first year resulted in modest sales of 2250 sets but the turning point came in 1952 when Jack Strauss, chairman of Macy's, the leading New York department store, played Scrabble on holiday. On his return to work, he was amazed to learn that Macy's did not stock the game and immediately ordered the situation to be rectified. In the year following Strauss's initiative, 4.5 million sets were sold and Scrabble spread to Britain and Australia.

A total of around 40 million Scrabble games have since been sold in 15 different languages and over 90 countries. More than half the homes in Britain have a set. There is a braille version while academics like to play Scrabble using only Latin words. Rude or offensive words are not banned from Scrabble except in Singapore where it is actually illegal to utter or write an obscenity. The highest number of points that can be scored on the first go is 126 — using either 'squeezy' or 'quartzy' while the highest-ever score in a competition is credited to Manchester's Dr Karl Khoshnaw in 1982 for 'caziques', the plural for a West Indian chief. The first ever World Championships were staged in 1991, although a British national contest had been in existence since 1971. Sadly, just before the presentation of the trophy one year, it was noticed that the inscription read: 'Scribble Championship'.

July 27, 1960
The Motor 53
GET INTO
THE SAFETY HABIT
with the
Britax
DIAGONAL
SAFETY BELT
Patents Pending
THE ONLY
DIAGONAL BELT
APPROVED TO BRITISH STANDARD
B.S. 3254
as recently announced
The world's most advanced safety belt.
Over 1,000,000 in use.
Patented metal-to-metal quick release buckle.
Full protection entirely independent of car seat.
Equally suitable for bench, individual or 'tip-up' seats.
Shock-absorbing Webbing of 100% 'TERYLENE'
Rear passenger space completely unobstructed.
Continuous development in U.S.A., Sweden, Germany and Gt. Britain.
MODELS FOR ALL CARS 84/- EACH
ORDER YOUR Britax BELTS NOW
Available through garages, stores, accessory shops and Halfords
or write for free booklet to :—
BRITAX (LONDON) LTD.
PROCTOR WORKS · BYFLEET · SURREY · Tel.: Byfleet 3145
BRITISH SAFETY COUNCIL
PROTEGIMUS
APPROVED
c19

Seat Belt

The car seat belt owes its origins to the work of Frenchman Gustave Désiré Liebau whose 1903 patent covered 'protective braces for use in motor cars and other vehicles'. Another pioneer was an American military doctor, Colonel Stepp, who demonstrated the merits of seat belts in a vehicle travelling at 124 mph (199 km/h).

Nevertheless, seat belts came into service in aeroplanes long before cars. They were not designed for use in private cars until the fifties with Illinois passing a 1955 legislation, requiring cars to be equipped with attachments to which belts could be fastened. Belts were first fitted as standard equipment in Swedish Volvos from 1959 but remained optional extras in most cars until the 1970s. Czechoslovakia was the first country to make seat belts compulsory, in 1969, the United Kingdom eventually taking the hint in 1983.

Self-assembly Furniture

Time was when the major problem facing a young married couple was stretching out the meat ration. Now it is how to fit the left side flange (B) into the right drawer wrap (D) using the cam studs (F). For the upsurge in the popularity of self-assembly furniture (or knock-down furniture as it is unfortunately known in the United States) has made do-it-yourself experts of us all — if only we can understand the instructions.

The concept actually dates back to 1850 when an American named Michael Thonet experimented with furniture made from flat boards and screws. However, the idea met with universal apathy and it was not until after the Second World War that self-assembly furniture began to catch on. Among the early pioneers was a Swede, Elias Svedburg, who designed a range of units for a Nordiska Kompaniet exhibition in 1946 but progress remained painfully slow. The public were simply not ready for a revolutionary change in something as traditionally basic and solid as furniture. There remained an underlying feeling that anything which was so easy to assemble might fall apart again just as quickly.

Entering the fray in the early 1960s were a couple of British entrepreneurs by the name of Noel Lister and Donald Searle. At the time, they ran separate businesses buying and selling things — one of them actually operated out of a caravan in a British Rail goods yard. Finally, they realised that they were wasting a lot of time and money bidding against each other at auctions. So they decided to pool their resources and start up a mail order business, selling almost anything they could buy — camping equipment, golf clubs, even home saunas. Taking the name of one of their mothers-in-law, they called their new company Mullard Furniture Industries. It soon became shortened to MFI.

Obviously, to be sent through the post, large items of furniture, such as cupboards, bookshelves and kitchen units, had to be packed in pieces in a box and then assembled by the purchaser. Thus, flat-pack furniture came to the UK.

In the late 1960s MFI opened its warehouse in Balham, South London, to the public. Here, customers chose what they wanted and took the boxes away. Gradually, more such warehouses were opened where products were displayed 'showroom style'.

By 1972 there were 25 MFI stores, but two years later the mail order operation was closed down, partly because a change of policy by British Road Services dispensed with van boys. As a result, there was a sharp increase in the amount of damaged merchandise being returned. From then on, MFI concentrated on out-of-town retail outlets.

Yet, although the business continued to expand (by the end of 1981 the number of MFI stores had risen to 116), there remained widespread suspicion about low-cost, self-assembly furniture. In some quarters, it was considered something of a joke. When Coventry City footballer Terry Gibson was asked in the club's programme notes about his greatest claim to fame outside soccer, he replied that it was once putting together an MFI wardrobe in less than four days.

The key to overcoming this prejudice was MFI's acquisition in the 1980s of the prestigious brand names Hygena and Schreiber. The quality and durability of the company's products have since improved beyond recognition. Even the instructions are now easy to follow. Pass the flange.

(left) The Motor magazine of 1960 urges the use of car seat belts.

Sindy Doll

'She dreams of wearing fabulous dresses, attending spectacular film premières and balls, becoming a pop star, working her way round the world and living in a country cottage with beautiful gardens and a pond.' It may be the goal for many a girl but Sindy has been able to realise her earliest ambitions. She has been there, done that, seen it . . . and managed to stay 18 for over 30 years.

Created by Pedigree in 1961 as one of a range of Mam'selle Dolls, she quickly saw off her sisters Patch, Poppet, Vicki and Mitzi to emerge in her own right as a British rival to Barbie. One of the most exciting things to happen to Sindy in the sixties was the acquisition of a movable waist so that she could do the Twist. Sindy's clothes have been designed by such famous names as Mary Quant, Vivienne Westwood and the Emmanuels, who made the Princess of Wales's wedding dress. The wardrobe designed by Mary Quant caused such a sensation that some of the outfits were sold in children's sizes.

Sindy's boyfriend Paul wore clothes by top men's outfitter Hardy Amies but, like Barbie's pal Ken, he proved something of a handicap to a girl wanting to make her way in the world. Indeed, after qualifying as a doctor, his popularity was at such a low ebb that he disappeared on his rounds for 20 years, finally making a comeback in 1987.

Sindy failed to notice his absence. She was too busy graduating from art student to air hostess, beautician and boutique owner. On his eventual return, there were plans for the two to marry but the wedding was called off, following a storm of protests from young gals who could not bear to see Sindy tied to the kitchen sink.

Perhaps the most worrying thing about one whose various careers demanded a well-scrubbed, even fragrant, appearance was that Sindy did not actually own a bath until 1972. If only Paul had been around to whisper in her ear . . .

Singing Telegram

On 28 July 1933 the world's first singing telegram was introduced by the Western Union Telegraph Company of New York. There were no gorillas, policemen or naughty nuns — just a straightforward rendition of a message — although even that was opposed by one executive for taking Western Union downmarket. But the service was so well-received by customers that it continued to operate, although from 1950, the singing was performed over the phone rather than in person.

A number of today's entertainers cut their teeth on singing telegrams. Chris Evans, presenter of *The Big Breakfast*, started out as the world's skinniest Tarzan while Julian Clary also found the call of the loincloth impossible to resist. He remembers: 'I was Tarzan or Gay Tarzan, depending on what the agency booked. You would slip in, change in the toilet and hide your own clothes above the cistern. Then you had to rush into the room, pick up the victim, sit them on your lap and make them eat a banana. Then you had to sing a song and hang around being jolly until they handed you your cheque in a brown envelope. That sort of thing makes you pretty fearless!'

Sindy in all her finery. No wonder Paul feels overshadowed.

Skateboard

Enterprising youngsters had been putting planks of wood on roller skates since the 1930s but, strangely, it took two surfers to create the modern urban sport of skateboarding.

It was 1958 when Bill Richards and his son Mark, who ran the Val Surf Shop in Dana Point, California, recognised that the street boards might also appeal to surfers, so similar were the techniques involved. They asked the Chicago Roller Skate Company to cut its roller units in two and send a batch of the divided parts. Val Surf then mounted these on square, wooden boards which they sold for around $8. The new sport was christened 'terra-surfing', acting as an agreeable diversion for surfers when there were no waves.

The Val Surf operation was very much a small-time affair but in June 1963, the Makaha Company began serious commercial exploitation of the boards and as the craze took off, received daily orders for 20 000 boards. The first American National Skateboard Championships were held at La Palma Stadium, Anaheim, California, in 1964. There were no downhill slaloms because the early boards were poor at turning while the wheels were incapable of rolling over anything larger than a cigarette butt without dumping the rider unceremoniously on his backside.

The safety factor of skateboarding became a matter for urgent concern. In New York alone, 50 skateboarders a month were being hurt, half of them breaking bones. *Good Housekeeping* reported: 'Seldom has a sport fad produced as many fractured arms, wrists and legs, concussions and lacerations as skateboarding.' The California Medical Association described boards as 'a new medical menace'. No fewer than 20 US cities banned the sport from streets and sidewalks and some

16th March, 1990

THE GUINNESS TIMES

SKATEBOARD SPEED RECORD SMASHED

HICKEY EXCEEDS THE SPEED LIMIT

American skateboard fanatic Roger Hickey, of Westminster, California, yesterday recorded the highest speed ever achieved on a skateboard, clocking 78·37 mph (126·12 km/h) on a 3 mile (5·5 kilometre) course near Los Angeles.

He set the record lying in a prone position on his skateboard, and hopes to set a speed record for a stand-up position later this year. However, skateboarding at great speed does have its dangers — Hickey has suffered 44 fractures over the years. Fortunately, the attempt was not made when members of the public were using the road, as the police would surely not have liked the fact that Hickey ignored the normal permitted speed limit in beating the record.

police departments requested stores to stop selling boards. Even in Portland, Oregon — the only US city to provide a road for boarders — police booked a skateboarding dog named Tiger. Since it was perfectly legal for dogs to skateboard, he was charged with not being on a lead! Such was the outcry against skateboarding that Makaha were now losing $75 000 in cancellation orders each day. In November 1965 skateboarding officially died.

It rose again, phoenix-like, in 1973, encouraged by the introduction of polyurethane wheels, more manoeuvrable and therefore much safer than the old clay wheels. Even so, when the craze hit Britain over Christmas 1977, there was no shortage of complaints from motorists and pedestrians alike. As a result, the West Midlands police charged 20 teenagers under a 1950s bye-law which forbade roller-skating on rights of way. It was a relief to all when the trend faded and we were able to head for the supermarket in peace without having to beware of youths doing a slalom through a line of trolleys.

(left) 'The Guinness Times' hails a new world skateboarding speed record.

(below) Probably even pigs could fly with Nimble sliced bread.

Sliced Bread

To many people, sliced bread is the greatest thing since . . . sliced bread. Originating in the United States around 1928, it was one of the first convenience foods, freeing harassed housewives and hurried husbands from the daily chore of hacking through a loaf.

Sliced bread was introduced to the UK in 1933 by Garfield Weston who later ran Associated British Foods which incorporated Allied Bakeries, makers of Sunblest. One of the first British brands was Spillers' Wonderloaf which appeared in 1937.

Following the grey loaves of the war, bread went into something of a decline, thick crusts becoming all too readily associated with poverty. But the march of the electric toaster in the 1950s increased the demand for sliced bread, the uniformly thin sections being far more acceptable than the old 'doorsteps'. More recently, the popularity of prepacked sandwiches has cemented the future of sliced bread. In fact it has reached the stage where tamper-proof seals have had to be fixed to the wrappers in order to prevent unscrupulous customers stealing the top few slices from the supermarket shelves. Needless to say, they leave their crusts.

Smarties have been a children's favourite since 1937.

Smarties

Throughout history, the world of big business has been littered with casualties, products which have fallen by the wayside or been sacrificed to make way for newer models. Into the latter category comes the light brown Smartie.

For 52 years, since the creation of the product in 1937, the light brown had joined the red, yellow, orange, green, mauve, pink and dark brown Smarties in bringing joy to millions of youngsters. But a threat loomed on the horizon, an overseas interloper eager to usurp the light brown's place in the tube. For the Germans had come up with a blue Smartie which was only on sale in that country plus France, Italy, Belgium and Holland.

The blue Smartie had proved a popular addition in those countries but at first the British remained steadfastly loyal to the light brown which had seen them through a World War, the Suez Crisis and the singing career of Little Jimmy Osmond. However, when the blue was temporarily introduced to the UK to celebrate Smarties' 50th birthday, its impact was immediate. Its kingfisher sheen made the poor old light brown look decidedly drab. In 1989, Nestlé Rowntree announced that the blue was here to stay. The light brown was no more. It was an ex-Smartie.

The chocolate sweets in the sugar coating have retained their popularity with successive generations to the extent that 16 000 are eaten every minute. No wonder 1960s Smarties advertising proclaimed: 'Wotalotigot'. And, according to teachers and playgroup leaders, the letters printed on the tops of the tubes have helped numerous youngsters with their spelling. All in all, it's a real success story — unless, of course, you happen to be a light brown Smartie.

Don't *wash* them..
..*watch* them

Persil
gets clothes *whiter*
than ever before...
...while you watch

If you only knew, there are women all round you, hundreds of them close neighbours, who do their washing while they cook their dinner!... They use Persil.

Now Persil *washes*, and Persil *whitens*. But more than all that —Persil *works*. Millions of oxygen bubbles come out of Persil and go bustling through the clothes, getting every thread and fibre clean; cleaner than even your patience and perseverance ever got them. White things white. Colours bright.

These bubbles do what your hands have always had to do in the past—and do it better; while you are free to get on with other jobs — merely glancing over now and again and giving the clothes a stir round.

The Amazing Oxygen Washer

Persil
REGISTERED

Persil will do all your washing; not only heavy whites, but coloured and dainty things too — artificial silks particularly.

JOSEPH CROSFIELD & SONS LTD., WARRINGTON

PER 176B-86

Soap Powder

At the end of the Boer War, Professor Giessler and Dr Bauer, both of Stuttgart, succeeded where others had failed — namely in producing a soap with a bleaching agent. Their solution was to mix ordinary soap with a percentage of a stable salt and as the mixture dissolved in water, the oxygen was gradually liberated.

In 1907 this, the world's first brand of soap powder, was marketed by Henkel and Company of Düsseldorf under the name 'Persil' (two of its vital ingredients being perborate and silicate). Almost simultaneously, Frenchman Jules Ronchetti combined sodium salts with soap to create his own powder. And at the same time as the Germans registered their trade mark Persil, Ronchetti registered a drawing of parsley, Persil being French for parsley.

Two years later, the German Persil was bought by Joseph Crosfield and produced at Warrington, Cheshire. Crosfield called Persil 'the amazing oxygen washer', further statements claiming that it 'produced a high degree of cleansing and bleaching efficiency, capable of removing most stains, yet not damaging the most delicate fibres nor the human skin', and that 'soap powder would do away with the dolly tub and washboard and the labour of rubbing clothes, because clothes soaked in Persil needed only soaking, boiling and rinsing'.

Despite such recommendations, soap powder was slow to catch on. At that time, bar soaps or specialist items such as Lux flakes, which had been around since 1900, were generally used for washing clothes and housewives were reluctant to change the habits of a lifetime. As an added inconvenience, all soap powders had to be stirred into a paste before being added to water. Persil was first marketed in half-pound packs costing 3½d., smaller packets priced at 1d. and 2d. being introduced just before the First World War.

In 1919 Crosfields joined forces with Lever Brothers and the sales of Persil took off, the advertising emphasising its care of natural fibres such as wool and silk which were then worn almost exclusively. By the start of the Second World War, the famous 'Persil Washes Whiter' campaign had begun, a typical example showing a schoolgirl in a sparkling white blouse standing next to her friend in a decidedly dull one, alongside the caption 'Someone's mother used her soap coupons wisely!' Among those who went on to wear the 'grubby' Persil shirt in the sixties was a young Simon Le Bon, later lead singer with the rock group Duran Duran.

More and more soap powders appeared on the market. Biological washing powders, combining detergents and enzymes, were introduced in Switzerland and Germany in 1936 although they did not invade the British market until 1968. The fifties and early sixties saw Persil slugging it out with the likes of Omo, Tide, Fairy Snow, Surf, Oxydol and Daz. The battle spilled over from the grocery shop shelves onto the television screens where Omo came with the secret formula WM7, Fairy Snow forced grey out and forced white in and Daz regularly proved its superiority over the mythical Brand X. Traditionally warming to the underdog, the British public sympathised with Brand X to such an extent that a Lancashire shop-owner even attempted to market a powder of that name.

(left) Hours of endless fun could be had watching Persil 'The Amazing Oxygen Washer'.

Tide turned Dad into a washday fan.

Soya Meat

It is a disturbing thought that while hunting for a substitute for leather upholstery in cars, Robert Boyer of the Ford Motor Company, Detroit, unearthed the process which makes soya meat. The result of Boyer's 1930s discovery was TVP (Textured Vegetable Protein), an artificial meat spun from soya fibres.

The soya bean is one of the oldest vegetables known to man, having been eaten in China around 2207 BC. Yet it was not until the 20th century that its high protein content was discovered — before that the plant had only really been used as an animal feed. Commercial processing began, converting soya into oil and cake. The first major factory was built by Augustus Eugene Staley at Decatur, Illinois, in 1922 and then with so many foodstuffs in short supply during the Second World War, including

S

Spam, Spam, egg, beans and chips.

meat, research was carried out to see whether soya could be used in human food. Acting on Boyer's chance discovery, the first edible soya protein was finally produced in the US around 1960 under the name of Boca Bits.

Soya has steadily eaten its way into the meat market, capitalising on health scares and rising prices. By 1978 the annual consumption had risen to 20000 tons worldwide. Among the delights available are soya burgers, pâté, sausage mix and vegetarian goulash.

Spam

'I ate my share of Spam along with millions of other soldiers. I'll even confess to a few unkind words about it — uttered during the strain of battle, you understand. But as the former commander-in-chief of the allied forces, I believe I can still officially forgive you your only sin: sending us so much of it.'

These were the words of President Eisenhower in a letter to the Geo. A. Hormel Company of Austin, Minnesota, shortly after the Second World War, echoing the views of millions of servicemen for whom Spam represented an almost daily part of their regular rations. There was even a school of thought which suggested that America change its name to 'Uncle Spam'!

And in his memoirs, Khrushchev admitted that during the war, 'without Spam we wouldn't have been able to feed our army'.

The war made Spam just as it did Vera Lynn. Spam was first developed by Hormel in 1937 (the name, combination of Shoulder Pork and hAM, was thought up by the brother-in-law of Hormel's chairman). It quickly became a great favourite of military cooks who served up the canned meat *ad nauseam* because it contained protein, was easy to digest and convenient.

It was not only soldiers who lived off Spam. It came to Britain as part of the wartime Lend Lease Act whereby goods and foodstuffs were given to the UK on the basis that they would be paid for when the war was over, and was often the only meat available. Indispensable until British meat rationing ended in 1954, it has gone on to become the most famous brand in the history of packaged food and has sold over four billion cans from Japan to Mexico.

A sizeable percentage was devoured by a six-year-old Dorset boy who developed an allergy to all meats except Spam and munched his way through six tins of the stuff every week for three years. He had Spam for breakfast, Spam for lunch and Spam for tea. He became so addicted that he developed a mental block against trying anything else and ultimately his parents had to send him to a child psychiatrist to get him eating normally again.

The current Hormel plant at Austin measures the size of 19 football pitches and contains an oven that cooks 450 cans of Spam a minute. A daunting prospect!

Alas, Spam was unable to carry its proud tradition into the Gulf War where it was announced that 'for the first time in decades, G.I.s are fighting a major war without their daily rations of Spam'. This was because it had been taken off the military menu at the request of the Saudi authorities, pork being a forbidden food and Spam having a 90 per cent pork content.

Yet in spite of the endorsements by world leaders, possibly the product's greatest claim to fame was via the Spam song on *Monty Python's Flying Circus* in a sketch in which a crew of Vikings took time off from raping and pillaging to sing the praises of Spam. Python member Michael Palin recalls: 'When we did the Spam song, I don't think we ever got permission from the company. We just went ahead. In the end, the Spam people were very keen and promised they would send us several tins of free Spam. We said: "No, that's alright. Thanks anyway . . ."'

Spangles

It used to be one of the most eagerly anticipated moments of the school day. Talk about the forthcoming maths test, last night's episode of *Thunderbirds* or what the P.E. master was doing with the games mistress in the locker room would all be temporarily suspended while the burning issue of the morning was addressed: What would be the Spangles mystery flavour?

Fiendishly disguised beneath a wrapper covered in a series of question marks, the mystery flavour taxed many a sweet tooth. It was one for Spangles specialists only.

Mars launched the boiled sweets in a tube in 1948 in the UK. The original variety was fruit flavoured, comprising orange, lemon, lime, blackcurrant (which everybody used to leave), apple, pineapple, grapefruit and strawberry. In their orange packet with yellow stripes and costing 3d., Spangles' advertising described them as 'Deliciously fruity — excitingly new', 'the modern way to buy sweets' and the 'sweet way to go gay'. It should be pointed out that in 1953 'gay' still meant 'happy'.

Further flavours emerged — mint, barley sugar, butterscotch and the much-missed acid drop — plus, from 1958, Old English, a collection of winter warmers consisting of treacle, toffee, mint humbug, aniseed, liquorice, barley sugar, butterscotch, rum and butter and peardrop.

But as concerns about tooth decay rose and the world became chocoholics, sales of sugar sweets plummeted and in 1984 Spangles came to a sticky end.

Spangles — gone but not forgotten.

S

Speaking Clock

Monsieur Esclangon, Director of the Paris Observatory, had become irritated by the amount of time his staff wasted on answering calls from the French public wanting to know the precise hour. So he designed the world's first speaking clock which came into service in Paris on 14 February 1933, voiced by broadcasting personality Marcel Laporte.

With 26 500 requests for the time received each week in the London area alone, Britain swiftly followed the French lead and on the afternoon of 24 July 1936, T.I.M. made its debut, installed in the basement of Holborn Telephone Exchange. The voice belonged to Jane Cain, an announcer for band leader Henry Hall. Incidentally, Jane was her stage name — she had been christened Ethel. Miss Cain, representing the Victoria Exchange, beat off 15 000 other hopeful telephonists in a nationwide contest to find 'the golden-voiced girl', thereby winning a handsome prize of ten guineas. The judges, who included poet John Masefield and actress Sybil Thorndike, were looking for someone 'as detached as the voice of a bird without trace of over-emphasis or personal advertisement, with nothing of the theatrical, and free from accent'.

Miss Cain remained the speaking clock for over 20 years with her 'beautifully-modulated voice, calm and unflurried'. The words used to make her announcements were recorded on four glass discs with 4320 permutations.

Two clocks were installed at Holborn in case one broke down but in 1942 it was decided that a duplicate pair should be provided elsewhere, lest the originals were damaged by bombing. The site chosen was Liverpool, a curious selection since the Post Office there had already been badly bombed. The clocks were placed on the second floor, a move which caused acrimonious correspondence since their designer had stipulated that they should be in a safe part of the country in a room with no windows and in a ground floor or basement with solid ground beneath. Within two years, the Liverpool clocks had been charred by fire and had to be renewed.

Soon 13 million callers a year were using T.I.M. Jane Cain was eventually succeeded by Pat Simmons whose

Jane Cain, Britain's first speaking clock.

S

voice told the time on no fewer than 65 million occasions. She remembered: 'Once I said something in a newsagent's, upon which a male customer asked: "Aren't you the speaking clock?"

'"Yes," I said.

'"What are you doing here? What happens if I ring up now and want to know the time?"

'He really thought I sat behind a desk all day repeating the time!'

Britain's first male speaking clock was Brian Cobby who began his reign in 1985. By then the winner's prize money had risen to £5000 — a far cry from Jane Cain's day.

The original French invention may have been supremely efficient in Paris but it was less reliable in the provinces. Just prior to the Second World War, a French government official asked the postal headquarters in Marseilles how they managed to maintain the accuracy of the speaking clock. 'It is easy, sir,' replied the senior engineer, 'I keep it adjusted according to the time signals broadcast by Radio Marseille.' The man from the Ministry then telephoned the radio station and asked how they knew whether their time signals were accurate. 'No problem,' came the reply. 'We simply ring up the speaking clock.'

S

Speedway

Rumours abound that something akin to speedway racing took place on a loose dirt surface at Pietermaritzburg, South Africa, in the spring of 1907 but the sport itself acknowledges the father of speedway to be New Zealander Johnnie S. Hoskins who introduced organised racing to Australia at the tail end of 1923.

One-time farmhand, boxer and photographer, Hoskins was 31 and broke when he stumbled across the small country town of West Maitland in New South Wales. Some friends fixed him up with a job as secretary of the local Hunter River Agricultural and Horticultural Society, the wages from which enabled him to buy an old motorcycle. The daredevil Hoskins wanted to race it but the only likely venue was the local trotting track where the town's annual show was staged and his superiors flatly refused to allow the hallowed turf to be used for bike racing. Hoskins pressed ahead regardless and one Sunday morning, he led his fellow enthusiasts onto the showground.

Being a typical Boys' Own story, the next step should have been that Hoskins roared to victory, scattering mud and his rivals in his wake. But in truth, he lost control of his machine after only a few yards and crumpled to the ground in an undignified heap.

Meanwhile, the deafening din had attracted a crowd. Hoskins anticipated instant dismissal from his post but instead he was told to organise more motorcycle races at the Electric Light Carnival on 15 December 1923, an occasion to mark the eagerly awaited arrival of electricity in West Maitland.

Over 60 riders turned up to compete for a first prize of £50. There was just one rule — that no competitor must remove his feet from the footrest. There were six entrants in the first race of the evening. Stripped of lights and mudguards, the machines accelerated towards the first corner but as they tilted, the inside footrests dug into the turf and brought down all six riders. They remounted and the meeting passed off successfully but the widespread disillusionment with those footrests caused the rule to be revised. From then on, the inside footrests were dismantled and the art of broadsiding was born.

Speedway spread through Australia like a bush fire. Within three years, there was a World Championship. Hoskins explained: 'We had run short of titles. We'd had the New South Wales Championship, the Australian Championship and just about every other championship. So I suddenly got the idea: World Championship. We had two Americans, a couple of Englishmen and a lot of imagination!' What fired the imagination was the prize money of £750 when in 1926 Australia, a working man's wages averaged less than £3 a week.

In May 1927 speedway came to Britain, at Camberley Heath in Surrey. But it was not exactly the sport we know today. The track was sand and the competitors rode the wrong way round — in a clockwise direction.

Stainless Steel

At the turn of the century, eating from steel cutlery was an unappetising prospect. Knives, forks and spoons would invariably be partly rusty, for keeping them in pristine condition required considerable effort. Not only did they have to be dried carefully after washing to prevent tarnishing but they also needed regular polishing with scouring powder in order to retain their shine. That the rusty spoon has become a relic of a bygone age is largely due to the endeavours of one man — Harry Brearley.

The youngest of eight children living in cramped conditions in Sheffield, Brearley's involvement with steel began when he used to take his father's packed lunch to the nearby works. Subsequently, Brearley junior joined the firm of Thomas Firth's as a cellar lad in their crucible steel melting plant. He did not last long and in 1882, at the age of 11, was sacked for being too young!

The following year he returned to Firth's as a bottle-washer in their chemical laboratory where he came under the wing of chief chemist, James Taylor, who encouraged him to attend night school. Brearley duly qualified as a metallurgist and after a spell in Russia, returned to a post as head of the newly merged Brown Firth research laboratories.

In May 1912 Brearley had cause to visit the Royal Small Arms factory at Enfield, Middlesex, in connection with the failure of rifle barrels due to internal erosion. He recommended using a steel with 15 per cent chromium, instead of the 5 per cent available at the time, since it had a higher melting point and a greater resistance to wear at high temperatures, both apparently essential factors in combating barrel erosion. On 20 August 1913 he made the first furnace cast of what later became known as stainless steel.

A dozen sample gun barrels were duly forwarded to Enfield but brought about little improvement. However, in the meantime Brearley had found a more commercial use for his process. During his experiments, he had observed that whereas the old carbon steel had rusted when left lying around in the laboratory, the cuts of chromium steel had maintained their brightness. Brearley reported that his new steel 'would appear specially suited for the manufacture of spindles for gas and water meters, pistons and plungers in pumps, ventilators and valves in gas engines and, perhaps, certain forms of cutlery'.

Brearley forged ahead with his plan for stainless steel cutlery but met with a mixed reaction. One of Sheffield's leading cutlers remarked that producing knife blades which would not corrode was 'contrary to nature'. Even one of Firth's directors is reputed to have uttered that 'rustlessness is not so great a virtue in cutlery, which of necessity must be cleaned after each using'. And when Brearley did manage to persuade a cutlery manufacturer to try some samples, the steel was so hard that it ruined the tools.

Eventually, satisfactory procedures were developed, although stainless steel's first major function was not in cutlery but on a loftier plane altogether — aircraft engine valves. Indeed, in 1916 the production of high chromium steels for other than defence purposes was prohibited by the British government until the cessation of hostilities.

By then, Brearley, angered by Firth's refusal to take out a British patent on his discovery, had resigned. Instead, he took out a United States patent whereupon Firth's, who had been making their own stainless steel, purchased a half share and the two parties were reunited.

Sheffield stainless steel went on to acquire worldwide fame. When the *Queen Mary* liner was launched in 1934, its kitchens sparkled in stainless steel while the *Daily Mail* Ideal Homes Exhibition of the same year featured *Staybrite City*, a 464-page catalogue listing the various uses of stainless steel. Today there are over 200 different varieties of stainless steel in existence, employed on such diverse items as kitchen utensils, spectacle frames and Concorde. The top 288 ft (88 m) of New York's impressive Chrysler Building has been clad in stainless steel since 1930.

Citing the earlier work of the Frenchmen Guillet (1905), Portevin (1909) and German scientist Monnartz (1911), doubts continue to be expressed as to who was the true inventor of stainless steel. For all the merits of their work (and of the three only Monnartz discovered the real effect of chromium on corrosion resistance), none of these gentlemen foresaw the commercial potential of their findings. That was left to Harry Brearley.

Rusty spoons were a thing of the past with stainless steel.

A 1920 Rowenta electric iron, forerunner of the modern steam iron.

S

Steam Iron

People have been trying to smooth out the creases in clothes for centuries. In the pre-iron age, a heavy stone heated near a hearth removed those unsightly creases from Neanderthal Man's loincloth. Then the first iron, a block of thick metal with a handle, came into operation with beeswax or candle grease used to smooth its passage over crumpled cloth. Electric irons were invented in France in 1880 but did not achieve any degree of popularity for another 40 years. Even then they were extremely heavy (weighing between 7 and 10 lbs (3–4.5 kg) — an 1895 model weighed as much as 14 lb (6 kg), heated up very slowly and had no thermostats until 1936 when the introduction of fabrics which melt easily made thermostatic control essential.

Although the first steam iron had been marketed in 1926 by the Eldec dry cleaning company of New York, acceptance of this new form of iron was not forthcoming until the 1950s, the decade which also witnessed the introduction of automatic temperature control. In 1953 Hoover launched its steam iron, able to dry iron fabrics which were still damp, and, at the touch of a switch, to emit jets of steam to dampen those which had become too dry. With the addition of a non-stick baseplate, these new lightweight irons (many of which weighed less than 1 lb) rapidly caught on. No longer did you have to go weight-training before doing the ironing.

Although for many years it remained necessary to iron over a damp cloth to raise the steam required for pressing trousers, improved technology has eliminated this inconvenience. Now 75 per cent of the four million new irons sold each year are steam models.

Stereo Record

In music circles, just as it was the compact disc which saw off vinyl, the LP which saw off the 78 and sanity which killed off Father Abraham and the Smurfs, so it was stereo that ended the reign of mono. But it was a long time coming.

Research headed by EMI physicist Alan Dower Blumlein in 1933 brought about the production by his company of the first stereo 78. Blumlein took out a patent on his invention yet, remarkably with hindsight, his work remained nothing more than experimental for over 20 years.

By the 1950s the advent of high-quality magnetic tape had enabled stereophonic sound to enter the American home. In the autumn of 1955 Ampex, the leading manufacturer of tape equipment in the US, hailed stereo as: 'The most exciting development yet in music listening.' For Christmas 1956, RCA released a selection of stereo tapes featuring the Boston and Chicago Symphony Orchestras but EMI and others remained adamant that stereo discs were not practicable, principally because of the cost. A stereo tape was priced at $18.95 whereas the same piece could be heard on a mono LP disc for just $3.98. And on top of that came the stereo equipment. Yet within two years, the American company Audio Fidelity and the British firms Pye and Decca were selling stereo discs using Blumlein's technique!

At the 1958 Radio Show, the British press waxed lyrical about the new 'High Fidelity' equipment. But buyers were more cautious, principally because most of the recordings were of poor quality since the industry had, after a wait of 25 years, been pushed into stereo production too quickly. Fuzzy distortion prevailed, one expert reporting instances of 'instruments wandering from one speaker to the other across a yawning chasm in the middle'.

The breakthrough was Decca's release of Wagner's opera *Das Rheingold*. Classical buffs eulogised over the sounds. Mono was on the way out.

The magic of stereo at the touch of a button.

Subbuteo

Peter Adolph was a keen ornithologist and so when he dreamed up a new table football game in 1947, he wanted to call it 'The Hobby'. However, because that was descriptive and could not be registered, he instead took part of the bird's Latin name (*Falco subbuteo subbuteo*) and called his game 'Subbuteo'.

Adolph set up a cottage industry near Tunbridge Wells in Kent and started selling the Subbuteo Assembly Set on a mail order basis. Early dispatches went out from a former hayloft perched above some stables. The teams were cardboard, the ball was cellulose and the nets were made of paper with wire frames. There was no playing pitch, just a piece of chalk and instructions to mark out the pitch on an ex-army blanket — one of the few things that was in plentiful supply in that immediate post-war period. The first edition cost 10s. 1d. (plus 6d. postage and packing).

Despite its lack of refinement, the game proved an instant success. Soccer itself was going through a boom period, devoured by a nation starved of its national sport for six years, and Subbuteo was seen as a realistic attempt to recreate the excitement of football on a table top. Part of its appeal was that two dozen different sets of team colours were available, covering every Football League club and many Scottish and international teams. Red and white striped shirts and white shorts denoted Stoke City and New Brighton; Plymouth Argyle, Southport, Hibernian and Eire played in green and white; and Blackpool shared their tangerine and white strip with Holland. By season 1949–50, a green baize playing cloth was introduced for 13s. 6d. while a referee and two linesmen could be bought for 1s. 6d. These days it costs several thousand pesetas and a holiday in Barbados . . .

With over six million fans in 50 countries, many of which have special Leagues, and its own World Cup, Subbuteo reflects the popularity of soccer. And it can be just as frustrating — particularly when Ian Rush topples off the table and goes up the vacuum cleaner or when the dog chews Gazza's head.

An early Subbuteo set demonstrates the statuesque defensive formation so faithfully copied by the England soccer team in recent years.

Sun Tan Lotion

Over hundreds of years, plant extracts had been used to protect the skin from the sun's harmful rays. For Victorian and Edwardian bathers, there was only a minimal risk of sunburn since the majority of the costumes left precious little skin exposed to direct light but with the skimpier garments of the 1920s, French fashion queen Coco Chanel created a trend in tans.

It began in 1925 after she had bought a house in the South of France and allowed her skin to darken. She looked so stunning that women across the world tried to emulate her. However, the craze caused medical problems for those who suffered prolonged exposure to the sun and the need became apparent for an easy-to-apply product which would encourage a tan while protecting the skin.

The answer was provided by Eugene Schueller's L'Oréal company who, in 1936, brought out the first mass-market sun tan lotion, Ambre Solaire. It was a tremendous success, especially since, as far as Britain was concerned, it coincided with the introduction of paid annual holidays. Soon millions of Britons were able to return from the likes of Skegness and Scarborough sporting a nice brown tan. Or was it rust?

Once it was: If you want to get a date, get a tan. Now it's: If you want to end up looking like a date, get a tan.

Superglue

It is somehow fitting that the modern substance which has caused so many accidents was discovered in exactly the same way.

Back in the 1950s scientists at the US photographic company Eastman Kodak were studying ethylenic monomers. In characterising a sample of ethyl cyanoacrylate for refractive index, the glass prisms of the refractometer accidentally became bonded together when monomer was applied. The researchers encountered enormous difficulties in prising the prisms apart and were thus alerted to the unique bonding properties of cyanoacrylates, or superglues as they came to be known.

Easy to use on metals, glass, plastics and rubbers and needing only one drop per square inch for firm bonding, the new product was marketed for industrial use in the late fifties by Eastman Chemical Products under the name of Eastman 910. But Eastman were not really sure how to sell their invention and at $100 for a one-pound bottle, progress was slow. Besides, Eastman 910 possessed a couple of undesirable qualities — it had a shelf life of only six months and at 212°F (100°C), its bonding power failed.

As further superglues appeared on the US industrial market (including such famous names as Loctite with its 404 SuperBonder), concern rose about the possible dangers of cyanoacrylates which, if improperly used, can cause eye irritation or adhere to the skin. In January 1974 America's Consumer Product Safety Commission ordered nine distributors to include stronger warnings on their packagings. The commission chairman said: 'It's a good, all-purpose glue. The problem is, maybe it's too good.'

The resultant hysteria in the American press soon subsided, only to resurface in Britain when superglue was introduced to the UK consumer market in 1976. Stories have abounded of hapless individuals with their fingers stuck together, some by accident, some by design — for superglue has become a weapon of the criminal wishing to immobilise his victim. One of the most remarkable incidents involved Englishman John Bloor who, in 1993, succeeded in supergluing his buttocks together.

Supermarket

The word 'supermarket' may sound cold and impersonal but it is a mite less embarrassing than the name of the forerunner of the concept. For how many wives could bring themselves to announce: 'Darling, I'm just off to the Piggly Wiggly'?

It was in a bid to economise on staff that two Californian shops, the Alpha Beta Food Market at Pomona and Ward's Grocetaria in Ocean Park, opted to go self-service in 1912. This new scheme quickly spawned a chain of self-service grocery stores in the same state, known as 'Humpty Dumpty Stores'. But these all retained counter service — that institution was not experimentally abolished until 1916 when Clarence Saunders introduced check-outs and a turnstile entrance at his Piggly Wiggly self-service store in Memphis, Tennessee. The move was such a success that within seven years, a further 2800 Piggly Wigglies sprang up across the United States.

Although these were undoubtedly the first supermarkets, the word itself was not coined until November 1933 when Albers Super Markets Inc. opened in the US.

Britain was slow to follow these new trends. Housewives liked the personal touch of counter service and it was only out of necessity, forced upon him by a shortage of staff due to the war, that Harold Wicker of the London Co-Operative Society opened the country's first self-service store, at Romford in 1942. Impressed by American supermarkets, Tesco boss Jack Cohen converted his tiny branch at St Peter's Street, St Albans, to self-service in 1947. After only a year, the shop returned to counter service amidst rumours of a spate of shoplifting, before going back to self-service successfully in 1949.

Having pioneered self-service in the UK, the London Co-Op then opened the first full-size supermarket, at Manor Park in January 1948. Although the Premier chain began operating at London's Earls Court in 1951, the supermarket remained a rarity in Britain during the first part of the fifties. But self-service stores flourished. Tesco alone converted 20 shops to the system in 1950 through a need to trim staff costs, since inflation was pushing up prices and wages faster than profits. Sales doubled, even quadrupled, causing British women to be warned against being 'lured into over-spending'. Retail-

The first Tesco self-service branch, at St. Albans.

ers claimed that the new shops kept the prices down but critics of self-service maintained that it encouraged pilfering and threatened the livelihood of small shopkeepers.

The supermarket finally got to grips with the British economy in the early 1960s — and with it came that most feared of machines, the supermarket trolley. The trolley had actually been invented as far back as 1937 when Sylvan Goldman introduced it at his Standard Supermarket in Oklahoma City. It was, as now, a peculiar contraption. The cart was made from a folding chair, a basket replaced the seat, the feet were mounted on wheels and the customer pushed the back of the chair.

Supermarket trolleys may look innocent enough but as we all know they can be lethal weapons in the wrong hands, particularly since their steering capacity is equal to that of the average Scotsman on Hogmanay. In Britain alone, no fewer than 7500 people were treated in hospital during 1993 for injuries caused by supermarket trolleys. And that did not include the countless bumps, bruises and minor lacerations which are all part of the weekly visit to the frozen food counter.

Synthesiser

One name will always be synonymous with the synthesiser — that of Robert Moog. Yet while his technological expertise popularised the instrument, it had actually been in circulation for the best part of a decade.

The first electronic synthesiser was the RCA Mark 1 developed by Olsen and Belar in 1955. The composer was able to programme it in advance by using punched paper rolls but it was a laborious exercise. It was a vast piece of equipment, virtually filling an entire wall, and like its successor, the more refined Mark 2 of 1959, was principally designed as a scientific exercise. Few musicians were allowed access to it.

Then along came Moog. He had been intrigued by electronic musical instruments as an engineering student at Cornell University and first exhibited electronic modules at the New York Engineering Society convention of 1964. Whereas previous synthesisers had to be changed and set manually by turning a dial or flicking a switch, Moogs operated on the principle of voltage control. The effect was the same but it was much quicker to achieve and more accurate.

Construction of voltage-controlled instruments was soon taking place in a number of countries. Composer Max Deutsch was one of the first to use a Moog but it only came to public attention on the Beach Boys' classic 'Good Vibrations'. Walter Carlos's 1968 piece, 'Switched on Bach', also helped increase the popularity of the synthesiser.

Until the early seventies, synthesisers could only play one note at a time so the range of sounds was limited. But further advances, plus more compact instruments such as the Mini-Moog, made them a firm favourite with rock bands. One of the pioneers was Keith Emerson, noted for sticking daggers in the keyboard and allowing the instrument to crash heavily onto the stage, thereby creating an explosive reverberation. One suspects it was not quite what Robert Moog had in mind.

Tampon

Hippocrates described them in the 5th century BC; Egyptians rolled their own from papyrus; and wealthy Byzantine ladies had them manufactured from finest carded wool. But the modern tampon was an inspiration of Depression-era America. Conceived by Earle C. Haas, a Colorado doctor and real-estate dabbler, manufactured by a distiller of slimming potions and marketed by a fast-talking laxative salesman, the modern tampon was a triumph of commercial zeal over establishment prudery.

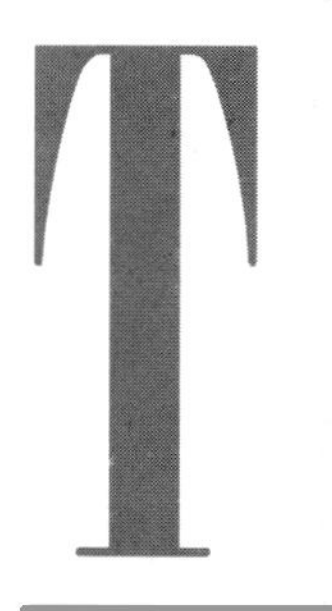

Before 1921 menstrual protection was left to a woman's imagination. Women used pieces of cloth or anything that would offer some form of protection and absorption. This was hardly satisfactory. The cloth had to be washed and reused, and was uncomfortable and unreliable. Then Lilia (now Smith & Nephew) launched the first disposable sanitary towel, Dr White's. It had loops at the end and required the use of a belt to hold it in place. The towel offered two major advantages over cloth — it was disposable and it stayed in position. However, it was still bulky and clumsy and many women preferred to use washable napkins instead, if only because they were cheaper.

Among those who hated sanitary pads was the wife of Dr Earle Haas. To help her cope with her monthly period, Dr Haas developed a tampon from compressed surgical cotton with a cord stitched through the length of it. Later, he designed a cardboard applicator to make insertion simpler, which is more like the tampon of today. The new device was so well received that within a year Haas had founded the Tampax Corporation. The first Tampax tampon was produced in 1933.

Even so there remained a degree of suspicion about Haas's invention. Some people maintained the quaint tradition of hanging out the bridal-night bedsheets speckled with blood to prove that the bride had been a virgin when she walked up the aisle. More realistic mothers, still wishing to convince the neighbours, achieved the same effect with a dead chicken. And for years the myth persisted that if a girl used tampons, she could not be a virgin.

So discreet for those 'difficult days'. A Tampax advertisement from the 1950s.

This fallacy was not diminished by the *Lancet*'s reaction when tampons arrived in Britain in the early 1940s. The medical magazine pronounced that virgins were 'incapable of using them'. The General Medical Council insisted that packs carry the warning 'Unsuitable for Unmarried Women', an instruction that was not removed until 1956.

Tampax tried to counter the fears via education and by advertising in women's magazines during the war. One advert from 1941 showed a series of drawings of women doing jobs usually associated with men — a bus conductress, a soldier changing a tyre — each bearing the slogan: 'In a man's job, there's no time for "not so good days".' Another read: 'Women's tasks today leave no room for disabilities. The active non-stop life of the war worker demands freedom of action never before known. In this, Tampax — sanitary protection worn internally — is woman's best ally.' By the end of that year, the Tampax slogan was: 'Women are winning the War — of Freedom.'

Around four million tampons are currently used every day in Britain alone. In 1993 men suddenly started buying them when singer Beverley Craven signed up with Tampax makers Tambrands to do five concerts around Britain. The only way to get tickets was to cut out tokens on Tampax packs. One male buyer, casting aside the customary embarrassment about purchasing tampons for wives and girlfriends, explained: 'It's worth spending a few quid on something for the girlfriend just so we can see Beverley.'

Tape Recorder

The origins of Richard Nixon's favourite invention can be traced back to 1898 when Danish engineer Valdemar Poulsen invented the Telegraphone, the world's first wire recorder. With poor reproduction and audible only through earphones, even Poulsen had to admit that the Telegraphone was not exactly state of the art technology. In his patent, he wrote that the best recording medium would probably be 'a strip of insulating material such as paper covered with a magnetisable metallic dust'.

The first tape recorder arrived 37 years later. Employing a plastic base tape coated with iron oxide, the Magnetophon, built by German company AEG, was demonstrated at the 1935 Berlin Radio Fair. It was marketed two years later, closely followed by the Soundmirror, a product of America's Brush Development Company.

But it was the Germans who set the pace during the war years, their tape recorders being used extensively for the broadcasting of propaganda messages. When the Allies liberated Luxembourg in the autumn of 1944, they uncovered a number of these machines and brought them home for detailed examination.

All recording studios switched to tape after the war and in 1948 the Wire Recording Corporation of America brought out the Wireway, a lightweight, portable magnetic tape recorder priced at $149.50.

Many customers remained sceptical about tape recorders. Since tape could be easily edited so that listeners were unable to detect any joins, many suspected that instead of getting whole concerts, they were being fobbed off with a patchwork of several separate performances. To allay public fears, some companies took the step of stating that their recordings were composed of complete, unedited 'takes'.

TCP

As with garlic, curry and cabbage, the moment you walk into a room you know instinctively when somebody has been using TCP. The familiar smell has been with us since 1917 when Count Callimachi, a Romanian biochemist working in London, invented what he hoped would be a cure for venereal disease. He named the liquid 'TCP' since he believed it contained trichlorophenol.

In fact, TCP proved ineffective against VD but its antibacterial properties were swiftly recognised. At first production was carried out on a small scale at a factory in Willesden. Bottles were filled by hand and delivered

That new-fangled contraption the tape recorder makes the front cover of a 1956 edition of Practical Wireless.

T

With all that TCP, at least nobody will get near enough to catch the cold from you!

to local chemists by a team of young female assistants on bicycles.

In 1923 production was taken over by British Alkaloids and 40 years later the brand was bought by the Pfizer Group. The first press advertising began in 1939 and wartime campaigns concentrated on keeping the British workforce healthy and productive under such slogans as: 'Here is a proved way of reducing winter illness absenteeism in industry.' Daily doses of TCP were also advocated for children as a preventative measure. Peacetime advertising was targeted at the family and British Alkaloids were one of the first companies to produce an educational booklet entitled *When You Have To Be a Home Doctor.*

Today TCP appears in over 40 per cent of household medicine cabinets worldwide. It is most commonly used for gargling, as a mouthwash and for children's cuts, grazes, bites, stings and recently pierced ears. Recent consumer research found TCP to be an ally around the home — reliable, versatile, tried and trusted. Where would we be without it?

Tea Bag

Seventy per cent of the tea we purchase today comes in tea bags but 60 years ago, they were virtually unheard of. For although tea was first imprisoned in a little muslin bag by San Francisco's Joseph Krieger in 1919, early use was confined to the catering industry. It was not until around 1935 that the tea bag made any impact on the US housewife.

Among the American manufacturers were Tetley Inc. of New York, for whom the tea bag accounted for about five per cent of overall sales. During the thirties, the splendidly named Tetley Ironside Tetley-Jones from Joseph Tetley & Co. in London visited the American side of the business to see what could be done to boost home sales. He was immediately impressed by the tea bag and returned to the UK ready to commence production.

However, the war intervened and it was not until 1953 that Tetley's finally introduced tea bags to Britain. At that time, instant coffee had made significant inroads into the British market — indeed it was so popular with young couples that it all but halted the growth of the tea industry. The muslin square proved the salvation of tea.

Tetley's first tea bags came in little envelopes rather like after-dinner mints. Costing just 1d. each (1s. 3d. bought a box of 16), they promised no leaves to empty away; no wasteful measuring; no strainer; no leaves in the cup; and no slop basin. Persuading the British to change their tea-drinking habits was a tough assignment but the 'new, quick, easy way to make delicious tea for ½d. a cup' quickly found favour. Added impetus was provided by Lady Isobel Barnett of BBC TV's *What's My Line?* who told the nation: 'Tea tastes so much better made this modern way.'

Even a Mr and Mrs Tex Ledger lent their testimony in the magazine *Practical Motorist & Motor Cyclists* by announcing that among the essential items they were taking on a motor-cycling trip to Australia were two rifles, one sub-machine gun, two automatic pistols and a supply of Tetley's tea bags!

Given such a recommendation, the tea bag could hardly fail.

Teddy Bear

It is doubtful whether any 20th-century innovation has given as much pleasure and comfort as the teddy bear. Teddies have fought in the Battle of Britain alongside RAF pilots and accompanied American G.I.s to Vietnam. They have been owned by such diverse individuals as John F. Kennedy, Prince Charles, Margaret Thatcher, Dustin Hoffman, Sir John Betjeman and Elvis Presley. When the latter recorded 'Teddy Bear', he was inundated with teddies from fans.

The story behind the birth of the teddy bear is almost as romantic as the toy itself. In November 1902 American President Theodore Roosevelt went bear hunting in Mississippi. After several days, he had failed to make a kill, causing his embarrassed hosts to scour the woods in search of suitable quarry. Finally, they flushed out a small grizzly bear cub which they drove towards the President's camp. However, Roosevelt decided he was not that desperate for the sight of blood and flatly refused to shoot the baby bear.

The American press gleefully latched on to the incident (omitting to mention that the cub had not exactly been spared, falling victim instead to one of the hunters' knives) and Clifford K. Berryman drew a cartoon

Tetley's pioneered the tea bag revolution in Britain during the 1950s.

in the *Washington Post* showing the President declining the opportunity to gun down the poor defenceless baby bear. The nation was touched.

The cartoon was seen by Russian immigrant Morris Michtom who ran a small novelty shop in Brooklyn, New York. That same month, he decided to cash in on the affair by asking his wife to make a stuffed toy bear from brown plush with button eyes and movable limbs. On one side of his shop window, Michtom displayed a copy of the cartoon and on the other side sat 'Teddy's Bear'. But not for long. For within five minutes, a customer had snapped it up. By the end of the day, Michtom had taken orders for a dozen more.

Legend has it that Michtom then wrote to Roosevelt seeking permission to use his name and received the reply: 'Dear Mr Michtom, I don't think my name is likely to be worth much in the toy bear business, but you are welcome to use it.' Michtom went on to form the Ideal Novelty and Toy Company and by 1903, was manufacturing teddies by the hundred.

But there was a rival claim to be the inventor of the world's first teddy bear — from the Steiff company of Giengen-an-der-Brenz in the Black Forest region of Germany. Richard Steiff had suggested making a cuddly bear with movable head and limbs after watching real bears at Stuttgart Zoo. The company had tried to interest the American market in 1902 but were firmly rebuffed, being informed that their bear was too thick, fat and clumsy. It was even described as a 'stuffed misfit'. Nevertheless, the new Steiff bear was shown at the 1903 Leipzig Toy Fair. It attracted little interest until on the last day of the Fair, a New York buyer told Steiff representatives of his dismay at not finding anything new. What he was looking for was something soft and cuddly, at which point Richard Steiff whipped out his bear. The American placed an immediate order for 3000 which was soon doubled. By 1907 Steiff's annual production had risen to 974 000 bears, most of them hump-backed and sharp-featured so that they looked more like Richard III than Winnie the Pooh.

The term 'teddy bear' was first coined in 1906 by the US toy-trade magazine *Playthings* and was actively encouraged by Roosevelt's aides who realised it enhanced the President's popularity. In the period leading up to the First World War, teddies were all the rage. There were teddy bear buckets, scarves, china, hammocks, even briefcases. Some bears wore expensive jewellery and were seen dining at fashionable Paris hotels with their proud owners.

Not everyone entered into the spirit. A Michigan priest denounced women who carried their teddies around with them, claiming the bear was 'destroying all instincts of motherhood and leading to race suicide'.

A collection of valuable old teddy bears (left, centre and right are Steiffs).

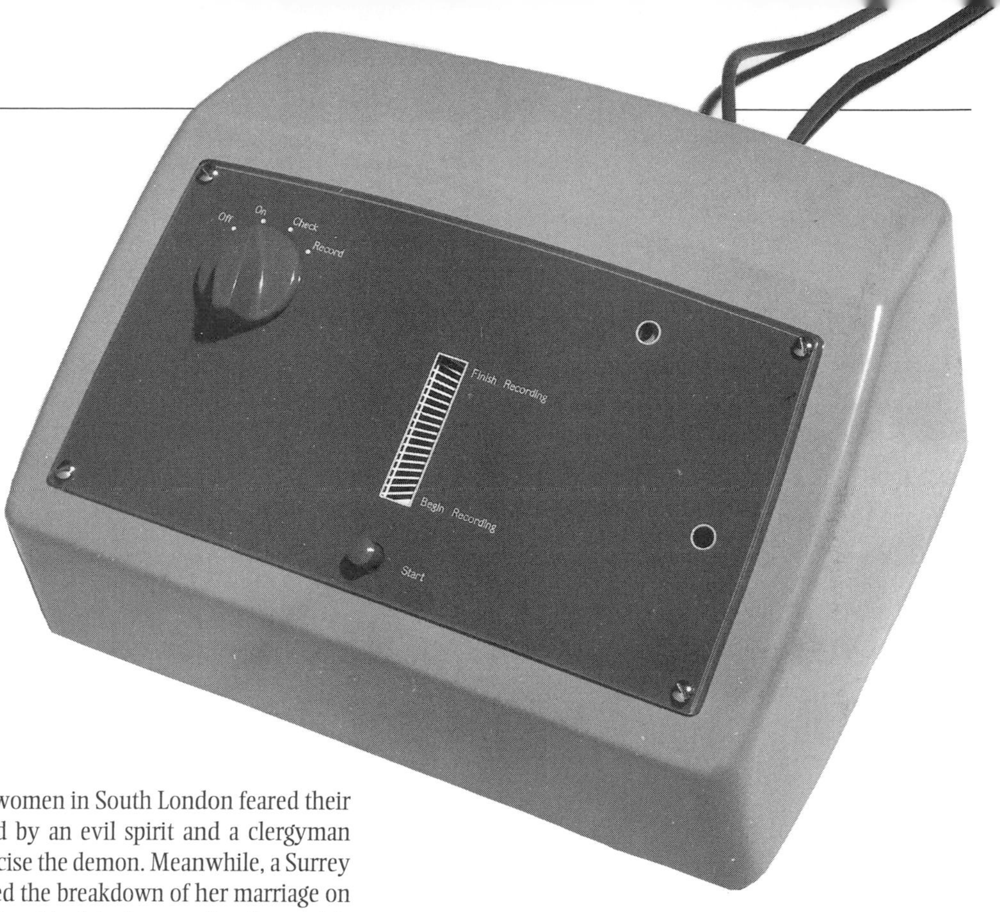

An early telephone answering machine.

More recently, two women in South London feared their teddy was possessed by an evil spirit and a clergyman was called in to exorcise the demon. Meanwhile, a Surrey woman partly blamed the breakdown of her marriage on the fact that her husband lavished more attention on his 21 teddies than he did on her.

A teddy bears' picnic at Longleat, Wiltshire, in 1979 attracted 2000 teddies and 8000 arctophiles (the correct name for collectors) while a rally at Philadelphia Zoo to mark the 80th anniversary of the teddy pulled in 25 000 visitors. Among them was the managing director of Steiff, complete with the company's 1902 prototype bear chained to his waist since it was reportedly insured for $40 000.

Over the years, teddy bears have been made from gold, silver, ivory, leather, walrus tusk, soap and chocolate. One of the saddest stories surrounded Mr Woppit, prized possession of speed ace Donald Campbell. The beloved bear was found floating on the surface of Coniston Water after Campbell's fatal 1967 crash while attempting a new world water speed record. A happier tale was that of Edward Bear who belonged to four-year-old Jamie Fowler of Wellington, New Zealand. In 1975, en route to a holiday in London, Jamie inadvertently left Edward on a seat in Los Angeles. A stewardess promptly sent the bear off in search of his owner, a 150 000-mile (241 400 km) journey which took in London, Copenhagen, Johannesburg, Hong Kong, Rio de Janeiro, Tahiti, Jamaica, Bermuda, New York and finally back to Los Angeles where he was reunited with Jamie on the return flight to New Zealand. Even then the drama was not quite over. For Edward, weighed down with labels, was again momentarily abandoned and was only reclaimed just before another helpful stewardess was about to put him on a DC10 bound for Singapore!

Telephone Answering Machine

T

The telephone was bad enough. It took us years to become accustomed to talking through a machine but now we have to talk *to* a machine. The reason is the answerphone, a piece of equipment which manages to reduce the most eloquent of souls to a tongue-tied, stammering wreck.

It was invented by American businessman Joseph L. Zimmerman to allay his worries about losing trade in his absence. Zimmerman's device was called the Electronic Secretary and in 1949 he formed a company of that name with George W. Danner. The Bell Telephone Company tried out a service in New York and Cleveland in 1950 before marketing the Bell 1A two years later.

In the UK, Ansafone Ltd introduced the Ipsophone, a Swiss answering machine which weighed a mighty 2½ hundredweight and took two men no less than three days to install. The more compact equipment which gradually appeared on the market particularly endeared itself to Orthodox Jews who were able to receive messages on the Sabbath without themselves activating electricity.

Of all the recorded messages, the most imaginative suggestion was surely that of lawyer Mogens Listrup, founder of Denmark's Progressive Party in 1972. He proposed abolishing the country's Ministry of Defence on economic grounds and substituting an answering machine with the message in Russian: 'We surrender.'

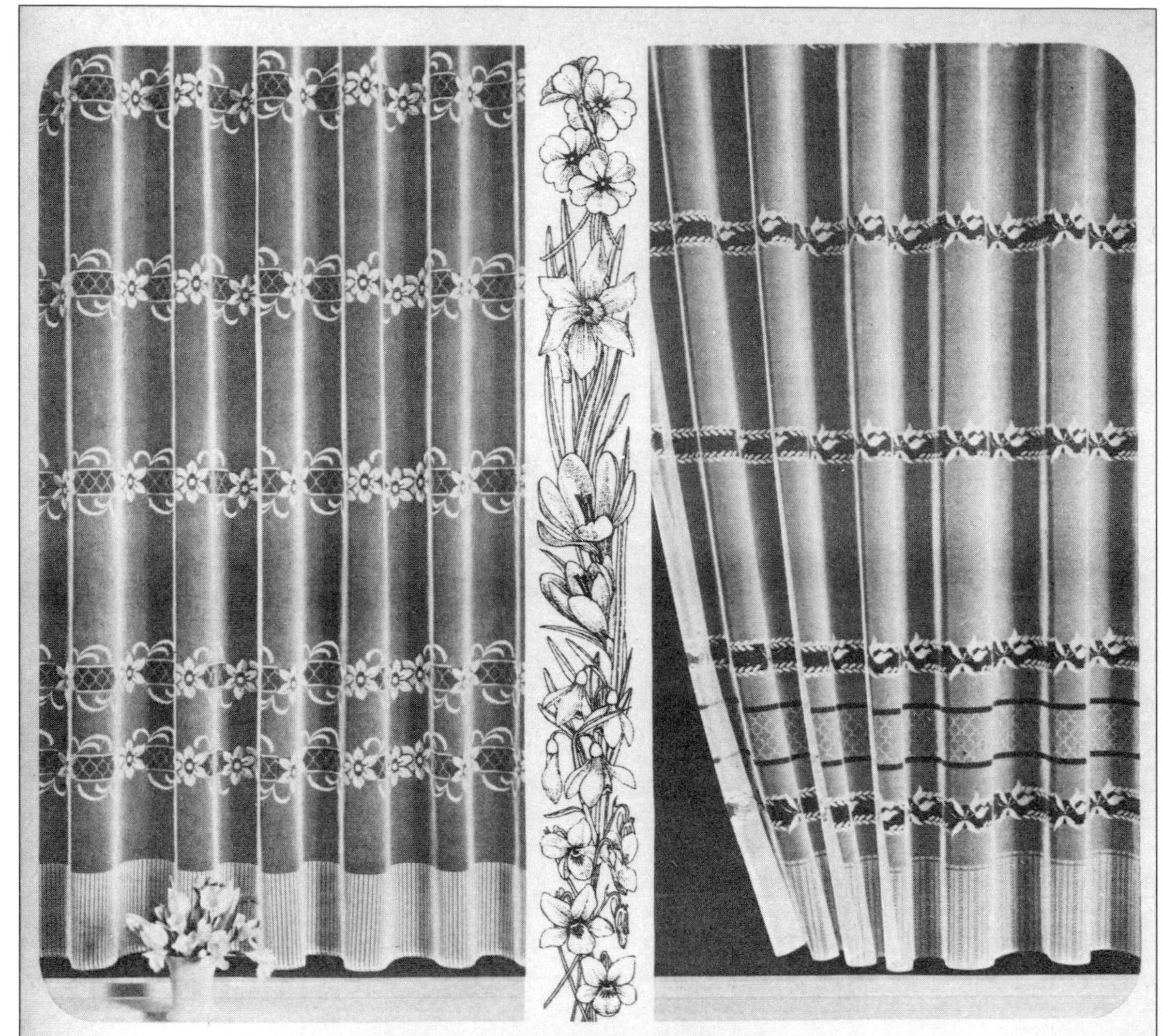

Fresh and lovely as Spring itself

Stiebel window nets in 'Terylene' Silver Seal

Stiebel of Nottingham are famous for their beautiful window nets and this Spring they offer you a fabulous choice of pretty designs and styles . . . all so light and airy. And however you prefer to buy them — whether ready-to-hang, as illustrated, or by the yard to make up — there are Stiebel nets in profusion to meet your requirements. In 100% 'Terylene' Silver Seal controlled quality, they're simply marvellous to look after; they wash easily, drip-dry, need little ironing and don't shrink.

SEE THEM AT YOUR LOCAL STORE NOW.

Designs illustrated above:

Left: CAMELIA B743 available in drop lengths 18" 24" 27" 30" 36" 40" 45" 48" 54" 63" 72" 81" 90". The 36" depth is approximately 5/11 a yard.

Right: MOSS ROSE B753 available in drop lengths 14" 18" 24" 27" 30" 33" 36" 40" 42" 45" 48" 54" 63" 72" 81" 90". The 36" depth is approximately 7/6 a yard.

68

Terylene net curtains — ideal for nosy neighbours.

Terylene

A research chemist with the Calico Printers Association in Accrington, Rex Whinfield found himself inspired by the work of Du Pont's Wallace Carothers, the man who invented nylon. Whinfield contemplated evolving a true synthetic fibre and, in a small laboratory shielded from the gaze of head office, he set about following up some of Carothers' work. His efforts were rewarded in the spring of 1941 when his colleague, James Dickson, added surplus ethylene glycol to the polymerisation process and produced a dirty brown resin from which promising fibres could be drawn.

As with many patents taken out during the war, the discovery was declared secret by the Ministry of Supply. The official public announcement was not made until 5 October 1946 in the *Manchester Guardian*, by which time the name Terylene had been coined and an exclusive licence negotiated with ICI for world manufacturing rights, except in the United States where Du Pont were licensed and the fibre was registered as Dacron.

The first Terylene articles, men's neckties, appeared early in 1948 followed by dresses, lingerie, shirts and knitwear where the fibre was seen as an alternative to wool. These garments were not always immediately successful. Shirts had a habit of harbouring dirt while stockings and socks also failed to compete with nylon, tending to go baggy very quickly. More specialist areas were examined, including mosquito nets, while a Terylene trawler net survived many trips to the fishing grounds off Grimsby, compared to the previous consumption of two nets per trip. Improved production methods cured a number of the teething troubles and as an indication that the new fibre was entering mass production, the first Terylene Union Jack was flown at ICI in 1952.

Thermos Flask

In 1892 celebrated Scottish scientist Sir James Dewar addressed the problem of maintaining gases and liquids at a constant temperature and concluded that the ideal solution was a glass vessel with double walls separated by a vacuum. He called this first vacuum flask a 'Dewar Vessel'. Over the next few years Dewar managed to 'silver' the inner surfaces of the glass by introducing a minute quantity of mercury as a gas. The gas condensed at lower temperatures and covered the glass with a heat reflective coating.

But no consideration was given to the commercial development of Dewar's vessel until one of his pupils, Reinhold Burger, returned to his native Germany to become a partner in the first company to manufacture

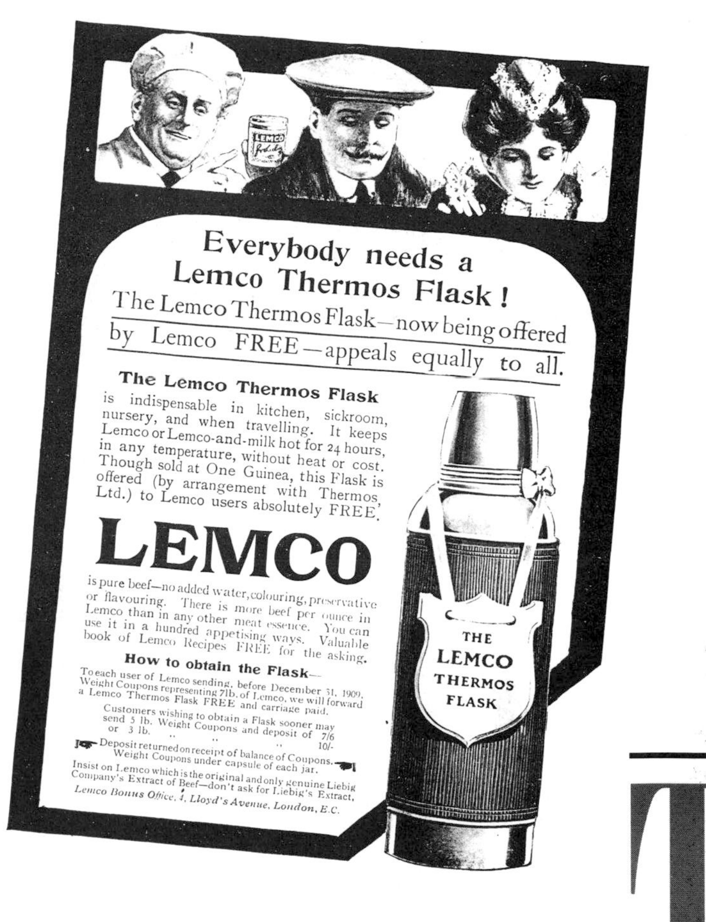

The Thermos flask appealed to all classes of society.

vacuum flasks for domestic application. The firm of Burger and Aschenbrenner began production in 1904 but felt they needed a name for their product. In the ensuing competition, a Munich resident suggested 'Thermos', derived from the Greek word *therme* meaning heat.

Early Thermos flasks were inclined to be expensive. Each was individually blown and the output per glass blower was only some nine or ten units a day. In 1908 a pint flask cost a guinea (21s.) but when Thermos Limited of London mechanised production three years later, the price was halved. Contemporary advertising depicted the Thermos flask in use in both the Tropics and the Arctic, describing it as 'a necessity for every modern household from Pole to Pole'. It kept food or drink hot for 24 hours in the coldest place, and cold for three days under the hottest sun. It was lauded as 'the bottle of the XXth century made for up-to-date people'.

During the Second World War, Thermos Limited was almost exclusively engaged in the production of flasks for the armed and civilian services. Wherever there was front-line action, the Thermos flask was there too. It was calculated that every time 1000 allied bombers went out on a raid, there were anything from 10 000 to 20 000 Thermos flasks in the air as well.

Tights

Before 1960 the only people to be seen wearing tights in public were ballet dancers or actors. Then Morley introduced brightly coloured woollen tights to the UK although they were designed for warmth rather than fashion and made little impact outside sportswear.

But Mary Quant in London and Valentino in Rome soon saw the possibilities of creating a fashion line. Quant said: 'The tights were a problem at first because you couldn't buy them in the colours I wanted. So I went to a theatrical manufacturer and persuaded him to make them in wonderful shades such as prune, ginger and bright mustard yellow with knickers and bras to match.'

It was the mini skirt which really sealed the arrival of tights, not just the woollen variety but also those in conventional stocking shades. Minis rose to such a height that a gap between stocking top and skirt became inevitable. Visible suspenders and bare thighs had prevailed among the can-can girls of the late 19th century but not even the most liberated sixties' teenager was brave enough to reveal all — particularly on a windy day. Released from elaborate suspenders, women found tights neater and more comfortable. They symbolised the new age of freedom. Feminists later stated that tights boasted the added advantage of providing greater protection in sexual encounters than the underwear of the 1950s.

As sixties' fashions became more daring, Mary Quant started designing tights with lace-effect patterns as well as in metallic silver and gold. The stocking was on the decline but it heroically maintained some sort of grip on the market, appearing regularly in fashion magazines until 1969 when a full-page advertisement declared: 'Annabella is not wearing stockings. She's wearing something much better, Charnos Hold-me-Tights.'

Millions followed Annabella's example and within a few years, tights controlled the market. One sector of the community who did mourn the demise of the stocking was the bank robber. There was a very real fear that if raiders wished to disguise themselves in future, they would be forced to go around in pairs!

Tizer

Few things conjure up the image of wizard wheezes, Billy Bunter and short trousers quite as much as Tizer. So it was no surprise that when soft drink giants A.G. Barr (famous for their Irn Bru) took over the Tizer brand for £2.5 million in 1972, the then chairman Robert Barr immediately insisted that the product should return to its original pre-war formula.

This proved no easy task and it took six months of research and detailed work by a team of chemists to blend the essences as they had been in the original formula. The biggest problem was that one essence — which became known as Essence X — was no longer available since the manufacturer had ceased trading. However, Barrs are now satisfied that today's Tizer is as close as humanly possible to the Tizer which was such a firm favourite between the wars.

Renowned for the 'taste which defies description', Tizer was the brainchild of Fred Pickup. In 1906 Fred and his brother Thomas started working in their uncle's soft drinks business but a year later they set up on their own near Portsmouth, selling half-gallon jars of brewed ginger beer and sarsaparilla. After a year of indifferent trading, they moved to Bristol where they traded in 'table waters'.

Leaving his brother behind in Bristol, Fred moved to Pudsey, Yorkshire, and bought a small firm which he renamed 'F. Pickup'. In 1919 he introduced his customers

(left) Tights look better here than they ever did on Batman and Robin.

(above) Tizer — an echo of bygone days.

T

to carbonated soft drinks. His unhappiness with the stone bottles led him to experiment and the following year he sold his drinks in pint glass bottles at his newly opened factories in Bradford and Leeds. This innovation was so successful that in 1922 Fred's business expanded to Manchester. And it was there, in 1924, that Tizer was launched.

Coined from the word 'appetizer', the new soft drink took off to such an extent that over the next 15 years, ten more factories were opened throughout the country. The mysterious red liquid swept the nation. It went on to become the acceptable drink to accompany jelly and ice cream or reading about the latest adventures of Dennis the Menace in the *Beano*.

Tizer now has a modern, lively image. It is widely available in clubs as an alternative to alcohol and there is even Diet Tizer to cater for the low-calorie market. But to many, the taste still harks back to days of yore. Now where's that catapult?

Traffic Light (electric)

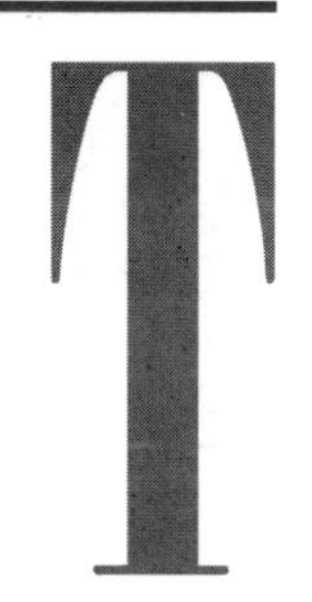

The first attempt at installing a traffic light system took place in London's Parliament Square in 1868. Revolving red and green lanterns, illuminated by gas, were manually operated by the police. Such a gentle task must have seemed a welcome break for the constabulary from tackling robbers and rioters — until, that is, the officer on duty was badly injured when the gas apparatus exploded. Consequently, the experimental set of lights was removed after just four years' service.

Electric lights were introduced in August 1914 by the American Traffic Signal Company in Cleveland, Ohio, at the crossroads of Euclid Avenue and 105th Street. The red and green lights were mounted on a 15-ft (4.5 m) high stand and were used in conjunction with a fearsome warning buzzer. Amber was added to the colours four years later in New York. The French shunned electricity and in 1923, attached to a lamp-post a manually operated light bearing the word HALTE on the glass. A gong warned motorists when it was about to be switched on or off.

Britain decided it was safe to return to traffic lights in 1926 when they were erected at the junction of St James's Street and Piccadilly in London. Automatic lights were brought in for a one-day trial in Wolverhampton on 11 February 1928 before being permanently adopted the following month by Leeds and then Edinburgh. Nevertheless, it was not an offence for British motorists to disobey signals until the Road Traffic Act of 1930.

Vehicle-actuated lights were installed in April 1932 at the junction of Cornhill and Gracechurch Street in the City of London although it was noted that these might prove ineffective with lightweight horse-drawn carts.

The traffic light is not usually top of any burglar's haul yet in one week three were dismantled and stolen from a roadside at Lincoln in the autumn of 1993. Police believed they were being used to liven up 'rave' parties.

Traffic Warden

The transformation of Clark Kent when he slips into the Superman cape or Bruce Wayne to Batman seems minor in comparison to that of the normally mild human beings when they don the uniform of a traffic warden. Suddenly they become all-seeing, all-knowing, intransigent individuals whose mission seems to be to inflict misery. Surely they only prowl the streets of our cities because they were considered too hard-line for the KGB.

'Meter maids', as they were known, were introduced in New York City by Mayor Robert Ferdinand Wagner where, after two weeks' intensive training, they made their debut on 1 June 1960. Within three months, the 'yellow peril' had reached the UK. As a result of the Road Traffic Act of 1960, traffic wardens were unleashed in the London borough of Westminster on 19 September. The first shift of 39 wardens set out at 8 a.m. and justified their presence by issuing 344 tickets that day. They started as they meant to continue, the first ticket being zealously issued by warden Frank Shaw to Dr Thomas Creighton who had parked his Ford Popular outside a West End hotel while treating a patient suffering from a heart attack. Shaw was unaware that the car belonged to a doctor and such was the furore in the press when the circumstances emerged that Dr Creighton was excused payment of the statutory £2 fine.

Nothing much has changed. In 1993 residents of Waltham Forest in East London protested about the alleged activities of a squad of private traffic wardens employed by the council. Locals claimed the wardens crept around at the dead of night, booking cars outside owners' homes. They were even said to have given a ticket to a funeral cortège. One councillor complained: 'They are rude and arrogant. Drivers have been booked while opening their gates or garage doors.'

Trampoline

Bouncing nets had been part of showbusiness acts such as The Walloons since around 1910 but the trampoline (taking its name from the Spanish *trampolin* meaning springboard) was not manufactured seriously until 1936.

That was when George P. Nissen and Paul F. Nissen, from Cedar Rapids, Iowa, founded the Nissen Trampoline Company. The prototype was called the model T.

The first Nissen tramp to be exported to the UK arrived at Loxford School, Ilford, Essex in 1949 and as the sport gained momentum, the inaugural world championships were staged in 1964. Standards of trampolining have progressed to such a degree that the record number of consecutive somersaults currently stands at over 3000.

Transistor Radio

When the cumbersome radio was first invented, the idea that it might ever become portable, let alone pocket-sized, seemed absurd. But portable radios appeared in the forties — even the British Royal Family owned them — and then the 1948 invention of the transistor at America's Bell Laboratories by William Shockley, John Bardeen and Walter Brattain paved the way for the transistor radio seven years later.

The TR-1, measuring 3 × 5 × 1¼ in (7.6 × 12.7 × 3.2 cm) and weighing 12 oz (340 g), was marketed by Regency Electronics of Indianapolis in October 1955. It was followed in June 1956 by the Model 710 from the British company Pye. Although designed in Pye's research laboratories under Dr Lax who constructed the prototype himself, it was released through a company subsidiary, Pam Radio and Television Ltd, since nobody was quite sure how well it would be received. In the event, it sold steadily despite the fact that these early transistor radios cost around 21 guineas — 50 per cent more than the average valve set. They were also prone to faults although, as mass production began, the number of defective sets was reduced from a startling 95 per cent to just two per cent.

The first pocket-sized transistor radio was Sony's TR-63, produced in Japan from March 1957, while the Philips model of the same year promised ten hours' play for a penny. Less economical was Roberts' mink-covered portable, unveiled at the 1959 British Radio Show and priced at £156.

Although fears still persisted about the quality of reception, a Philips transistor which accompanied the Cambridge West Greenland Glaciological Expedition of the late fifties achieved good long-range reception in a deep gorge, using a 20-ft (6 m) length of flex hung between the tents and connected to the earth terminal. And as those who wanted a peaceful afternoon at the seaside were soon to discover to their cost, there was nothing wrong with the reception of the pop sounds of Radio Caroline on Brighton beach.

The world's first pocket-sized transistor radio, the Sony TR-63.

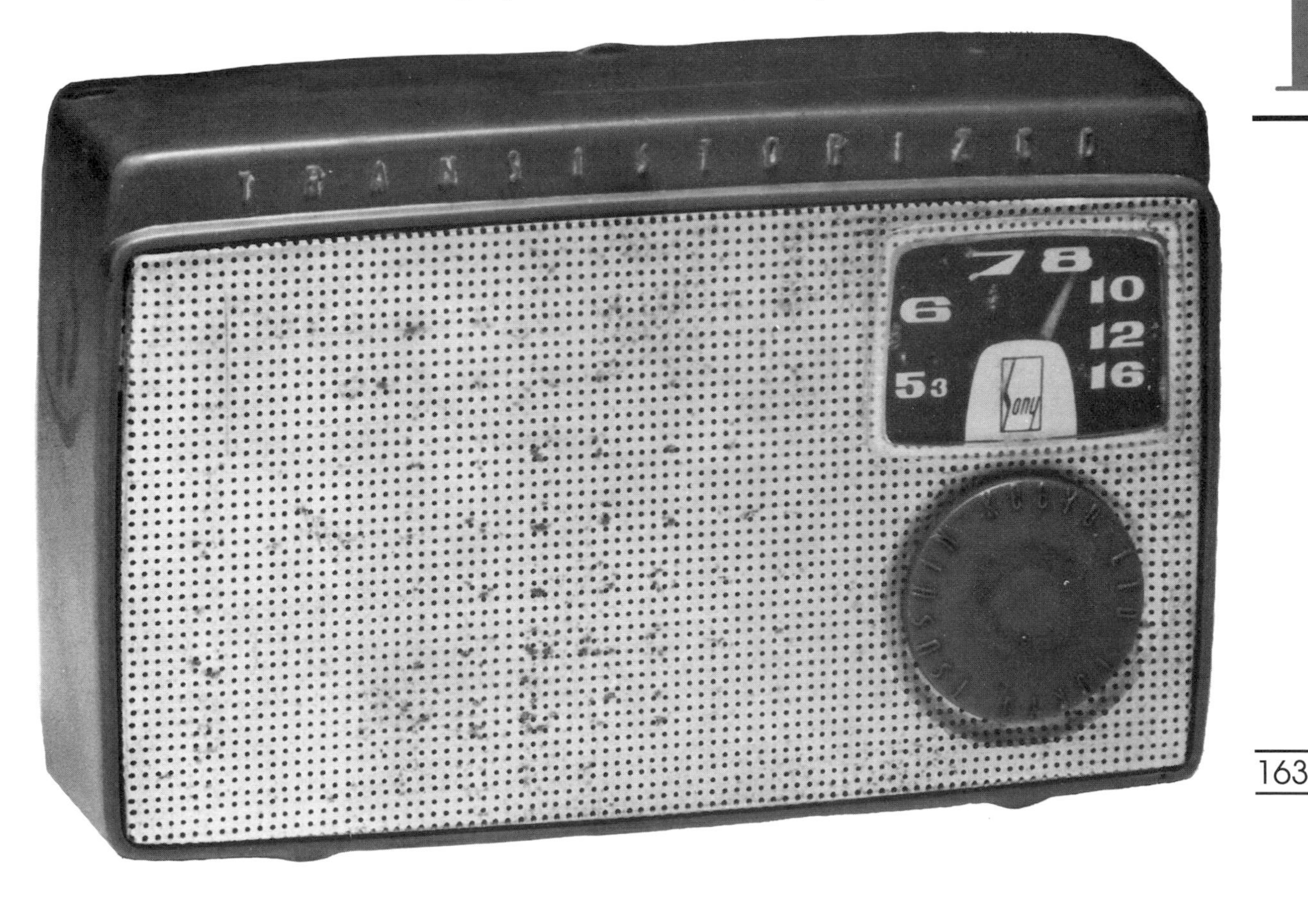

Trivial Pursuit™
GENUS III EDITION
Genus
Genus
Genus
Genus

Trivial Pursuit

Who was Anastasia and Drizella's stepsister? Which Briton's photo appeared on Pakistani birth control posters because she only has two children? And who was England's first and only Pope? The answers (Cinderella, Princess Diana and Nicholas Breakspear) are among the thousands of nuggets of information supplied by the world's fastest-selling board game, Trivial Pursuit. In 12 years, it has sold nearly 60 million sets (including versions in Arabic and Russian), on average one being sold every six seconds somewhere in the world. If every game sold were piled high, the tower would stand some 500 times taller than the summit of Mount Everest — and statistics do not come any more trivial than that.

The game was formulated in 1982 by three young Canadians — newspaper photographer Chris Haney, sports writer Scott Abbott and former ice hockey player John Haney. It took them just 45 minutes to think up the concept but another four years to get it marketed. It was originally called Trivia Pursuit (Chris Haney's wife Sarah added the 'l') and calling their company Horn Abbott after Chris Haney's nickname of 'Horney', they made 1100 prototypes. A loss of $45 000 was made on that first batch, to the dismay of 18-year-old unemployed artist Michael Wurstlin who had designed both board and logo in return for five shares in the company. He was a little happier by the end of 1985 when two Trivial Pursuit shares were worth over $1 million. But the strain involved in getting the game off the ground took its toll on Chris Haney. He ended up in intensive care suffering from stress and was unable to speak to anybody for weeks.

Just occasionally there has been a distinct lack of communication between question and answer in Trivial Pursuit. For example:

'For which club did Kevin Keegan first play professional football?'

Answer: 'Cuba'.

And . . .

'What was the Beatles' first hit record?'

Answer: 'Danny Blanchflower'.

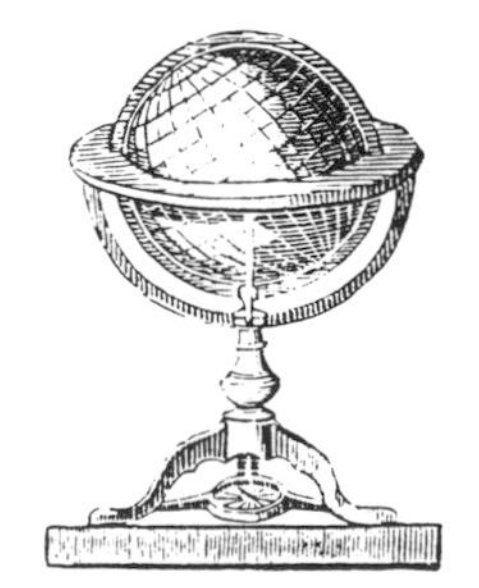

(left) After an uncertain start, Trivial Pursuit became one of the success stories of the eighties.

T-shirt

Whether it be FREE NELSON MANDELA or I GOT DRUNK IN BLACKPOOL, anything meaningful that had to be said about the latter part of the 20th century was proclaimed from the front of a T-shirt. Yet it is ironic that the single event which established this icon of American youth was the Japanese bombing of Pearl Harbor.

'Lightweight shortsleeve cotton undervests' had been part of US Navy attire at the turn of the century and young American soldiers brought back similar French Army garments from the First World War. Although this apparel was widely worn among athletes at American universities, the vest was dealt a crushing blow when Clark Gable appeared without one in the 1934 film *It Happened One Night.* Virtually overnight it became unmanly to wear a vest.

That is, until in 1942, still reeling from Pearl Harbor, the US Navy issued specifications for a knitted cotton undershirt with a round neck and short sleeves set at right angles to the front and back panels. The Navy called it a 'T-Type'.

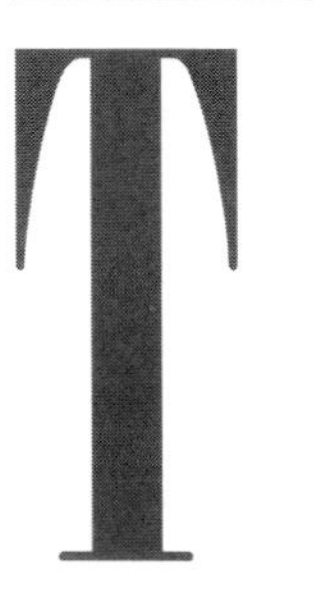

The T-shirt quickly became more than a vest. Whilst the authorities boasted of its 'greater sweat absorption under the arms', soldiers and marines were more concerned with the effect it had on girls. It graduated to off-duty wear in the evenings and from plain white to having the names of camps and individual divisions printed on the front. And because it saw so much active combat, nobody dared call it unmanly.

After the war, T-shirts appeared portraying heroes of the day such as Joe DiMaggio, Davy Crockett and Roy Rogers. Then, in 1951 a moody Marlon Brando wore one in *A Streetcar Named Desire.* He was acclaimed for his 'sensual, unfeeling, mean, vindictive performance' and the T-shirt immediately gained rebel status, a position confirmed two years later by the same actor in *The Wild One* where he wore his T-shirt beneath a black leather jacket.

The introduction of the plastisol transfer in 1963 enabled customers to select a design and watch it being put on their T-shirt within minutes. Politicians were quick to grasp the potential message-power and in 1968 the British government used models wearing T-shirts proclaiming WE DON'T SMOKE to promote an anti-smoking campaign targeted at teenagers.

The saddest thing about T-shirts is that they were not invented earlier. The 12 disciples would surely have worn them, William the Conqueror could have had special ones made to commemorate the Battle of Hastings, while the MAGELLAN'S WORLD TOUR 1519 T-shirt would undoubtedly have become a prized possession.

Tupperware

Some vote for the Democrat Party, others for the Republican Party. But each year in the United States, around 90 million people vote for the Tupperware party.

The modern social gathering takes its name from Earl Silas Tupper who, as a chemist with the Du Pont company of America, was working on plastics in the period leading up to the Second World War. In response to a request for some waste material, Du Pont gave Tupper a chunk of solid black polythene slag, a by-product of oil refinery. After prolonged experimentation, he succeeded in converting the uncompromising substance into a light, flexible, non-breakable plastic, modelling what came to be known as the famous Tupperware seal on the upturned lid of a tin of paint. In 1938 he founded the Tupperware Plastics Company and production was able to begin at the end of the war in 1945.

Tupper was particularly excited about the unique water-tight, air-tight seal which was able to keep food fresher for much longer than existing containers. However, the seal very nearly proved his downfall since demonstrators at retail stores were unable to operate it. As a result, nobody bought Tupperware until a group of direct sellers demonstrated the seal effectively. Suddenly, sales soared and Tupper, realising that this was the way ahead, bravely removed all of his products from store shelves in 1951 and concentrated instead on direct selling via home demonstrations.

One of Tupper's demonstrators was a lady named Brownie Wise and it was she who instigated Tupperware parties, first in the US and then from 1960, in Britain. These informal get-togethers were an instant hit with housewives, not only broadening their social circles but also creating new job opportunities. Today it is estimated that a Tupperware party starts somewhere in the world every 2.8 seconds.

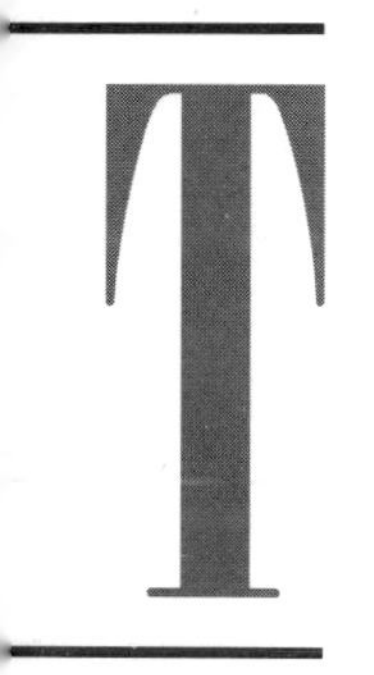

An array of Tupperware, just waiting to party.

Passengers sample the delights of the Underground escalator at Marble Arch.

U

Underground Station Escalator

As the new century dawned, a familiar sight in early-morning London was that of the city's workers emerging from railway stations, their faces and clothes blackened with smoke. The reason for their dishevelled appearance was that they had been travelling on steam underground trains which were no respectors of the need for a sparkling white shirt for the office. Then, in 1906, electric systems were introduced. Underground travel, which had always been a faster and more economical way of crossing London than bus or horse-drawn cab, now became clean as well. The novelty was such that 37 000 passengers travelled on the first day of the Bakerloo Line that year.

The major drawback to journeying by underground train was the seemingly endless flights of stairs which had to be negotiated at either end. So, thought was given to the installation of escalators, a late 19th-century invention from America. When the Piccadilly railway was constructed in 1906, a 'double spiral continuous-moving track', built by the Reno Electric Stairways & Conveyors Ltd, was set in one of the lift shafts at Holloway Road station. The track moved at 100 ft (30 m) per minute but, although apparently in good working order a week before the official opening of the railway, it was mysteriously never opened to the public.

Thus the honour of being the first London Underground station to install escalators passed to Earls Court on 4 October 1911. Two 40-ft (12 m) Seeberger escalators linked the District and Piccadilly lines, notices on the wall advising passengers: 'Please do not sit on the stairs. Step off with the left foot first.'

To reassure the public of the safety of this new device, sectional views were published and, more intriguingly, a man with a wooden leg, 'Bumper' Harris, was hired to go up and down the escalators. 'Bumper' was obviously convincing, for the *Illustrated London News* reported: 'London's new amusement — up and down the escalator,' adding: 'Passengers on their way to the City have been seen to leave a train, go up with the stairs and down with the stairs — and catch the next train.' Nowadays the authorities have curtailed such reckless practices by ensuring that at any given station, only one escalator is in working order.

Vacuum Cleaner

By trade, Hubert Cecil Booth built factories, bridges and 'big wheels' for amusement parks but it was the result of his observations at London's St Pancras railway station in 1900 which earned him a place in 20th-century history.

Booth was watching a spectacularly unsuccessful demonstration of railway carriage cleaning by use of compressed air. A huge air blower was placed over one open carriage door to blow dirt into a bag placed over another. The ensuing activity merely served to create clouds of dust which floated up before settling again in less accessible places.

Discussing this ineptitude in a restaurant in Victoria Street with other witnesses, Booth believed the solution was to suck dirt into a receptacle rather than trying to blow it away. To underline his point, he placed a handkerchief over the back of his plush seat, put his lips to it and sucked. He almost choked but a ring of black spots on the handkerchief proved the principle to be sound. Even more surprisingly, he was not asked to leave the restaurant.

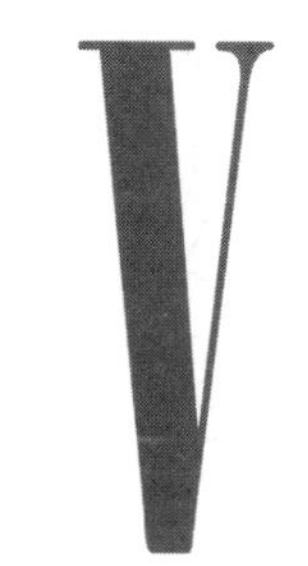

A prototype machine was built and in 1901, Booth patented his mechanised lips as an 'apparatus for the extraction of dust from carpets etc.'. The patent referred to the term 'vacuum cleaner', wording taken by Booth from a French inventor who, attempting to extract dust from his laboratory using an electric motor linked to vacuum bellows, had succeeded in blowing himself up. As a result of the explosion, his widow had also been forced to pay for repairs over a large area of Lyons!

In 1902 Booth formed the Vacuum Cleaner Company Ltd. He decided not to sell his cleaners to the public but to provide a service, which was just as well since his first model was so large it was nicknamed the 'Puffing Billy' and needed a team of men to operate it. No householder could have coped. Having the carpets cleaned necessitated the stationing of a horse-drawn van outside the customer's house. Mounted on the back of the van was a powerful vacuum pump, driven by a petrol motor, and from which 800-ft (244 m) long hoses snaked their way through the first-floor windows to remove the offending dust. Apart from being cumbersome, the appliance was extremely noisy and frightened passing horses, which led to Booth being sued by cab proprietors.

The making of Booth's invention was the 1902 coronation of Edward VII at which the vacuum cleaned the blue carpets of Westminster Abbey. So impressed were the King and Queen that they asked for a demonstration at Buckingham Palace and later ordered two cleaners, one for the Palace, the other for Windsor Castle. Unable to resist the prospect of royal patronage, Booth made an exception to his 'no sales' rule. Now that the vacuum cleaner was used in such elevated circles, it became a novelty among the upper classes. Society hostesses threw tea parties at which the entertainment consisted of Booth's white-uniformed employees cleaning the carpets and upholstery. Booth even provided visible inspection tubes in order that guests might watch the dirt being sucked up.

Booth's cleaner had become the first viable alternative to the Bissell carpet sweeper and in 1906 he decided the time was right to begin sales. His first model for domestic use was the Trolley Vac, powered by an electric motor but still weighing 100 lb (45 kg) and very expensive. Cheaper at £4 was the double-bellowed Baby Daisy of 1910 which required the concerted efforts of two men to work it. An even more unusual model was the rocking chair vacuum cleaner, a piece of equipment clearly designed by a man. The idea was that the man of the house sat in the chair, the movement from which activated a suction pump. This in turn inhaled the grime through a hose and nozzle which his good lady moved around the room. The reasons given for its failure to catch on were that having to rock the chair so frantically made the man giddy and that he became disenchanted with having to move the chair from room to room.

Meanwhile across the Atlantic, Chapman and Skinner of San Francisco had produced the first portable vacuum cleaner in 1905. Then, two years later, J. Murray Spangler, an asthmatic janitor from North Canton, Ohio, tried to make his job easier by inventing a labour-saving cleaning device. Powered by an electric motor, it consisted of a tin can, a broomstick and an old pillowcase as a dust bag. Curiously, this contraption was the forerunner of the modern upright cleaner.

It attracted the attention of H.W. Hoover, a local harness-maker who, fearing that the arrival of the automobile would hit the carriage trade, was looking for alternative ventures. Spangler sold the design to Hoover and in 1908, the latter marketed it as the Electric Suction Sweeper, priced at $75. It was so successful that Hoover was able to export to Britain by 1919, that year selling some 2250 machines at a cost of £25 each. In 1926 Hoover introduced the principle of 'Positive Agitation', achieved by the inclusion of a motor-driven metal agitator equipped with a row of soft sweeping brushes and two highly polished steel beaters. This led to Hoover's famous slogan: 'It beats as it sweeps as it cleans.'

Hoover also pioneered the vacuum cleaner salesman whose house calls helped increase the number of machines in the UK from 200 000 in 1930 to 400 000 by 1939. Three-quarters of these were paid for on hire purchase since the rates were very low at the time. A peculiar side effect was that two old vacuum cleaners plus other odds and ends formed the prototype iron lung in 1927!

Not all vacuum cleaner demonstrators are as efficient as either the Hoover representatives or indeed Hubert Cecil Booth. In 1993 reports came in of an Australian salesman who, attempting to illustrate the quality of his equipment, confidently tipped a pile of dirt on to a family's brand-new carpet. When the cleaner failed to remove the sooty mound, the salesman was attacked by the irate couple and ended up in hospital.

The first Hoover vacuum cleaner, the Model 'O', made before the First World War.

V

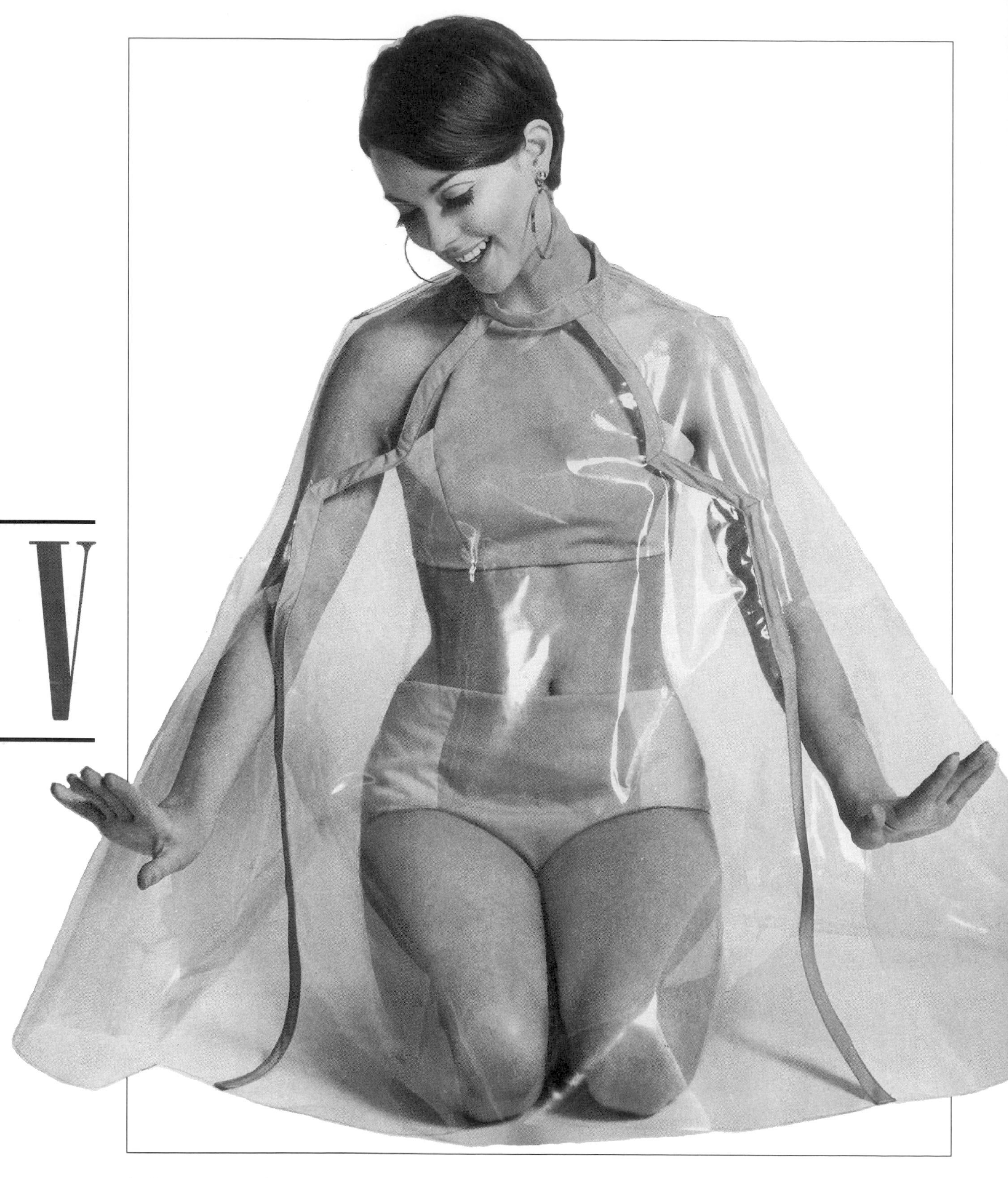

In the 1960s, London's Hornsey College of Art staged a competition to show the many uses of Velcro. The winner was this transparent PVC cape, fastened against the elements with Velcro.

Velcro

In 1950 while hunting in the woods at the foothills of the Juras in his native Switzerland, 43-year-old Georges de Mestral noticed that his trousers and the ears of his faithful dog were covered in burrs, picked up by brushing against burdock weed.

De Mestral was intrigued and on returning home, examined the tenacious little burrs under the microscope. He observed that the outer skin of the burrs comprised numerous tiny hooks with which they attached themselves to anything that happened to be passing. Just a few months previously, he had been annoyed when a firmly jammed zip on his wife's dress had ruined an evening out and was seeking an alternative system of fastening, one which did not require meshing metal teeth or sliders. Armed with his new discovery, de Mestral immediately began to consider the possibility of re-creating the hooked surface of the burr in textile form.

After early struggles during which he made only moderate progress, de Mestral was introduced to Jakob Müller, the world's leading manufacturer of narrow fabric looms. Their association soon bore fruit and in 1956 de Mestral patented his invention under the name 'Velcro', from the French words velours and crochet, meaning hooked velvet. Velcro consists of two nylon tapes, one covered in thousands of tiny loops, the other in thousands of tiny hooks. When pressed together, the hooks grip the loops forming a tight, secure closure.

In 1957 de Mestral, who later diversified his talents by inventing an asparagus peeler, opened his Velcro factory at Aubonne. Today the hook and loop fastener is manufactured in the United States, Britain, Germany and Spain, and each year enough Velcro tape is produced to stretch twice around the world. It has widespread uses in industry and recreation and has even inspired its own sport. In 1990 one Rodney Fletcher, landlord of the Black Swan Tavern in Rotorua, New Zealand, encouraged customers to don Velcro-covered tracksuits, bounce on a trampoline and try to stick themselves to the highest point possible on a Velcro-covered wall. Originally christened 'sticky', it has spread to Britain under the name of 'fly-jumping'. Clearly an Olympic sport of the future . . .

Velcro has also scaled Everest on rucksacks and when Neil Armstrong and Buzz Aldrin landed on the Moon in 1969, they wore Velcro on their spacesuits. Nowadays it is virtually impossible to go anywhere — in a plane, in a car, to hospital or receiving a 'Jim'll Fix It' badge — without somehow feeling in the grip of Velcro. And to think it all started with that walk in the woods.

(right) A 1931 advertisement for Vicks VapoRub.

Vicks VapoRub

Raised on a farm in North Carolina, Lunsford Richardson became a pharmacist and purchased a drugstore in the quiet backwater town of Greensboro. Many of the local farmers were too poor to afford proper medical advice and so they consulted Richardson about their aches and pains. He began selling home remedies under the label 'Vicks' — he had been attracted by a magazine advertisement for Vicks Seeds and Vic also happened to be the name of his brother-in-law.

Richardson formed the Vick Chemical Company and in 1905, introduced Vicks Magic Group Salve, an ointment containing the new Japanese drug menthol which had proved efficacious in treating the croup of his eldest child. The product was later renamed Vicks VapoRub.

Vicks was soon combating colds right across America. In 1946 it was claimed that 94 million Vicks packages were being used annually, a survey revealing that 89 out of every 100 young mothers in Seattle swore by the product. And the Vicks success story did not end there. For it threw up that essential fashion accessory, the inhaler. No nostril is complete without one.

V

Video Game

An engineering student at the University of Utah, Nolan Bushnell used to spend much of his spare time playing a game called Spacewar on the college computer. In the evenings he worked in an amusement arcade and, seeing the customers playing on the pinball machines, was convinced that they would be equally addicted to Spacewar if it could be converted into an arcade game.

Since the main-frame college computer cost $4 million, Bushnell was obliged to wait for the 1971 invention of the microprocessor which could be easily fitted into an arcade machine. He worked hard to develop his new game and in June 1972, he and an associate each put in $250 to found the company Atari, named after an expression from the Japanese game of Go, similar in intent to the chess term 'check'. In November the game was ready. Devised and built by Bushnell, it was called Pong and was an electronic version of table tennis.

Bushnell installed the solitary game of Pong in a bar in Sunnyvale, California. The customers were hooked on it — in fact they started coming to the bar to play Pong rather than to drink.

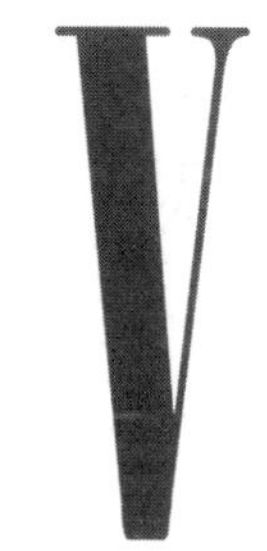

But by 1974 Atari was still on the verge of bankruptcy when Bushnell introduced an adaptation of Pong which could be linked to a television set. It was called Home Pong. Fears that anyone would want a product with such a name in their house were swiftly allayed and by 1975, sales had risen to $40 million.

Pong soon became obsolete in the face of more advanced games, including Atari's Pac-Man and the Japanese Space Invaders. By 1982 some 20 per cent of US homes owned a video game.

The invention which Bushnell intended to be an obsession has turned out to be exactly that. Today's compact computer games prove irresistible to children and parents alike. Indeed marriage guidance counsellors in Britain have been dealing with an increasing number of video 'widows' whose marriages are being wrecked by their husbands' addiction to their children's video games.

Video Recorder

It is the moment you have been waiting for. The episode of *Miss Marple* recorded from earlier in the week is nearing its nail-biting climax. All the suspects are gathered in the drawing-room and she names the murderer as . . . Big Bird. A combination of bewilderment and despair gives way to the realisation that the vital last minutes of *Miss Marple* has been lost to *Sesame Street*. The video has been programmed incorrectly.

The frustrations of being the owner of a video recorder were far from the minds of John Mullin and Wayne Johnson when they demonstrated the first model at the laboratories of Bing Crosby Enterprises, Beverly Hills, in November 1952. The idea was not developed commercially, however, with the result that a video recorder did not appear on the market until April 1956 when Ampex of California brought out the Ampex VR-1000, a machine the size of a wardrobe. This was the culmination of research work carried out by Charles P. Ginsberg, Charles E. Anderson and 19-year-old student Ray Dolby, soon to invent his own sound system. To accompany the machine, 3M produced Scotch 179 video tape.

The VR-1000 was not intended for home use. Neither was the BBC's mighty VERA (Vision Electronic Recording Apparatus), which consumed more than 10 miles (16 km) of tape per hour. The first domestic video recorder did not arrive until the Sony CV-2000 of 1965. In January 1970 *The Times* said: 'Anyone with cash to spare for a piece of status-bolstering gadgetry in a luxury class beyond the reach of most, can now buy himself a Philips home video recorder for £275.'

The following year, Philips introduced the first video cassette recorder, the Philips 1500. As prices have tumbled, a video recorder is now as much a part of the furniture as a television set or a refrigerator. Some people even know how to set it.

Volkswagen Beetle

The Volkswagen Beetle was Hitler's car. Yet it owed its ultimate fame to the British occupational forces who, confronted with the prospect of little means of private transport, rebuilt the bombed Volkswagen factory at Wolfsburg and resurrected the Beetle. Without them, this appealing little car would have died with the war. More to the point, there would never have been *Herbie the Love Bug*!

It was in 1931 that Austrian car designer Dr Ferdinand Porsche, working in Stuttgart, had the idea for a people's car with a hump-backed appearance and a rear engine. At the time Germany was in the grips of depression and Dr Porsche found it difficult to interest manufacturers in such a revolutionary vehicle.

Then, in 1933, at the Berlin Motor Show, Hitler declared: 'A nation is no longer judged by the length of its railway network but by the length of its highways.' His speech provided a fillip for the motor industry and at a meeting with Dr Porsche, he emphasised that he, too, was keen on creating a 'Volkswagen' ('people's car'). Whilst publicly the Führer continued to underline the new car's civilian potential, privately he wanted to ensure that it was capable of fulfilling his military aims and ordered the German Ministry of Transport to instruct Dr Porsche that it must be capable of carrying three soldiers and one machine gun plus ammunition.

Backed by Hitler's money, three prototypes were built and road tested in 1936. One crashed and had to be rebuilt while another collided with a deer and returned to base with dinner on the back seat. Opel's plans to build a people's car of their own were scuppered when the authorities took control of all iron and steel supplies. So it was left to Dr Porsche to launch his model in 1939. Hitler called it the KDF Wagen, standing for *Kraft Durch Freude* ('Strength Through Joy'). It was available in just one colour, blue/grey. A special savings scheme, whereby stamps were paid over a period of years, was introduced to make it more affordable to the populace since the price amounted to around four months' average wages. A total of 336 668 Germans enrolled in the scheme but only 630 KDF civilian cars were built during the war — and they went exclusively to Nazi officials.

Following the intervention of the British Army, the Volkswagen, as it had become known, was retrieved from the rubble of battle-scarred Germany. When it was first seen in the UK in 1946, a report criticised the 'excessive engine noise, lack of power, poor braking and poor general finish'. Apart from that . . .

But these obstacles were overcome and the Beetle (a nickname it had earned from the 1930s) proceeded to capture the hearts of the world's drivers. It even won over the Americans who generally wanted large Cadillacs in the fifties. Indeed the 'Bug', as the Americans called it, became so popular that a black market operated towards the end of the decade.

The Beetle earned a reputation for remarkable durability. In 1963 a vehicle christened 'Antarctica 1' spent 12 months at Australia's research base at the South Pole. Shortly after its return, the same car won the Australian BP Rally, conducted in the heat of the outback!

Beetle owners delight in adapting their loved ones. They have been converted into snowploughs, Rollswagens (with a Rolls-Royce bonnet) and welded together to form a 23½-ft (7 m) long Beetle, able to carry 21 Swiss passengers. Since the gear lever was 13 ft (3.9 m) behind him, the driver needed an assistant to change gear. There is all manner of Beetle merchandise — toilet roll holders, doorbells, lamps, toy telephones, cigarette lighters, bottles filled with schnapps. But the *pièce de résistance* must surely be the Beetle beauty contests where proud owners display their vehicles. Swimwear is optional.

Owners have their Volkswagen Beetles painted in many different colours and designs.

V

Walkman

An ardent golfer and lover of music, Sony chief executive Akio Morita sought a lightweight, compact machine which would enable him to enjoy both of his pleasures simultaneously. Clearly, trying to strike a five iron while carrying a portable cassette recorder was impractical but in 1979 his company came up with the Walkman boogie-pak, described as 'the first gadget to combine hi-fi and high fashion'.

It had been a long haul. Mitsuro Ida and his electronics engineering team at Sony had been trying to redesign a small portable tape recorder called the 'Pressman', so that it gave out stereo sounds. Having accomplished that, they were dismayed at not being able to create a model which recorded. Many within Sony were by no means convinced that the personal stereo would sell for apart from its inability to record, there was a fear that customers would find the headphones annoying. But without bothering to conduct the usual market research, Morita gave the go-ahead and the first Walkman went on sale in July of that year. While competitors dithered for almost 12 months, unsure of whether the concept would be a success, Sony were busy making improvements which ensured that they would always stay one step ahead of the opposition. Within four years, they had reduced the Walkman to half its original size. In its short history, around 100 million Walkmans have been sold worldwide — and not all to golfers.

Wall Can Opener

During the Napoleonic Wars, the blockaded French needed a method of feeding their far-flung Army, forcing Napoleon to offer a prize of 12 000 francs for a solution. The answer was the tin can.

Having invented the tin can, thought had to be given to a way of opening it. The lids were sealed with solder and the tins came with instructions to 'cut round on the top near to the outer edge with chisel and hammer'. Such a hazardous operation meant that while Napoleon's soldiers were fed, many of them went into battle with only nine fingers.

Thus the can opener was born. The first models were decidedly ornate, made in cast iron and in the shape of a bull's head, possibly to denote that their major task would be to open tins of bully beef, or corned beef as we know it today.

By the 20th century, designs had become plainer. Rotary can openers gained a foothold in the US but as household appliances multiplied in the 1920s, it was believed that an opener attached to a wall would greatly enhance the average American kitchen. So in 1927 the Central States Manufacturing Company of St Louis marketed the world's first wall can opener.

Waste Disposal Unit

Another device to be created by the First American Kitchen Revolution of the 1920s was the waste disposal unit. In 1929 J. Powers of GEC, Bridgeport, Connecticut, invented a 'grinding unit' to fit under a small auxiliary sink. Electrically powered, it was seen as a boon for removing food waste and was eventually produced commercially in 1935.

Although the waste disposal unit was one of the few domestic appliances to be designed primarily for the home rather than for the catering or hotel industry, it did not find a ready market with the housewife of the day. Families rejected it as being too noisy and also too dangerous for small children who were always likely to lose a wayward limb along with the household waste.

Waterproof Watch

When wristwatches first appeared at around the turn of the century, they were the subject of much ridicule. More vulnerable to shock, dust and humidity than fob watches, they were considered wholly unreliable. The general perception was that they had little future.

But the Rolex company of Geneva, founded by Hans Wilsdorf in 1905, had other ideas. Nine years later, a Rolex watch was the first ever to be given a Class 'A' certificate by Britain's renowned Kew Observatory. This proved that wristwatches could be as reliable and precise as the marine chronometers of the day.

Wilsdorf set about developing a waterproof watch. In 1926 Rolex watches housed in a new case were immersed in water for three weeks. Their timekeeping showed not the slightest variation, the problem of a watertight winder having been solved by inventing the screw-down winding crown, a sophisticated design which has been continuously improved ever since. The case was called the 'Oyster', a name which was to assure lasting protection of the movement against water and dust.

The following year, Wilsdorf demonstrated the waterproof qualities of the watch by handing one to young London typist Mercedes Gleitz before she set off on her attempt to swim the English Channel. She duly swam the Channel with the Rolex Oyster strapped to her wrist, both swimmer and watch emerging unscathed from the murky waters.

Into the typing pool. London secretary Mercedes Gleitz begins her 1927 swim of the English Channel with a Rolex waterproof watch strapped to her wrist.

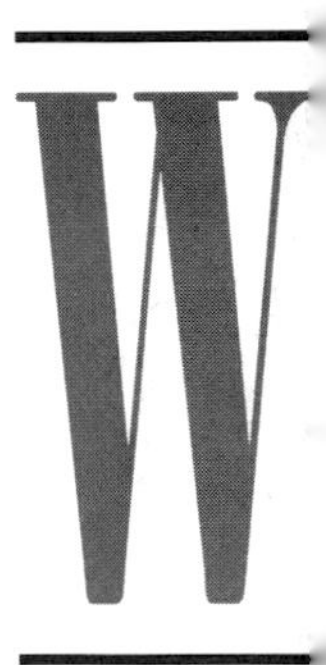

The Swiss company subsequently built on their achievements with such high-performance models as the Submariner (1953), designed for diving and underwater exploration, and the Sea-Dweller (1971) which catered for professional divers and came equipped with a valve allowing helium and other gases to escape and to protect the watch from decompression.

Water Skis

'If there was anything new or dangerous I could figure out, I wanted to try it. I decided that, if you could ski on snow, you could ski on water.'

These were the words of fearless 18-year-old Ralph Samuelson of Lake City, Minnesota, who in 1922 became the first person to demonstrate the art of water skiing. His first attempt was on snow skis behind the family boat but he found them to be too thin and instead cut down two pine boards, which he had bought for a dollar each from a local timber yard, and curved them at the tips by steaming them for three hours in his mother's copper boiler. Halfway down the skis, he attached a leather footstrap.

Samuelson called them 'water skis' but his natural confidence was dented when, not realising that he had to raise the tips from the lake surface, he found himself swallowing considerable amounts of water. He later said: 'It took me at least three weeks and 25 tries before I mastered it. Everyone, of course, thought I was completely nuts.'

The family boat could only reach 20 mph (32 km/h) so Samuelson had to keep criss-crossing in order to maintain any speed. When he was towed by a faster boat, it left him plastered with engine oil. In 1925, he planned to go jumping from a floating dock. Unfortunately, he omitted to wet the dock beforehand with the result that his skis stuck at the summit, the bindings ripped out and Samuelson was launched over the top into the water below. He remedied the situation by greasing the ramp with a pound of lard, after which he thrilled the spectators with leaps of up to 60 ft (18 m).

The Wabasha County Leader of 28 August 1925 reported: 'Last Sunday afternoon at the Lake City bathing beach 2000 people were given a real thriller when Ralph Samuelson of this city did water skiing behind a seaplane that sped through the water at a dizzy pace and at times flew a few feet above the water. Ralph Samuelson again demonstrated his right to be termed "the best water ski rider in the Northwest".'

By the 1930s the sport had reached the French Riviera. Among early practitioners were David Niven, Errol Flynn and Lord Louis Mountbatten who was in the habit of going to dinner on water skis. If invited to dine out on another destroyer, he would roll up his trousers to the knee, take off his socks, hang his shoes around his neck, descend from his own ship, don his skis and be towed over to the neighbouring vessel by a boat driven by an officer!

Wheel Clamp

Named after its town of origin, the dreaded Denver Boot hit London on 16 May 1983. For a 12-month experimental period, 300 clamps lurked ready to pounce on illegal parkers in Westminster, Whitehall, the Strand, Kensington and Chelsea.

Motorists finding a yellow clamp attached to their car had to go to Hyde Park car pound and pay £19.50 plus a £10 parking fine. Once the money was paid, a mobile crew would be alerted by radio and the clamp removed. Drivers were strongly advised not to try to remove the clamps themselves since experts proved that the car was far more likely to fall apart before the clamp did.

The first victim was a Turkish businessman whose Mercedes was clamped. In the first three weeks, no fewer than 77 embassy cars fell prey to the new regulations, causing foreign diplomats to protest. In an attempt to defuse the situation, the Foreign Office announced: 'Diplomatic cars are permitted a maximum of three parking spaces outside their embassies. We have given an undertaking to try to obtain more parking spaces for them.'

Loathe them or hate them, wheel clamps have certainly been instrumental in clearing up some of London's parking problems.

The dreaded wheel clamp wreaks havoc on the streets of London.

Windscreen Wiper

One of the earliest forms of car windscreen wiper was the potato. Drivers would carry half a potato in the car and smear it over the windscreen at the first hint of rain. As a result, the droplets would run together and a reasonably clear view could be obtained. The major drawback with this method was the need to keep stopping the car whenever the screen required rubbing. Also, in prolonged wet spells, considerable amounts of potatoes would be used up which explained why families rarely had chips while it was raining.

In the very first models, the majority of car windscreens were made in two sections so that in wet or foggy weather, the upper half could be tilted open to afford a clear view through the gap. This was satisfactory at low speeds but as engine power increased and windscreens became larger, new methods were sought. One was the potato. Another less edible technique was invented in 1911 by Prince Henry of Prussia who came up with the idea of a strip of rubber mounted on a metal frame to be manually moved up and down the windscreen by the driver. However, with only two hands, this made driving in the wet a tricky proposition. An advanced version of the Prince's innovation was manufactured under the name of the 'Gabriel'. Here the wiper was operated by pulling a string.

The first automatic wipers appeared in the United States in 1916 as standard fitment to the Willys Knight. They worked by suction from the engine but had a tendency to go fast when driving slowly and reduce to a crawl when they were most needed at high speeds.

In 1923 the first electric wiper unit, the Berkshire, was produced in the United States. In Britain it cost £2. 15s. including the motor. But electric wipers were notoriously unreliable and for many years suction prevailed. One of the problems was that the electric motor was often fixed in an inaccessible spot beneath the instrument panel. Consequently, mending a broken wire could necessitate dismantling half of the car.

Windsurfing

Californian businessmen Jim Drake and Hoyle Schweitzer enjoyed sailing and surfing respectively. The two friends regularly discussed the possibility of a sailing surfboard but always struggled over the matter of steering. Then, while driving home from an aeronautics design meeting, Drake hit upon the idea of a movable mast.

He produced two versions. One only enabled the mast to lean backwards and forwards and was therefore impractical, the other had a universal joint. The problems with the latter were that it was difficult to raise the sail and once under way, it tended to make the tail of the board sway from side to side in a fishtail effect. Drake overcame these hurdles by attaching a rope to the boom in order to raise the sail and by adding a tailfin under the board to cure the fishtail. Due to its shape, Drake's boom was called a wishbone.

Schweitzer, meanwhile, had been busily building a large enough surfboard to bear the mast and sail. By 1969 he was sailing it. His exploits created such commercial interest that he decided to patent the idea. Schweitzer's early models were made from expensive fibreglass but when he stumbled across cheaper plastics, mass production was able to begin. The demand was enormous, especially from Holland and Germany, and the sport of sailboarding or windsurfing expanded so quickly that by 1984 it was granted the accolade of inclusion as an Olympic sport.

However, doubts began to emerge with regard to the originality of Schweitzer's invention. A 1965 article by American Newman Darby in the magazine *Popular Science* was produced. Headlined 'Sailboarding: An Exciting New Water Sport for High-speed Water Fun', Darby's piece claimed it was 'a sport so new that fewer than ten people have yet mastered it'. And in 1982 Schweitzer's patent was challenged by Englishman Peter Chilvers who said that he built the first sailboard in Hayling Island back in 1958. Chilvers, who had been content with sailing alone and had never marketed his discovery, saw his claim to priority of invention upheld.

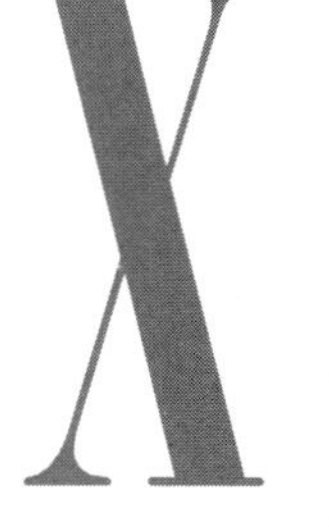

X-Certificate Film

The annual report of the British Board of Film Censors for 1926 stated that the following were among those subjects to be cut: 'White men in a state of degradation amidst native surroundings; American law officers making arrests in this country; officers in British regiments shown in a disgraceful light; workshouse officials shown in an offensive light; girls and women in a state of intoxification; suggestive, indecorous and semi-nude dancing; men leering at the exposure of women's undergarments; marital infidelity; degrading exhibitions of animal passion; passionate and unrestrained embraces; indecorous bathroom scenes; men and women in bed together; "crook" films in which sympathy is enlisted for the criminals; breaking bottles on men's heads; and brutal fights carried to excess, including gouging of eyes, clawing of faces and throttling.'

Described as a collection of 'ex-Colonels and maiden aunts in long, flowered frocks', the BBFC also banned any form of relationship between coloured men and white women but not between white men and coloured women. This sexist distinction arose from the belief held at the time that black men were more biologically capable than white men of sexually satisfying a white woman.

One BBFC script-reader objected to the line: 'Plenty of number nine's doctor?', adding: 'I do not know what it means but coming from an ex-Sergeant Major, I suspect the worse!'

Attitudes changed after the Second World War. The BBFC became more liberal which, in the circumstances, was hardly difficult. They passed the top half of Jane Russell's breasts in Howard Hughes' *The Outlaw*, gang warfare in *Brighton Rock* (starring Richard Attenborough) and sexual repression among nuns in *Black Narcissus*. This loosening of the chastity belt plus the arrival of the shady 'spiv', increases in crime and the divorce rate (following a spate of hasty wartime marriages) all served to create a climate for the 'X' film.

It was introduced to Britain in January 1951, encompassing the old 'H' for horror category and limiting admission to those over 16 years of age. It meant that at last a film could be passed that was not suitable for accompanied children. The first film to receive an 'X' rating was *La Vie Commence Demain* ('Life Begins Tomorrow'), a French film which opened in London on 9 January 1951 and which was considered unsuitable for youngsters because of a scene dealing with artificial insemination. Under the old system, the film would either have had to be cut for British screening or been banned altogether.

The new category immediately became associated in the mind of the public with sex. The major cinema circuits relied on a family audience and were convinced that excluding children from any programme would not only reduce box office receipts for that film but, in the long run, disrupt the family habit of going to the cinema. Consequently, 'X' films were confined to tiny independent cinemas who were willing to show *risqué* foreign films to small audiences. The larger distributors avoided the new certificate like the plague. Only eight films from 1951 were given an 'X' certificate and Rank released just 14 throughout the whole of the 1950s. Many local authorities objected to the new classification too and, possibly for rather dubious motives, demanded to see all 'X' films before they would allow them to be screened.

The minimum age for admission to an 'X' film in Britain was raised to 18 in 1970, and 12 years later the certificate was replaced by a simple '18'.

Y-Front

At the turn of the century, long johns were all the rage in the undulating world of men's underwear. The Edwardians favoured coloured outfits in blues, reds, lavenders and stripes, although they religiously wore white on Sundays.

In 1910 American underwear manufacturers Coopers Inc. of Kenosha introduced a one-piece garment in which two flaps of fabric overlapped in an 'X' shape. It was called the Kenosha Klosed Krotch.

Its lightweight nature marked a pleasant change from the old heavy materials, a trend that continued after the First World War when the one-piece was replaced by the two-piece. With more efficient heating methods, there was no longer the need to be lagged in thick underwear.

The fascist regimes of Germany and Italy helped to create the macho-man look of the 1930s in which knee-length drawers were superseded by brief buttoned shorts but it was a magazine photograph of a pair of swimming trunks on the French Riviera which inspired Coopers to bring out the world's first Y-Front in 1934. With an inverted Y feature at the crotch and no buttons, the garment's factory name was 'Brief Style 1001' although it was later christened the 'Jockey'.

The story of the launch of the Y-Front is the stuff of which marketing legends are made. A huge window display had been booked for the prestigious Marshall Field store in Chicago but just as it was about to be unveiled, the city fell victim to Arctic blizzards. The store management reasoned that customers would hardly be interested in skimpy underwear at 12 below zero and promptly gave instructions for the display to be altered and all advertising to be cancelled. But the display removal men were delayed by the snow and nobody remembered to scrap the advertisements. It was fortuitous both for Marshall Field and the Y-Front since the entire stock of 600 was sold out by noon and a further 1000 pairs were shifted over the next eight days.

Despite the threat of Bugs Bunny boxer shorts, the Y-Front has continued to hold a place very close to man's heart. And who would have thought that it played a vital part in the war effort? For the reclamation of rubber was essential during the war years, causing the Hawick firm of Lyle & Scott, who held the UK franchise for Y-Fronts, to appeal in advertisements: 'As a Y-Front wearer may we ask you, in the National interest, to return elastic bands from your old Y-Fronts to your Y-Front retailer.'

A caped crusader models Y-Fronts.

JOCKEY®
What the well-dressed undergraduate is wearing
Y-FRONT– of course
THE ONE AND ONLY
Coopers
Y-FRONT
underwear
IN GREAT DEMAND AT ALL GOOD MEN'S SHOPS
Made in Gt. Britain exclusively by
HAWICK, SCOTLAND and IDEAL HOUSE, ARGYLL STREET, LONDON, W 1
Y

WORLD
YO-YO
CHAMPION

Yo-Yo

The principle of the yo-yo has been around for centuries. A similar implement was used as a toy by the ancient Greeks while in the 16th century, a yo-yo-like device weighing 4 lb (1.8 kg) and with a 20-ft (6 m) thong served as a fighting weapon in the Filipino jungle.

It was after seeing young Filipinos playing with a harmless version of the above in the early 20th century to cries of 'yo-yo' (which means 'come come') that Chicago toy-maker Donald F. Duncan decided to introduce the yo-yo commercially in 1929.

He started an instant craze, the yo-yo reaching Britain within three years. Among the pioneers were Canadian brothers Pat and Henry Conlin. When 16-year-old Joe Young became Canadian yo-yo champon, the brothers brought him to England as a prize. In London, he demonstrated his skill at a cabaret, with the result that almost immediately dancing was abandoned for the evening while everyone present tried to make the 'little devil on the end of a string' perform tricks. The Conlins promptly cabled Canada for 20 000 gross of yo-yos. Not all were impressed. 'It's too childish,' stated the chairman of a big store after witnessing a demonstration. 'You don't imagine people are going to waste time trying to make a top run up and down a string like this, do you? Why . . . it's more difficult than it looks. Let me try again. Hold on, I'll get it in a minute . . . Hang it, it's worse than golf.' And so the firm's board meeting was delayed for an hour while the chairman played yo-yo! In 1932 *Tit-Bits* magazine reported that the brothers were selling around 300 000 yo-yos a week. The yo-yo has enjoyed spells of overwhelming popularity ever since, as young and old attempt to loop-the-loop. In March 1990 the woodwork class of Shakamak High School, Jasonville, Indiana, constructed a yo-yo 6 ft (1.8 m) in diameter and weighing 820 lb (372 kg). It was launched from a 160-ft (48.8 m) crane and, against all the odds, managed to yo-yo 12 times.

(left) A picture of concentration. Intrepid world yo-yo champion Arthur Pickles demonstrates his successful technique.

Zip (in clothing)

The concept of the zip dates back to the 1890s but it was neither perfected nor used in clothing until the 20th century.

It was in 1893 that Whitcomb L. Judson, a Chicago engineer, took out a patent for a 'slide fastener'. The principle of two metal chains which could be joined together with a slide fastener was sound but the appliance had an unfortunate habit of jamming or flying open without warning. It was therefore just as well that Judson envisaged using his fastener on boots rather than trousers.

Judson's invention caught the attention of one Colonel Lewis Walker who founded the Automatic Hook and Eye Company to market it. Given the limitations of the product, it is scarcely surprising that sales were practically non-existent.

But Walker persevered and in 1902 an improved model under the name of 'C-Curity' was introduced by his new Universal Fastener Company. This too failed to catch on — literally.

Finally, in 1913, Gideon Sundback, a young Swedish engineer from Hoboken, New Jersey, produced something resembling the zip we know today by putting identical units on parallel tapes and by attaching the metal locks to a flexible backing. In 1914 Sundback was granted a patent for 'separable fasteners' and his product was marketed by Walker as the Talon Slide Fastener.

When the US entered the First World War in 1917, its Army and Navy ordered zips for clothes. The zip was now well and truly on its way and in 1919 was marketed in Britain by Kynoch of Birmingham as the Ready Fastener. It was initially used in sports clothes but there remained a number of sceptics, particularly since the early zips were extremely heavy. To calm public fears, a huge zip was put on show at the Wembley Empire Exhibition of 1924. By the end of the exhibition, it had been zipped and unzipped three million times without catching.

The zip was used on women's dresses from 1930 and in corsets a year later. But even as late as 1935, salesgirls in America were advised to 'explain its use and operation' to their customers.

The turning point for men came in 1934 when the Prince of Wales, George Duke of York and Lord Louis Mountbatten all appeared with zips on their trouser flies. Men therefore decided it was safe to risk zips on trousers although the fashion was considered too avant-garde for some. The suitmakers of London's exclusive Savile Row were decidedly unimpressed. It was buttons for them — they considered the zip to be perfectly vulgar.

SOME INVENTIONS THAT FLOPPED

Cheek Pads

In an attempt to remove any look of facial emaciation, Thomas Best of Chicago patented a pair of cheek pads in 1902. They fitted between the cheek and jaw and contained rubber air chambers so that they could be inflated to the desired size.

Child-spanker

A formidable weapon which would have outraged child welfare officers was the paddle-shaped spanker patented in 1953 by George Jorgenson of Norfolk, Virginia. The blade of the paddle was round and, according to its inventor, large enough 'to contact a substantial area of the rump of a child'. Jorgensen's concession was to make the handle jointed so as to give way if the parental clout became too severe.

Chocolate Medicine Spoon

In 1937 the aptly named Constance Honey of Chelsea patented a chocolate spoon for giving medicine to reluctant children. Basically, her idea failed because it was too popular. She would tell her young relatives: 'I'd give you your medicine but I haven't a spoon left in the house!'

Floating Soap

Hartlepool housewife Sarah Fox found bathtimes a nightmare with four small children. The bars of soap turned gooey as they slipped underwater and then the youngsters slipped on them when standing up to get out. So Sarah set out to make a floating soap. Early attempts — including inserting a table tennis ball inside a soap bar — sank without trace but then she hit on a buoyancy technique. This involved grating soap, microwaving it and finally putting it through a food processor. Sarah and her husband ploughed cash into marketing attempts but shops showed no interest and the big soap companies did not even reply to her letters. In 1992 she was forced to abandon the project. She said: 'I still believe I've come up with one of the greatest innovations of modern times but, sadly, nobody appears interested. It seems mankind doesn't want to benefit.'

Hedgehog Flavoured Crisps

In 1984 Welshpool publican Phil Lewis was discussing crisp flavours with some romany customers. They told him of an old gipsy delicacy — hedgehog baked in clay — and suggested it might make a change from cheese and onion or salt 'n' vinegar. So, Lewis set to work in his kitchen and produced the world's first hedgehog flavoured crisps. The recipe was a closely guarded secret but was said to be so authentic that you could almost see the tyre marks on the bag. Customers approved, likening the taste to smokey bacon, but as the venture attracted more and more publicity, animal lovers protested and Lewis was forced to abandon the snack for more traditional flavours. Bensons Crisps bought him out in 1988 and keep Hedgehog on as a brand name rather than a flavour. But they were considering reintroducing the distinctive taste of hedgehog to mark the tenth anniversary.

THE ACME
MUSTACHE GUARD.
Solid Comfort while Eating.
No Use for Napkins.
Neat and simple, easily and quickly adjusted. Does not interfere with free use of mouth.
WORKS PERFECTLY.
Made of gold and silver plate. Can be carried in vest pocket. Every genteel person should have one. Two sizes, large and medium. Mention size when ordering. Price $2.00. Sent by mail to any address. Sold only by the
Acme Novelty Co.,
Omaha, Neb.

'Every genteel person should have one' — the Acme Mustache Guard.

Moustache Guard

Thomas Ferry of Wilmington, Delaware, invented a moustache-guard in 1901. He said it was 'designed to hold the mustache away from the lips and to prevent the lodgment of food thereon while eating'. It consisted of a number of upwardly pointing teeth inserted through the moustache from below 'to support the long flowing ends of the mustache which otherwise might droop down in the way'. An elastic tape was then strapped around the lip hair.

Pedestrian Bumper

To reduce pedestrian casualties in 1960, David Gutman from Philadelphia came up with a special bumper designed to be fixed to the front of a car. Not only would it cushion the impact but it also had a huge pair of claws which would grab the pedestrian around the waist to prevent him dropping to the street.

Sinclair C5

January 1985 saw intrepid British electronics genius Sir Clive Sinclair unveil his solution to the nation's traffic problems — a single-seat, electric tricycle called the C5. The battery and pedal-powered machine was capable of travelling 20 miles (32 km) before recharging and cost a modest £399. But at just 31 inches (79 cm) high, the fragile, lightweight C5 looked terrifyingly vulnerable when tested among London's buses and juggernauts. Sir Clive remained bullishly optimistic, predicting that by the end of the century 'the petrol engine will be seen as a thing of the past'. Within two months, production of the C5 had been suspended for good.

Sir Clive Sinclair aboard his C5.

Solar-cooled Hat

'It is well known that cooling the top of the head will have a cooling effect on the entire person,' stated Chicago's Harold W. Dahly in his 1967 patent for a solar-cooled hat. Unfortunately, any benefits of the headgear, which operated by means of a solar-powered fan inside the top of the hat, were outweighed by the fact that it made the wearer look totally ridiculous.

Snoek

With food rationing at its height, one of the unsavoury dishes introduced to Britain in 1948 was a South African fish called snoek. Edible fish are not exactly noted for their beauty (how many cod do you see on *Blind Date*?) but the blue snoek was so hideous that its picture on the can label completely put people off either buying or eating it. In the end, snoek became a national joke instead of a national dish.

Strand Cigarettes

Based on a Frank Sinatra film, the 1960 television commercial for Strand cigarettes (3s. 2d. for a packet of 20) was an illustration of advertising that, far from boosting sales, actually caused the product's demise. It showed actor Terence Brook as a mysterious man lighting up on a deserted street corner and promised: 'You're never alone with a Strand.' The advert was hugely popular, Brook became a celebrity overnight and 'The Lonely Man Theme' reached number 39 in the UK charts. But much as the public loved the commercial, they did not buy the product which was soon discontinued. The theory was that viewers believed that if they smoked Strand, they would end up as lonely as the chap in the commercial.

THE BEST OF THE REST

A Mrs Natalie Stolp from Philadelphia had observed with discomfort that flirtatious young men 'frequently avail themselves of the crowded conditions of cars and other means of transportation to annoy and insult ladics, ncxt to whom they may happen to be seated, by pressing a knee or thigh against the adjacent knee or thigh of their feminine neighbour'. Her 1914 patent sought to stem the rising sap by attaching a spring to the lady's underskirt which responded to pressure by releasing a short, sharp point into the offender's flesh.

* * *

What child could have resisted an American doll from 1952 which came complete with removable plastic stomach, heart, liver, lungs, kidneys and intestines?

* * *

In 1966 American Thomas J. Bayard invented a vibrating toilet seat, acting on the belief that physical stimulation of the buttocks is effective in relieving constipation.

* * *

Earl M. Christopherson of Seattle patented a 1960 device to enable people to look inside their own ears.

* * *

In the 1980s three French women, Dominique Peignoux, Yvette Guys and Françoise Dekan, marketed a contraption that was tucked inside a baby's nappy and played 'When the Saints Go Marching In' as soon as it became wet.

* * *

In 1919 John Humphrey of Connecticut invented an unusual alarm clock, one which would rouse a sleeper from his slumbers by hitting him. The apparatus consisted of a timepiece attached to an adjustable rod with a rubber ball on the end. When the alarm on the clock went off, instead of a bell ringing, the rod would be activated, causing the ball to hit the desired area of the sleeper's anatomy. Humphrey deemed his device to be of great benefit to deaf people or invalids who might be upset by bells . . . but presumably not by being whacked over the head with a ball.

Acknowledgements

The author would like to thank the following for their assistance in compiling this book: adidas (UK) Ltd; Alcoholics Anonymous; Aluminium Federation Ltd; Argos Distributors Ltd; Atari Corporation UK; Barclays Bank plc; A.G. Barr plc; Bayer plc; BBC; Birds Eye Wall's; Biss Lancaster plc; Mark Borkowski PR; British Adhesives & Sealants Association; British Aerosol Manufacturers' Association; British Alcan Consumer Products Ltd; British Cellophane; British Paper & Board Industry Federation; British Patent Office; British Plastics Federation; British Shoe Corporation; British Telecom Museum; Broadstone Communications; Cartmell Public Relations; Central Council for British Naturism; Chanel Ltd; Combe International Ltd; Courtaulds Textiles (Holdings) Ltd; Disposable Nappy Association; Drambuie Liqueur Company; Electrolux; Fisons plc; Flymo Ltd; Formica Ltd; Gaymer Group Ltd; GEC; Gillette (UK) Ltd; Goblin Ltd; R. Griggs Group Ltd; Guide Dogs for the Blind Association; Hasbro; Hoover Ltd; Hotpoint; Humbrol Ltd; Ice Cream Alliance; ICI; Infoplan Public Relations; Johnson Wax Ltd; Kenwood Ltd; KFC (Great Britain) Ltd; Kimberly-Clark Ltd; Kraft General Foods; Lego UK Ltd; Lever Brothers Ltd; Littlewoods Pools; LRC Products Ltd; L'Oréal; Luncheon Vouchers Ltd; Lyons Tetley Ltd; Mars Confectionery Ltd; McDonald's Restaurants Ltd; MFI Furniture Centres Ltd; National Dairy Council; National Museum of Photography Film & Television; National Savings; Nestlé UK Ltd; Newforge Foods Ltd; Nottinghamshire Library Services; Pentel Stationery Ltd; Polycell Products Ltd; Polaroid (UK) Ltd; Procter & Gamble Ltd; RAC Motor Sports Association Ltd; Ransomes Sims & Jefferies Ltd; RAPRA Technology; Rawlplug Company Ltd; Reader's Digest; Reckitt & Colman Ltd; Rolex; Rowenta (UK) Ltd; Science Museum; Selectus Ltd; SmithKline Beecham; Smith & Nephew plc; Sony Consumer Products Company UK; Spear's Games; Stainless Steel Fabricators Association; Sternstat Ltd; Stransky Thompson Public Relations; Tambrands Ltd; Thermos Ltd; 3M United Kingdom plc; Unicliffe Ltd; Waddingtons Games Ltd; Wander Ltd; Wearne Associates.

SELECT BIBLIOGRAPHY

Collecting Teddy Bears — Pam Hebbs (Collins, 1988)
Person to Person — Peter Young (Granta Edns, 1991)
Drop by Drop: the Loctite Story — Ellsworth S. Grant, 1983
Machines in the Home — Rebecca Weaver and Rodney Dale, 1992
Hearth and Home — Sheena Brooke (Mills and Boon, 1973)
The Guinness Book of Movie Facts and Feats — Patrick Robertson (Guinness, 1988)
The Shell Book of Firsts — Patrick Robertson (Ebury Press and Michael Joseph, 1983)
Famous First Facts — Joseph Nathan Kane (H.W. Wilson Co., New York, 1981)
The Hornby Companion Series — Bert Love and Jim Gamble (New Cavendish Books, 1986)
In Praise of Teddy Bears — Philippa and Peter Waring (Souvenir Press, 1980)
The Eyes on Tomorrow: The Evolution of Procter & Gamble — Oscar Shugill, 1980
Mothers of Invention — Ethlie Ann Ware and Greg Ptacek (William Morrow, New York, 1988)
The Launderette Story — Stanley S. Bloom (Duckworth, 1988)

PICTURE ACKNOWLEDGEMENTS

adidas (UK) Ltd, p. 6
Autocar Motoring Archive, p. 176
Barclays Bank plc, p. 31
Birds Eye Wall's, Photograph: Mark Berry Photographic, p. 58
Birds Eye Wall's, p. 66, 82
Biss Lancaster plc, p. 155
Bob Thomas Sports Photography, Photograph: Mark Thompson, p. 65
British Aerosol Manufacturers' Association, p. 8
British Alcan Consumer Products Ltd, p. 16
British Telecommunications plc 1922, p. 43, 55, 127, 143, 157
Central Council for British Naturism, p. 108
David Bond, p. 21, 78, 100, 160
Drambuie Liqueur Company, p. 47
Fisons plc, p. 70
Flymo Ltd, p. 60
Formica Ltd, p. 64
Gaymer Group Ltd, p. 15
Girl Guides Association, p. 68
R. Griggs & Co Ltd, p. 46
Guide Dogs for the Blind Association, p. 71
Guinness Publishing, Cover flap, p. 30, 136 (*above*)
Hasbro, p. 7, 134
Hoover Ltd, p. 169
Humbrol Ltd, p. 10
ICI, p. 114
Jockey, p. 179
John Frost Newspapers, p. 11, 17, 26, 34 (*below*), 37, 50, 51, 53, 54, 59, 62, 73, 75, 76, 80 (*below*), 87, 90, 92, 93 (*left*), 106 (*left*), 110, 112, 123 (*left*), 129, 132, 133, 136, 138, 145, 147, 152, 154, 158, 159, 171, 173
KFC (Great Britain) Ltd, p. 86
Kenwood Ltd, p. 61
Kraft General Foods, p. 123
Luncheon Vouchers Ltd, p. 91
Mars Confectionery Ltd, p. 94, 142
Mary Evans Picture Library, p. 183
McDonald's Restaurants Ltd, p. 95
National Motor Museum, Beaulieu, p. 74
Nestlé Uk Ltd, p. 83
Courtesy of New Musical Express, copyright IPC Magazines Ltd, p. 121
Newforge Food Ltd, p. 140
Parker, p. 164
Perrier UK Ltd, p. 113
Phillips Electrical, p. 89
Phillips Fine Art Auctioneers, P. 156
Pictorial Press Ltd, p. 52, 84
Photograph: Mark Cameron, p. 57
Photograph: Jeff Carlick, p. 65
Polaroid (UK) Ltd, p. 118
Popperfoto, p. 25, 77, 80/81 (*above*), 105, 106 (*right*)/107, 109, 113, 115, 167, 180, 184
Procter & Gamble Ltd, p. 45
RHM Foods Ltd, p. 22
Ransomes Sims & Jefferies Ltd, p. 104
By kind permission of Reader's Digest, p. 126
Robert Opie, p. 12, 14, 27, 28, 33, 34 (*above*), 38, 41, 42, 48, 49, 69, 72, 81 (*below*), 93 (*right*), 97, 99, 101, 103, 117, 119, 120, 125, 128, 137, 139, 149, 153, 161
Rolex, p. 175
Rowenta (UK) Ltd, p. 146
Scouts Association, p. 25
Selectus Ltd, Photograph: Robert Belton, p. 170
Slingsby Aviation Ltd, p. 79
Sony Consumer Products Ltd, p. 163
Spear's Games, p. 131
Tesco Stores Ltd, p. 150
Thermos Ltd, p. 5
Waddingtons Games Ltd, p. 148
Wearne Associates, p. 166

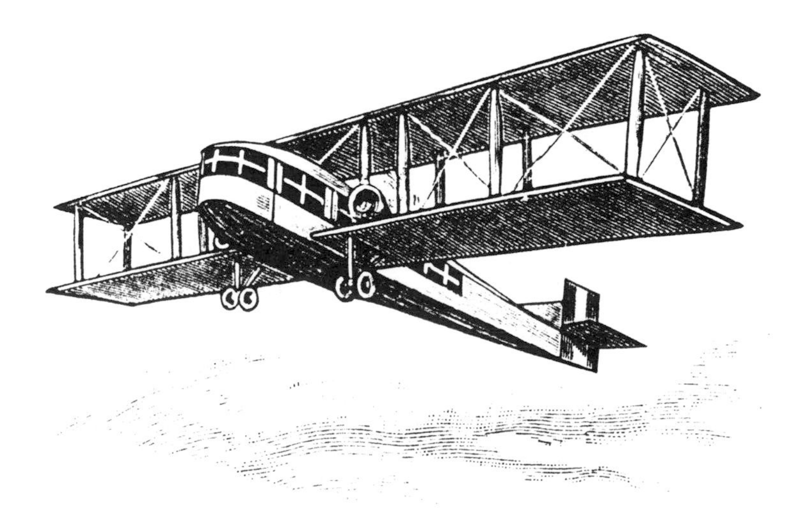

Index